WHAT CAN WE REALLY KNOW?

●▲■

The Strengths & Limits Of Human Understanding

WHAT CAN WE REALLY KNOW?

●▲■

The Strengths & Limits Of Human Understanding

DAVID R. ANDERSEN

FOREWORD BY
ANGUS J.L. MENUGE

ACADEMIC

Published by:
1517 Publishing
PO Box 54032
Irvine, CA 92619-4032

Publisher's Cataloging-In-Publication Data
(Prepared by Cassidy Cataloguing Services)

Names: Andersen, David, author. | Menuge, Angus J. L., writer of foreword.
Title: What can we really know? : the strengths and limits of human
    understanding / David R. Andersen ; foreword by Angus J. L. Menuge.
Description: Irvine, CA : 1517 Publishing, [2023] | Includes bibliographical
    references and index.
Identifiers: ISBN: 978-1-956658-54-5 (paperback) |
    978-1-956658-58-3 (hardcover) | 978-1-956658-59-0 (ebook)
Subjects: LCSH: Knowledge, Theory of (Religion) | Knowledge, Theory of. |
    Religion—Philosophy. | Theology. | Realism. | God—Knowableness. |
    Philosophy and science. | BISAC: PHILOSOPHY / Epistemology. |
    RELIGION / Philosophy. | RELIGION / Christian Theology / General.
Classification: LCC: BT40 .A54 2023 | DDC: 230.01—dc23

Printed in the United States of America.
Cover art by Zachariah James Stuef.

Dedication

To my loving and beautiful wife, whose tenderness could soften the hardest heart, and who is one of the greatest gifts I've ever received. Thank you for inspiring all that is best in me and for modeling a life of devotion and gratitude.

Contents

X   CONTENTS

Foreword

Angus J. L. Menuge

Aristotle is famous for his account of moral virtues, like courage and justice. Yet Aristotle also recognized intellectual virtues, such as practical wisdom, and today there is a thriving discipline called virtue epistemology. This approach to the theory of knowledge focuses on the attitudes that aid us in finding as much truth, and rejecting as much error, as possible. One of these attitudes is intellectual humility, the central motivation and guiding theme of David Andersen's wonderfully insightful book. This is a welcome antidote to the epidemic of misplaced certainty and cultic deference to "experts" that plagues our age.

Why is intellectual humility so important? Why, for example, is it better to be like Sam Gamgee than it is to be like Saruman? First, notice that Sam, a lowly gardener, has a realistic sense of his own limitations. He does not claim to know all sorts of things that are beyond his capacity to know. Second, Sam listens to the testimony of others who may be better placed to know than he is. Third, Sam is a critical consumer, wisely concerned about the character and reliability of his advisors. In this way, Sam is both open to discovering new truth, yet healthily skeptical of even expert advice. He is also quick to admit that he got something wrong (as when he thought Frodo had been killed by Shelob), and he readily revises his beliefs in light of new evidence. Saruman, by contrast, represents the false certainty that fuels our emerging omnicompetent scientocracy. He asserts the godlike wisdom required to remake the world. Yet in his pride he overreaches, ignoring factors right under his nose, like the waking Ents, that will ensure the failure of his plans. He overrates the messages of Sauron that feed (and redirect) his guiding narrative, while shutting out those like Gandalf who try to disabuse him of his delusions.

Yet humility is not enough. One might be so humble that one despairingly concludes that truth is completely inaccessible, falling into a debilitating skepticism. This is unreasonable because we have ample evidence that scientific knowledge has increased, even if the best-confirmed scientific theories are still liable to falsification. So, humility must be balanced by a proper (chastened) confidence—confidence that truth exists and that our minds are sometimes able to discover it. This confidence is rooted in the prescientific natural faith that the world is orderly, our minds are rational, and that there is an affinity between the way we think and the way the world works. This is not a blind faith, as it has been vindicated time and again by the discovery of theories that increase our ability to predict and control phenomena.

By contrast with humility and proper confidence, false certainty is a disease of the mind. What we most need is an accurate diagnosis of its sources and an identification of effective remedies. That is the main focus of the first eight chapters of Andersen's book. These chapters provide an accessible introduction to the theory of knowledge and the philosophy of science, and they ultimately advocate critical realism. Critical realism is the sensible view of most ordinary people and of the many working scientists who have not succumbed to scientism. It recognizes the inevitable human and social contribution to knowledge: we are creatures of our times and our thinking is shaped and limited by the concepts available to us. Thus, in Mendel's times, scientists could not entertain the thought that genes are DNA. Yet at the same time, critical realism rejects the extreme constructivist claim that all we have are different narrative conceptions that make no contact with the world as it is. Limited as our concepts always are, that does not prevent them from revealing partial truths about the real world. That theories are routinely falsified and superseded does not prevent them from disclosing insights into what is going on behind the manifest image of appearances.

One way that this book encourages the humility and confidence that it advocates is via its dialectical mode of exposition. Repeatedly, we learn of several opposing views and conclude that while none is entitled to full certainty, there are more reasonable alternatives. In the process, we are given ample reason to reconsider the culturally dominant idea that the "experts" have vast and infallible knowledge. This book can be read as a series of pins that puncture overinflated balloons of certainty, together with more modest and robust replacements.

On the sobering side, Andersen shows that both philosophers and psychologists have thoroughly exposed our intellectual frailty.

It may surprise non-philosophers that after a few thousand years of intense analysis, philosophers cannot provide a definition of knowledge for which there are no reasonable objections. This does not mean that we do not know anything, but that knowledge itself is one of those things that we only partially know. There are several basic features of knowledge beyond dispute but a healthy disagreement about what more is required to distinguish it from true belief. Turning to science, we learn that the best historians and philosophers of science have concluded that there is no clear demarcation line between science and non-science. We can identify paradigmatic examples of each, but every attempt to provide necessary and sufficient conditions for a theory or practice to qualify as scientific is vulnerable to counterexamples. Further, scientific realists have sometimes made overconfident claims about scientific confirmation. Confirmation of a theory does not show it is approximately true, since theories that have mostly false predictions can still be right in some cases. And since there can be multiple theories that make the same true prediction, it is a fallacy (affirming the consequent) to claim that one of these theories is made more credible. More generally, antirealists have leveled a number of powerful objections to scientific realism that need to be taken seriously. Yet, as Andersen shows, one should also be skeptical of the skeptics. A chastened critical realism provides good reason to believe that ultimately falsified theories may still identify real objects and processes in nature.

Cognitive psychology has also delivered a few slices of humble pie. Experts are sometimes tempted to think of themselves as the watchmen of our culture, issuing apocalyptic warnings and draconian edicts to control the populace. They should beware of the psychologists who watch the judgments and reasoning of the watchmen. The fact is that even the experts routinely acquiesce to cognitive biases that deviate from ideal logical and statistical reasoning. Experts who should know better draw conclusions that ignore the baseline, concluding a man is most likely a philatelist because he has representative stereotypical mannerisms, but ignoring the prevalence of stamp collectors in the general population. And they naturally overrate risks that are easily available to their consciousness, while underrating others. Thus, after a terrorist attack using an airplane, experts may advise driving even though driving is statistically much more dangerous than flying. Most humiliating of all, Andersen unpacks the research of Philip Tetlock on the

accuracy of expert predictions. It turns out that the experts never outperform rather crude extrapolation algorithms, and that humble non-experts
are often more successful. One reason for this may be that experts are proud
of the models they have developed, and tend to ignore or reinterpret the
data that does not fit, while humbler souls are more open to a variety of
variables. Often enough, a humble hobbit may get it right when Saruman
gets it wrong.

But this is not a counsel of despair. Precisely because we can detect
limitations and biases in our thinking, we can develop procedures to counteract them. We can identify and consider all of the available explanations
of the data. We can ensure that the baseline and potentially confounding
variables are taken into account. We can allow our theories and models to
be challenged by critics just as we challenge theirs.

A good illustration of the value of this approach is the debate between
theists and non-theists over the best account of reality. This is the focus of
the remaining four chapters of Andersen's book. He considers various views
of our knowledge of God, rejecting presuppositionalism and Plantinga's
view that religious belief can be properly basic, requiring no independent
ground. Turning to an evidentialist approach, Andersen explores the
remarkable resurgence of natural theology. The new wine of recent scientific discoveries in cosmology and biology, mixed with the sophisticated
tools of formal logic and probability theory, has reinvigorated the classical
cosmological and teleological arguments for God's existence. Andersen can-
vasses some of the best skeptical objections, but argues that theists are ready
with persuasive rejoinders. What is striking about these new arguments for
God is that they employ the best tools we have developed to counteract the
bias identified in the earlier part of the book. They are models of cogent
reasoning that consider the full range of competing hypotheses and seek
to infer the one best explanation. They do not rely on any presuppositions
that bias the investigation from the start but allow all of the hypotheses to
compete on a level playing field.

To be sure, knowing that God exists is not much use if one does not
know who God is. And there is also the worry that some arguments may
establish the existence of a supernatural entity but fall short of establishing
that this entity is what we mean by God. So, in the last chapter, Andersen
considers the case for the resurrection of Jesus. If successful, such an argument supports both the existence and identity of a God worthy of wor-
ship. In dialog with skeptical challenges, such as swoon and hallucination

theories, Andersen makes the case that a historical resurrection is the best explanation of several well-attested historical facts.

This book's balance of intellectual humility and reasonable hope is an oasis in the barren lands of dogmatic scientism. May it enlighten, encourage, and refresh its readers!

Introduction

In his classic defense of liberty, F. A. Hayek commented that if old truths are to retain their hold they must be restated in the language of successive generations. What may have been communicated well at an earlier time can become worn with use and cease to have the same effect as it once did. Though the underlying ideas may still be as valid as ever, the language in which they're stated can fail to convey the same conviction. This, he suggests, may be an inevitable consequence of the fact that no statement of an ideal can be complete. Hence, articulation of an idea must be continually adapted to the current climate, in terms that resonate with the concerns of contemporary recipients.[1]

Questions of the nature of human knowledge are perennial. But, as Hayek reminds us, our contemporaries may bring new concerns to the old questions of the status of human knowledge and judgments. While countless volumes have already been written on the subject, this topic will forever be a work in progress—even though much, if not all, of what we can say simply repeats the contributions of prior generations. Still, to be relevant, it must address present controversies and set out clearly what it affirms and denies. This volume attempts to do just that by placing the problem of knowledge and judgment within a broad context, one that grapples with the concerns of philosophers, research psychologists, theologians, and, to a smaller extent, even economists.

Much of the twentieth and twenty-first centuries were (at least partly) situated between two visions of what and how much can be known. First,

---

[1] F. A. Hayek, *The Constitution of Liberty: The Definitive Edition* (Chicago, 2011), 47-8.

there were those who argued for an objective basis of at least some of what we claim to know, whether it was grounded in human reason or empirically in the external world. Against them were those who insisted that all knowledge is a social construct and therefore relative, e.g., as articulated in postmodernism and social constructivism. To be fair, these debates have been waged along a vast continuum and reflect the endless variety that the idea of a continuum implies. Indeed, they've been discussed at least since the time of the ancient Greeks.

Yet attitudes about what we can know, and how certain we can be, have turned in a peculiar direction in just the past few years. Attempting to describe this development, Ilana Redstone has suggested that much of today's discourse—e.g., within the university, science, the media, law, medicine, and social media—is caught in the grips of what she calls the "certainty trap," which manifests itself as an intolerance of beliefs that deviate from prevailing views.[2] She notes that two things seem to be driving this: a blind certainty about the unquestionable truth of the intellectual fashions of the day and a failure to recognize the profound limits of human knowledge.[3] Its pervasive presence can be felt with the dramatic rise in the tendency to express disdain, both for the position with which one doesn't agree and the moral character of the person who holds it.[4] It is also detectable in other alarming trends, such as the now too common practice of "canceling" lectures by academics who don't conform to current intellectual trends and passions. At least part of the problem is that ideological diversity within educational and cultural institutions has become an increasingly rare phenomenon, which has reinforced a group-think that solidifies trendy ideas.

Correcting these trends might prove to be more challenging than one would like; however, as Redstone also notes, certain barriers stand in the

---

[2] We should note, however, that current attitudes have been in the making since at least the early decades of the twentieth century. See, for example, F. A. Hayek's remarks in *The Fatal Conceit: The Errors of Socialism*, ed. W. W. Bartley III (Chicago, 1989), 52-4.

[3] Ilana Redstone, "The Certainty Trap," https://www.tabletmag.com/sections/news/articles/the-certainty-trap, and "America by Gaslight," https://www.tabletmag.com/sections/[sectionSlug]/articles/america-gaslight-ilana-redstone.

[4] That such attitudes have plagued human history is easy to show. Edmund Burke, for instance, once commented similarly that, "It is no excuse for presumptuous ignorance that it is directed by insolent passion." Quoted in Thomas Sowell (who documents many other references of this type) in *A Conflict of Visions: Ideological Origins of Political Struggles* (New York, 2007), 64.

way of understanding truth. The one most relevant here is what she refers to as the *settled question fallacy*, which occurs when we behave as though certain questions have definitive and clear answers when they, in fact, do not. Consider, for instance, the highly charged issue of racism, which has come to dominate so much of the public conversation. While very few scholars reject racism as an important variable, systemic racism is widely touted as the definitive cause for the vast majority of disparities in group outcomes—meaning that, absent discrimination, all intergroup differences would cease to exist –without reference to other variables that have measurable effects, such as age, preferences, priorities, and effort.[5] A particularly pernicious form of the settled question fallacy occurs when one side of a controversial issue claims that a question is no longer up for debate. When this occurs, proponents portray a false degree of confidence which is caused by an unwillingness to acknowledge the limitations of our knowledge—a situation that often leads to coercion, judgment, or ostracism as the prime mechanisms for achieving stated goals. Perhaps nowhere was this more apparent than in the rapid consolidation of then-controversial positions during the COVID-19 pandemic. Questions that were previously open and highly debatable were suddenly considered to be definitively answered and no longer open for discussion; these positions were then solidified within an ever-changing orthodoxy.

    Though the certainty trap may seem especially pronounced at present, it isn't completely unlike prior searches for certainty. Beginning with the foundationalism of Descartes, which assumed that there are foundational or basic beliefs that guarantee their own truth and from which other non-basic beliefs can be derived, many Enlightenment thinkers insisted that any true knowledge would be infallible. The basic beliefs of which that knowledge is composed functioned as axiomatic, self-evident truth that required no demonstration or justification.[6] During the twentieth century, the same trap vexed logical positivism, though in somewhat different ways. For instance, on the basis of certain *a priori* assumptions regarding the foundations of knowledge, A. J. Ayer could strike down any metaphysical statement—including those concerning the nature God—as meaningless and therefore unworthy of attention.[7] Thus, the overconfidence afflicting today's culture

---

[5] For a critique of this popularized argument, see Thomas Sowell, *Discrimination and Disparities* (New York, 2019).
[6] Alister E. McGrath, *A Scientific Theology*, vol. 2, (Grand Rapids, 2002), 21ff.
[7] Alfred Jules Ayer, *Language, Truth and Logic* (New York, 1946).

can be seen as a continuation of the human tendency to regard present knowledge as more certain than it is—which, in effect, is the tendency to downplay or deny our ignorance.

Ignorance and the Beginning of Wisdom

Along with countless philosophers before him, Hayek began his monumental study on liberty by stressing the Socratic maxim that the recognition of our ignorance is the beginning of wisdom. We must become aware, he argues, of our necessary ignorance of much that helps us achieve our aims—meaning that most of the intellectual advantages we have rest on the fact that individuals benefit from more knowledge than they realize. Yet ignorance too often is glossed over and treated as a minor imperfection that can be more or less disregarded. The truth is that human beings didn't simply impose a pattern on the world created by their minds, as if it were by some omni-competent endowment. Rather, the mind is itself a system that continually changes as a result of our endeavor to adapt to our environment, which means that human knowledge isn't something that stands outside of nature, nor is it independent of experience.

To demonstrate this, Hayek notes that there are two respects in which our conscious knowledge is only part of the conditions that enable us to achieve our aims. The first is that the mind is itself a product of the civilization in which it has grown up and it's unaware of much of the experience that has shaped it (e.g., the habits, language, traditions, and moral beliefs that are part of its makeup). Second, the knowledge that any individual consciously applies is only a small part of the knowledge which, at any one time, contributes to his action. "When we reflect," he says, "how much knowledge possessed by other people is an essential condition for the successful pursuit of our individual aims, the magnitude of our ignorance of the circumstances on which the results of our action depend appears simply staggering."[8] Since the sum of knowledge possessed by all individuals doesn't exist anywhere as an integrated whole, the problem becomes figuring out how to profit from this knowledge, which exists only as isolated, partial, and conflicting beliefs of all people.[9]

---

[8] F. A. Hayek, *The Constitution of Liberty: The Definitive Edition*, 73-82.
[9] For Hayek, this serves as a prime reason that any reliance on the central planning of society is doomed to failure.

While this would seem difficult to deny, one of the great ironies is that, even though the best minds have seen that the range of acknowledged ignorance will grow with scientific advance, popular beliefs have gone in the opposite direction; even among scientists, there's an assumption that the range of our ignorance is steadily decreasing and that we can aim at more comprehensive and deliberate control of human activities. But this contradicts the fact that the growth of our knowledge constantly reveals new realms of ignorance. This is partly because the more knowledge increases, the more it's divided into specialties, which in turn increases the necessary ignorance of the individual. No matter how much of an expert she may be in one ever-narrowing domain, she is bound to be ignorant of vast areas of most others. Moreover, such a division of knowledge implies that those solving problems (scientific, societal, etc.) have no way of predicting who will discover new ways of solving them. Precisely because every individual knows so little and because we rarely know which of us knows best, we rely on the independent and competitive efforts of the many. Humiliating to human pride as this might be, our necessary ignorance of so much means that we have to deal not with certainty, but with probabilities and chances.

Our Task: Balancing on the Tightrope

As with so many mistakes in life, intellectual errors often occur when one truth is elevated at the expense of other equally important truths, leaving only a reductionism that turns a blind eye to the nuance inherent in a complex world. Such errors can be easy to make, because simultaneously holding two truths that seem to be in tension is taxing for even the strongest minds. Difficult as it is, if we're to avoid an artificial conception of reality, we need to be mindful of the key variables. This means that we must walk a bit of a tightrope when discussing what and how we know what we claim to know, how certain we can be, and—even more vexingly—whether some aspects of the world may simply be unknowable.

To maintain our balance, we'll affirm two ideas that often seem at odds. The first is that human beings have the remarkable ability to gain knowledge about the world and can represent the workings of nature through abstract thought. The second is that their knowledge is a social product, which means that it's fallible, culturally conditioned, and comes with some built-in constraints. Taken in their raw forms, these two principles tug at one another in opposite directions, with the first pulling us toward the certainty trap and the second toward radical skepticism or a blanket denial of objectivity (e.g., as in social constructivism). Affirming both, however, this book will resist all reductionist approaches that artificially elevate any single idea and will invite us to view the topic of epistemology in a holistic way.

In order to do this, it will be necessary to provide context for our topic. Toward that end, this book will provide an overview of the debates within two independent but closely related branches of study: namely, the relevant branches of philosophy as well as the recent social scientific research on judgment and decision-making. Because philosophers have been discussing the problem of knowledge since at least the time of the ancient Greeks, we'll begin with a brief introduction to the problems they consider, focusing particularly on contemporary concerns. (Note: Because these chapters provide only a high-level overview, they're not intended for professional philosophers who could no doubt write a much more extensive introduction than the one offered here.) Next, we'll explore relatively recent research that aims to understand how humans actually make judgments, and compares this with how they ought to make judgments. As we examine some of the core controversies, it will become clear that common contemporary claims to certainty are unfounded and that a healthy dose of humility should be at the heart of all claims to knowledge. Just as importantly, however, we'll see that there are solid reasons to believe that we do in fact have at least some justified knowledge of the world and of God.

Looking Forward

To begin our examination, chapter one will discuss some of the basic debates within the field of epistemology (which examines how we know what we know) and ask questions such as: Do we derive knowledge from our senses, or does it arise via human reason? If from our senses, do they give us an accurate picture of the way the world really is, or do our minds simply construct a world consistent with our social context? Also, what does it mean to have what philosophers call justified belief? While chapter one focuses primarily on the individual knower, chapter two explores the effects of social interactions and social systems on our claims to know. Since so much of what we know is transmitted by others, we'll ask when our beliefs that are based not on the evidence of social science can be considered justified. In a complex society like ours, information is vast and spread out in a fragmentary way across multiple institutions and groups. Given this, how can the non-expert know whom to trust, and how can even experts who rely on other experts distinguish the wheat from the chaff? The issues addressed will highlight the fact that our knowledge has some important built-in constraints, given the social way knowledge is often mediated.

Next, because scientific knowledge is (rightly) considered to be one of humankind's greatest achievements, chapters three through six will discuss the central debates within the philosophy of science. The questions that will occupy our attention include the following: What is science, and what separates its claims from those we consider to be non-scientific? What is the aim of science, and do its theories give us truth about the inner workings of nature, or are they merely fictions that allow us to make useful predictions? Just as importantly, is there an upper limit to scientific knowledge, and how certain can we ever claim to be? We'll discover that the bulk of the debates discussed in these chapters occurs between two rival camps: realism and antirealism, the former of which affirms that science gives us a literally true picture of the world, while the latter questions whether such claims are justified. Chapter seven will conclude our discussion of science with an exploration of critical realism, which seeks to maintain both that science can give us a true picture of the world *and* that much of our knowledge is a social product, and therefore fallible.

Because of its relevance to our topic, chapter seven will examine the extensive experimental research into the judgment and decision-making literature. Known also as the heuristics and biases program, these researchers seek to understand empirically, via experimental procedures, how people actually make judgments, and then compare that to how they ought to make them. It becomes evident that human knowledge, as manifested in judgments and decisions, is limited by internal constraints that aren't easily (if ever) corrected. Subsequently, chapter eight will conclude our non-theological overview by noting the not-so-obvious fact that much of what we claim to know comes in the form of prediction. This being so, it will examine how or if such "knowledge" can be legitimately included in what we can claim to know. Though we deal with expert judgment in various chapters, chapter eight will discuss the comprehensive research of Philip Tetlock, which spanned the years 1984 to 2004, on the accuracy of expert predictions. Given our cultural reliance on expert forecasts, this chapter will ask how justified we can be in trusting such pronouncements. What the research will show is that knowledge of the future, while potentially valuable in some respects, is constrained by certain factors inherent in the human condition.

Rounding out our analysis, the final four chapters will deal with the question of our knowledge of God. With the failure of certain attempts to bar claims to knowledge of God before they begin, debates between theists and critics have tended to take on a more *a posteriori* form (i.e., they are based on concrete evidence), centering around particular arguments and evaluating specific evidence for or against. Thus, these chapters explore various arguments for God's existence, including Alvin Plantinga's case for Reformed Epistemology; the argument from Big Bang cosmology and origin of life research, which challenges the traditional Darwinian account of evolutionary development; and a case for the historicity of the bodily resurrection of Jesus of Nazareth. In addition to laying out the arguments themselves, we'll also examine the logical form they typically take and discuss exactly what and how much each one claims to show.

Chapter 1

What Is Knowledge?

Until June of 1979, scientists were convinced that bacteria can't grow in the stomach, because stomachs are acidic. Because stomachs are acidic, they must be sterile, it was thought—a fact so well known it was practically dogma in the field of medicine.[1] Then, Robin Warren (a pathologist at the Royal Perth Hospital in Australia) discovered *H. pylori*, when he began to notice through his microscope bacteria that were curved like croissants and that flattened the brushy surface of the stomach's lining. Colleagues couldn't see it initially, but after magnifying them to one thousand times, and then with an electron microscope, they eventually saw what Warren was referring to, but they still didn't see his point. The dogma of the sterile stomach insisted that bacteria couldn't live in the gut, so even though others had sporadically noticed it (dating all the way back to 1875), experts knew that whatever it was it couldn't be bacteria. The trouble is that they were wrong, and Warren was right.

The concern in this chapter is the larger question of how any of us, not just Warren's skeptical colleagues, knows what we claim to know. The question isn't simply what justified *them* in being certain that the stomach is sterile, but how we can know that *we're* justified in our beliefs. Is it possible that we're more like Warren's colleagues, holding dogmatically to long-standing assumptions? These are the types of issues that philosophers have been grappling with for centuries in a field called epistemology (the theory of knowledge). Cutting to the heart of what it means to know, they've considered questions such as: What is required for a belief to be

---

[1] Kevin Ashton, *How to Fly a Horse: The Secret History of Creation, Invention, and Discovery* (New York, 2015) 91-95.

considered not only true, but justified or grounded in good reason? From what source(s) do we derive our knowledge: from our senses or our minds? If from our senses, do they give us an accurate picture of the way the world really is, or do our minds simply construct a world consistent with our social context? And should our musings on such things have any connection to what can be empirically demonstrated, such as through the methods of the natural sciences?

These are the problems we will explore in this chapter. As we'll see, it's not just that such issues lie at the heart of what it means to know, but also that they provide the appropriate point of departure for our later discussions about how we actually form judgments, what we can know from science, and if there are inherent constraints on what we can know of God. (Note: Because our present aim is to provide an overview of the topic as seen by philosophers, and that in a single chapter, we'll have to bypass a great deal of material. Ambitious, no doubt, but necessary.)

Given all this, let's begin with the traditional approach to what does and does not constitute knowledge.

Traditional View: Knowledge is Justified True Belief

What are the prerequisites for knowing something, as opposed to just believing it or wishing it to be true? Philosophers have discussed various requirements, but the classical expression—called "justified true belief" (JTB)—involves the three following components:[2]

S knows that p if and only if

1. p is true;
2. S believes that p;
3. S is justified in believing that p.

Let's unpack each of these in turn. First, a statement must be true, which implies that what isn't true can't be knowledge. If someone claims to know that someone is dead, after which that same person turns up very much alive, then he really didn't know it. *Thinking* you know something isn't the same as knowing it. Knowing is thus different from believing, wondering,

---

[2] Jonathan Jenkins Ichikawa and Matthias Steup, "The Analysis of Knowledge," The Stanford Encyclopedia of Philosophy (Summer 2018 Edition), ed. Edward N. Zalta, https://plato.stanford.edu/archives/sum2018/entries/knowledge-analysis/.

speculating, or hoping, all of which merely describe a person's state of mind. But the requirement for truth isn't enough. It was true that bacteria were in the stomach long before Robin Warren discovered it; despite this, physicians and researchers couldn't say they knew it. Why? Because knowing involves not just a statement's truth, but a person's awareness of its truth, which is the second requirement. We'd think it strange for someone to say, "I know that the earth is round, but I don't believe it."[3] Still, even having a proposition be true and believing it to be so isn't enough for someone to *know* that it's true. Suppose a person believes there's going to be a tornado tomorrow in his home town. Not only is the sky clear and the weather calm, but weather forecasters predict nothing of the kind. To everyone's surprise, however, a tornado rips through the town anyhow. His statement turned out to be true and he believed it, but did he *know* it? The same holds for the person that has an overabundant confidence in his predictions. He believes that the next throw of dice will be double-sixes. The throw is made and it's double-sixes. Did he really know it? Most would agree that lucky guesses aren't knowledge.

Thus, to know requires a third component, which states that there must be good evidence for believing a proposition. A person with knowledge must not only believe p, he must have good *reason* for believing p—otherwise his belief is just a lucky guess. In other words, you must have justified belief if you want to claim you know something. But since evidence is a matter of degree, how much evidence is adequate? How do I know the chair exists on which I sit? Don't I know that I've lived on earth for a certain time, and that it's been here long before I was born? Do I know who my parents are? Do I have sufficient evidence for any of this for me to say that I *know*? After all, as Bertrand Russell suggested, it's possible that the earth was created five minutes ago, complete with memories.

Consider another example that was offered by John Hospers.[4] Do you know there are chairs in the room next door? You walked by ten minutes ago and they were there, but can you say you know they're there now? Isn't it possible that in the last few minutes someone came and emptied the chairs out of the room, or that you were mistaken in what you saw? It might be argued that only when the evidence is complete, so that nothing could place the statement in doubt, can we say we know. In that case, you didn't really know the chairs were next door at the time you made the statement. To see

---

[3] John Hospers, *An Introduction to Philosophical Analysis* (New Jersey, 1988), 21ff.
[4] John Hospers, *An Introduction to Philosophical Analysis*, 23-4.

how this is so, consider two scenarios. In the first, you say the chairs are there, go next door, and indeed they're there. In the second, you say the chairs are there, go next door and, to your surprise, the room is empty. The only difference between the two is that in the first case the chairs were there and in the second they weren't. Yet at the point you made the statement, the evidence in the two cases *was exactly the same.* You surely didn't know the chairs were there in case two, when they weren't there; so you didn't know either in the first case when they were. One might suggest that your educated guess wasn't exactly knowledge.

At this point, a distinction could be made between a weak and strong sense of what it means to know. In the weak sense, you did know because you believed a proposition—for good reasons—that turned out to be true. But in the strong sense, you didn't know because your evidence (even though good) was incomplete. There was still more evidence you could have had. In this sense, you don't know until there's nothing more that could cast doubt on your claim to know. Thus, in the strong sense, you can't know anything that you're not perceiving right now, not even that there *is* a room next door.

But is even seeing for yourself enough? People have had hallucinations. Sometimes they think they're seeing one thing instead of another, or they see what they want to see (a phenomenon experts call schema-based errors). An example of the latter was demonstrated in an experiment involving rooms people had visited before; in this case, it was the graduate student office. When asked to recall the room and what was in it, participants frequently reported books that weren't there. Pre-existing schemas created the *expectation* of seeing books, so participants included them in later recollections. They retroactively included the plausible presence of books in their memories.[5]

The skeptic might react to such cases by saying that, if we admit our senses are sometimes faulty, then perhaps they *always* are. While this is theoretically possible, most philosophers nevertheless agree that we know some things about the world and that the bar skeptics erect is unreasonably high.

Problems with the Traditional View

Although most philosophers agree that each component of the JTB theory is *necessary* for knowledge, there's a consensus that the components aren't

---

[5] William F. Brewer, "What is Recollective Memory?" in *Remembering Our Past: Studies in Autobiographical Memory*, ed. David C. Rubin (Cambridge, 1995), 44-45, 50.

collectively *sufficient*.[6] This is because there appear to be cases of justified true belief that still fall short of knowledge. Consider two counterexamples to the JTB theory. First, imagine that we're looking for water on a hot day and suddenly see water, or so we think.[7] As it turns out, we're not seeing water but only a mirage. However, after reaching the spot where we think we saw water, we get lucky and find water right under a rock. Can we say we had genuine knowledge of water? The answer seems to be no. We were just lucky.

Our second counterexample, and perhaps a bit more difficult to follow, was proposed by Edmund Gettier:[8]

Suppose Smith has good evidence for the false proposition

1. Jones owns a Ford.

Smith's evidence may be that, according to his memory, Jones has at all times in the past owned a Ford and that Jones just offered Smith a ride while driving a Ford. Now imagine that Smith has another friend, Brown, of whose whereabouts he's completely ignorant.

Suppose that Smith infers from number 1 the following three disjunctions (Note: A disjunction is a compound statement formed by joining two statements with the connector "or," so that a disjunction is false if and only if both statements are false; otherwise it's true.[9])

2. Either Jones owns a Ford or Brown is in Boston.
3. Either Jones owns a Ford or Brown is in Barcelona.
4. Either Jones owns a Ford or Brown is in Brest-Litovsk.

---

[6] Jonathan Jenkins Ichikawa and Matthias Steup, "The Analysis of Knowledge," The Stanford Encyclopedia of Philosophy (Summer 2018 Edition), ed. Edward N. Zalta, https://plato.stanford.edu/archives/sum2018/entries/knowledge-analysis/.
[7] Jonathan Jenkins Ichikawa and Matthias Steup, "The Analysis of Knowledge," The Stanford Encyclopedia of Philosophy (Summer 2018 Edition), ed. Edward N. Zalta, https://plato.stanford.edu/archives/sum2018/entries/knowledge-analysis/.
[8] Edmund L. Gettier, "Is Justified True Belief Knowledge?" *Analysis*, vol. 23, no. 6, 1963, 121–123. *JSTOR*, www.jstor.org/stable/3326922.
[9] I'm indebted to Professor Lex Newman (University of Utah) for pointing out that, though the Gettier problem gets its traction from cases of "inclusive" disjunction (e.g., "x and/or y" as defined above), there are also cases of "exclusive" disjunction (e.g., "x or y, but not both").

Since (1) entails (2) through (4), and since Smith recognizes this, his beliefs (2)-(4) are justified. Now suppose that Brown, by sheer coincidence, is in fact in Barcelona. But is Smith's belief knowledge? The answer seems to be no because it was mere luck that it turned out to be true. Thus, it seems that even true beliefs that are justified can still be lucky, and therefore inconsistent with knowledge.

Reliabilist and Causal Theories of Knowledge

In order to prevent lucky guesses from counting as knowledge, many philosophers have added to the traditional view a condition that should be included with truth and belief—and replace justification—as components of knowledge. One of those is the idea of reliability. What seems problematic about lucky guesses is that they're formed in a way that it's unlikely they should turn out to be true. Knowledge reliabilism argues that it's unreliability, and not lack of justification, that prevents such beliefs from amounting to knowledge. Thus, reliabilist theories incorporate a reliability condition into knowledge, stated as follows:[10]

S knows that p if and only if

1. p is true;
2. S believes that p;
3. S's belief that p was produced by a reliable cognitive process.

This view replaces the justification component of the JTB theory with a reliability clause. Proponents argue that those who think that knowledge requires something *other than* reliably produced true belief are adding unnecessary requirements. If we have a reliable belief-generating mechanism and we act on the beliefs generated, what additional benefit does the idea of justification confer?

The attractiveness of reliabilism can be illustrated with an example (proposed by Richard Feldman). Two bird-watchers, a novice and an expert, together see a pink-spotted flycatcher on a branch. Both form a belief that it's a pink-spotted flycatcher. The expert is justified in believing this but the novice isn't, as the latter jumps to the conclusion out of excitement.

---

[10] Jonathan Jenkins Ichikawa and Matthias Steup, "The Analysis of Knowledge," The Stanford Encyclopedia of Philosophy (Summer 2018 Edition), ed. Edward N. Zalta, https://plato.stanford.edu/archives/sum2018/entries/knowledge-analysis/.

Reliabilism says that the crucial difference between the two lies in the difference between their respective belief-forming processes.[11] The expert connects what he sees with his vast experience with pink-spotted fly-catchers, but the novice does no such thing; he just guesses. Meaning that the expert's method of identification is reliable, whereas the novice's isn't.

Similar to reliabilism, causal theories of knowledge replace the justification component in the JTB theory with a condition requiring a causal connection between the belief and the fact believed, as follows:

S knows that p if and only if

1. p is true;
2. S believes that p;
3. S's belief that p is caused by the fact that p.

Although some have suggested that reliabilism and causal theories fare better than the JTB theory with respect to the Gettier cases mentioned above, many argue that they don't. None of the theories thus far completely succeed in stating sufficient conditions for knowledge. While the debate over this will no doubt continue, some have suggested that, unless we're to surrender to radical skepticism (in which case we don't know *any* of what we ordinarily think we do), some forms of luck ought to be considered compatible with knowledge.

What About Our Concepts? Rationalism vs. Empiricism

Having described the traditional theory, we need to take a step back and ask an even more fundamental question: where do we get the very concepts that form the basis of our claims to know? The two most prominent answers to this—known as rationalism and empiricism—part company based on whether concepts originate from sense experience or whether we get at least some from pure reason. As you'll see, each position can affect how a person sees justified belief.

We'll begin our discussion with rationalism, which in general argues that we can by pure reason know at least some substantive (non-trivial) truths about the real world.[12] More specifically, rationalism

---

[11] Alvin Goldman and Bob Beddor, "Reliabilist Epistemology," The Stanford Encyclopedia of Philosophy (Summer 2021 Edition), ed. Edward N. Zalta, https://plato.stanford.edu/archives/sum2021/entries/reliabilism/.
[12] Paul Helm, *Faith and Understanding* (Grand Rapids, 1997), 5-6.

adopts one of at least two claims. The first is the intuition/deduction thesis, which says that some propositions are knowable by intuition alone, while others are knowable by being deduced from intuited propositions.[13] According to this view, intuition is a form of rational insight in which we intellectually grasp a proposition and just "see" it to be true in a way that forms a true, justified belief. In order to understand how rationalists make the move from intuited truths to others based in them, it will help first to explain how philosophers see deduction (and, conversely, induction).

Deduction is a process in which we derive conclusions from premises through valid arguments, such that the conclusion must be true if the premises are true. The following commonly cited example will help.

1. All men are mortal.
2. Socrates is a man.
3. Therefore, Socrates is mortal.

A deductive argument makes the claim that its conclusion is supported by its premises *conclusively* such that, if the premises are true, then its conclusion *must* be true.[14] A deductive argument can either be correct or not correct; when it is correct, logicians call it valid (if not, then invalid). When an argument is valid and all of its premises are true, then it's considered sound. If a deductive argument isn't sound—i.e., if the argument isn't valid or if not all its premises are true—it fails to establish the truth of its conclusion, even if the conclusion is true. In contrast, inductive arguments make no such claim and are based solely on probability; their premises support their conclusions, but always fall short of certainty, as the following illustrates:

1. Most corporate lawyers are conservatives.
2. Angela Palmieri is a corporate lawyer.
3. Therefore Angela Palmieri is probably a conservative.[15]

---

[13] Peter Markie, "Rationalism vs. Empiricism," The Stanford Encyclopedia of Philosophy (Fall 2017 Edition), ed. Edward N. Zalta, https://plato.stanford.edu /archives/fall2017/entries/rationalism-empiricism/.

[14] Irving M. Copi and Carl Cohen, *Introduction to Logic*, eleventh ed. (New Jersey, 2002), 42-50.

[15] Irving M. Copi and Carl Cohen, *Introduction to Logic*, 44.

As you can see, the difference between deduction and induction lies in the *relation* between the premises and conclusion, with the former having a necessary connection and the latter only a more or less probable connection.

Returning now to our first rationalist thesis, proponents argue that intuition and deduction provide us with *a priori* knowledge, meaning knowledge that's gained independently of sense experience (with *a posteriori* knowledge being after, or based on, sense experience). Mathematics often serves as an example of *a priori* knowledge—for example, that 2+2=4 or that the number 3 is prime and greater than two. Other examples might include statements such as "All bachelors are unmarried males" or "All vixens are female."[16] One thing to note is that these statements are true by definition and don't establish that there *are* any bachelors or vixens in the real world (which is something that only sense experience can do).[17] But claims that certain *a priori* knowledge gives us substantive truths about the real world can get more controversial, as some philosophers have included knowledge of ethical truths and metaphysical claims such as the existence of God. And, as you might guess, the more items rationalists add to a list of *a priori* truths, the more controversial it becomes.

The second rationalism claim is the innate knowledge thesis, which says that we have some truths as part of our rational nature. Our innate knowledge isn't learned through either sense experience or intuition and deduction, for the simple reason that they're part of our nature. Though experiences may trigger a process by which such knowledge springs to consciousness, the experiences don't give us the knowledge itself. It's been with us all along.[18] How? Some rationalists suggest that we gained the knowledge in an earlier existence, while others argue that it was provided by God

---

[16] Bruce Russell, "A Priori Justification and Knowledge," The Stanford Encyclopedia of Philosophy (Summer 2020 Edition), ed. Edward N. Zalta, https://plato.stanford.edu /archives/sum2020/entries/apriori/.

[17] Many philosophers have drawn a distinction between analytic statements (e.g., "All bachelors are unmarried") and synthetic statements (e.g., "There is a book on this table"), the former true by definition and the latter an empirical claim open to falsification. While the analytic-synthetic distinction is common, it was challenged by W. V. Quine in "Two Dogmas of Empiricism," in *From a Logical Point of View: 9 Logico-Philosophical Essays* (Cambridge, 1953), 20-46. See also Hilary Putnam, "The analytic and the synthetic," in *Mind, Language and Reality: Philosophical Papers,* vol. 2 (Cambridge, 1975), 33-69.

[18] Markie, Peter, "Rationalism vs. Empiricism," The Stanford Encyclopedia of Philosophy (Fall 2017 Edition), ed. Edward N. Zalta, https://plato.stanford.edu /archives/fall2017/entries/rationalism-empiricism/.

at creation, while still others say it's part of our nature through natural selection.

One consequence of rationalism is its denial of skepticism for at least some areas of knowledge. If we claim to know some truths with *a priori* certainty, as rationalists do, then we obviously reject skepticism concerning those truths. Also, rationalism is committed to a position known as foundationalism: the view that we know some truths apart from basing them on any others, and that we then use this foundational knowledge to know additional truths.

On the other end of the spectrum is the empiricist thesis, which argues that we have no source of knowledge other than sense experience. It rejects the rationalist theses above in that, insofar as we know something, our knowledge of it is *a posteriori*, dependent on sense experience, which is our only source of ideas. Empiricism doesn't hold that we automatically have empirical knowledge, only that it can be gained (if at all) by experience. Having said this, it's important to point out that rationalism and empiricism need not conflict at all times. We can be rationalists in math and empiricists in all or some of the natural sciences. They conflict only when speaking oppositely about the same subject. The seventeenth-century empiricist John Locke rejected the innate knowledge thesis, but adopted the intuition/deduction thesis with regard to our knowledge of God's existence.[19] One could similarly argue the same for our knowledge of morals and yet retain empiricism elsewhere.

Nevertheless, when speaking to the same subject from opposite directions, the terms rationalism and empiricism are important, especially as they relate to our knowledge of the external (mind-independent) world. Here, the rationalist holds that some truths concerning the external world can and must be known *a priori*, that some of our ideas required for that knowledge must be innate, and that this knowledge is superior to any that sense experience could provide.[20] The empiricist replies that our knowledge of the external world, along with our ideas about it, are gained only by experience, which is the sole source of information. As David Hume (1711-1776) argued, intuition and deduction can provide us with knowledge of necessary

[19] John Locke, *An Essay Concerning Human Understanding,* vol. 1, collated and annotated by Alexander Campbell Fraser (New York, 1959), 37ff. John Locke, *An Essay Concerning Human Understanding,* vol. 2, 306ff.

[20] Peter Markie, "Rationalism vs. Empiricism," The Stanford Encyclopedia of Philosophy (Fall 2017 Edition), ed. Edward N. Zalta, https://plato.stanford.edu/archives/fall2017/entries/rationalism-empiricism/.

truths, such as those of mathematics and logic, but it isn't substantive knowledge of the external world. It's only knowledge of the relations of our own ideas.[21] (Note that while we'll later examine evidence that the mind plays a role in the acquisition of knowledge, this fact doesn't require the adoption of the innate concept thesis.)

Before leaving the idea of certainty and probability, we should note that much of contemporary philosophy embraces a position known as fallibilism, i.e., the thesis that no belief can ever be rationally justified in a conclusive way. According to this view, there will always remain possible doubt as to the truth of a belief, which includes not only our commonsense views but also our most cherished scientific claims.[22] For most philosophers, it also means that people can know things on the basis of inductive, perceptual, or testimonial evidence—as opposed to the more strict requirement that knowledge can only be based on deductive arguments in which the evidence entails what it is evidence for.[23]

Appearance and Reality

Although there's controversy concerning whether we can gain substantive (*a priori*) knowledge via reason alone, most philosophers give at least some weight to the knowledge gained with our senses. Nevertheless, there are times when our senses lead us astray and cause us to make errors of judgment. Things aren't always what they appear, which means that we need to make a distinction between appearances and reality itself. This is usually shown in several ways.

First, there are illusions, of which we can cite the following examples. (1) The stick immersed in the water looks bent, but you pull it out and it's straight; (2) The trees in the distance look grayish-blue, but you still believe they're green; (3) The train tracks appear to converge in the distance yet you know they remain parallel; (4) The two parallel lines in the Muller-Lyer illusion (one with arrows pointing inwards, the other with arrows pointing outwards) are obviously different, with the bottom line

---

[21] David Hume, *An Essay Concerning Human Understanding*, ed. Anthony Flew (La Salle, 1988), 71ff.

[22] Stephen Hetherington, *Internet Encyclopedia of Philosophy*, https://iep.utm.edu /fallibil/.

[23] Richard Feldman, "Fallibilism and Knowing That One Knows," *The Philosophical Review*, vol. 90, no. 2 (Apr., 1981), 266-7.

longer than the one above it.[24] However, when you measure them with a ruler, you see that they're identical in length. Now, if asked about their length, you can say you know the truth. Even so, you still see one line as longer; (5) You place one hand in hot water, the other in cold water; then you place both hands in lukewarm water. The lukewarm water feels warm to one hand and cold to the other, but we believe the water is lukewarm all the time—it just seems hot or cold.[25] When we believe that something appears to have one quality but actually has a different quality, we're misled by perceptual illusions.

The upside is that we deal with them often enough that we're accustomed to them. A lifetime of experience with depth perception tells us that, if two objects look identical in size but one appears farther away, then it must be larger than it actually looks.[26] Except in extreme cases, most philosophers would say that (normally) seeing an object gives you situational justification for believing something about it. The evidence of the senses usually provides justification for your beliefs with content appropriate to that evidence.[27] If your experience is of a brown expanse, you're justified in believing there's something brown before you; if it's of something warm in your hand, you're justified in believing there's something warm in your hand. Thus, when a visual belief arises in a way that you believe something either because you see *that* it is so or see it *to be* so, normally the belief is justified.

But what about hallucinations? Sometimes people perceive things that aren't there at all. While illusions and hallucinations have some commonalities, as long as we know the nature of the error, it doesn't make that much difference what we call it. What matters is that the error doesn't lie in our senses, but in our *judgments*.[28] Perceptual errors are errors of judgment. Fortunately, the same senses that can lead us into mistakes also enable us to correct the mistakes. If a momentary experience leads us to a mistaken judgment, further experience leads us to discover that the original judgment was mistaken.

---

[24] Daniel Kahneman, *Thinking, Fast and Slow* (New York, 2011), 26-7.

[25] John Hospers, *An Introduction to Philosophical Analysis*, 52-3.

[26] Gerald Zaltman, *How Customers Think: Essential Insights Into the Mind of the Market* (Boston, 2003), 65-7. Note Zaltman's discussion of the "larger" creature chasing the "smaller" one.

[27] Robert Audi, *Epistemology: A Contemporary introduction to the Theory of Knowledge* (London, 2000), 19, 24-6.

[28] John Hospers, *An Introduction to Philosophical Analysis*, 53-4.

Commonsense Realism and Phenomenalism

From what we've seen, it's hard to deny that we're sometimes led to errors of judgment because things aren't always what they appear to be; appearances and reality aren't always identical. But having made such a distinction, an even trickier question becomes unavoidable: is the physical world as we normally perceive it an exact copy of the physical world as it really is, or is the reality "out there" different from our perception of it? Various answers have been offered, which, as we'll see, not only come to some surprising conclusions but can have some rather serious consequences. (Note: the phrase *sense data,* as used below, refers to what we immediately perceive whenever we're perceiving something, without regard to whether there's anything "out there" that corresponds to our perception.)

Commonsense realism is the view that the sense data people have when their senses aren't impaired are accurate copies of the physical world—and that the physical world isn't *constituted* by sense data in any way. Accordingly, there is a real physical world that causes us to have the perceptions we do, which are exact copies of the qualities that are really present in those objects.[29] An object that appears to be blue really is blue; an object that appears to be hard or cold or smooth really is such. The physical world exists and in no way depends on our observation of it for its existence. Thus, if all perceivers disappeared, the physical world as we perceive it would still exist.

At odds with commonsense realism, phenomenalism maintains that the physical world is the inferred totality of our sense data, and doesn't exist apart from sense data. Thus, the physical world is completely dependent on the perceptions of a perceiver for its existence. If all perceivers disappeared, the physical world would cease to exist. While phenomenalism garners some support in professional circles, many argue that it's reductionistic and fails to account for much of what seems to be true about our experience. Throughout this book, we'll focus on a more nuanced view known as critical realism, i.e., the view that the sense data we have directly when perceiving the physical world are in some ways similar to the characteristics objectively present in the physical world, and in other ways dissimilar. But before we discuss this, we first need to explore another option that's taken root in some academic and cultural circles.

---

[29] William H. Halverson, *A Concise Introduction to Philosophy* (New York, 1981), 105ff.

Retreat to Relativism

Commonsense realism is often seen as naïve, given the fact that sometimes our senses deceive us. A stick immersed in water looks like it's bent, and there's no point of view you can adopt to make it look any other way. The only reason you know it's not really bent is because it's straight when removed from the water. Or, think about the mirage that a desert traveler sees. He sees it just as clearly as we see real trees and stones, but because he can never reach and drink the water, he calls it an illusion.

But what if our senses don't really give us an accurate understanding of the real world at all? What if we're unable to garner any objective knowledge of things "out there" and are instead chained to subjective viewpoints, shaped either by our own constructions or that of society? Going the opposite direction of commonsense realism, postmodernism argues that everything, including the natural sciences, is a human construction. Knowing reality in an objective way is unachievable;[30] all knowledge is therefore relative. Because of this, postmodernists adopt a position known as anti-realism, which denies that we can know the world as it is and only can understand it as it has been socially constructed at a particular time. The natural sciences, along with all human knowledge, are held to be culturally or socially constructed, which can be deconstructed to expose and eliminate the power structures holding them up. Sociologist Harvie Ferguson thus claims that the major developments in physics are the result of the "bourgeois consciousness."[31] Modern physics, it follows, has nothing to do with representing the inner structure of the physical world, but rather simply reflects deeper sociological forces.

Postmodernists will argue the same for other areas, including religion (and especially Christianity), which, being a social construction, can simply have its ideas and rites explained by patterns of power. Jacques Derrida's "there is nothing outside the text" encapsulates the postmodern denial that words refer to a reality beyond words; this is extended to the rejection of the idea that scientific theories refer to anything in the real world. Since being bound by evidence seems troubling to postmodernist thinkers, realism (whatever its form) is thought to demean us by denying the creativity and freedom they regard as the hallmark of excellence. Rather than inhabiting a world inherited from those before us or being accountable to evidence, we

---

[30] Alister E. McGrath, *A Scientific Theology*, vol. 2, (Grand Rapids, 2002), 55-6.
[31] Alister E. McGrath, *A Scientific Theology*, vol. 2, 178-9.

construct our own worlds. Along similar lines, social constructivists argue that communities construct ideas and values to suit their own needs. These aren't considered responses to reality, but rather a construction reflecting the interests and agendas of specific social groups. Thus, scientists generate ideas that suit their own interests and advance their own agendas and power structures.

Having said this, a caveat is in order since there's an important difference between the weak and strong constructivist program.[32] The former holds that the development of scientific theories can't be explained solely with reference to the external world, but needs to account for at least some social influences. The latter, more radical position, holds that the external world plays no role in the development of scientific theories. The former is true in an obvious sense, in that the observer's historical and social location determines his access to the external world, both in terms of available technology and the social factors that play a role in the reception of scientific theories.

Though we'll have more to say on this, there's little doubt that social factors condition the manner in which reality is represented. The news media, for example, claims to offer its consumers an objective view of the world, while in reality it delivers a socially and ideologically conditioned narrative. Yet sociologists arguing for strong constructivism go beyond such observations and argue that social phenomena simply don't have any objective existence at all, but must be interpreted and provided meaning by those encountering them. All knowledge of the world, including the natural sciences, is a human construction rather than a mirror of an independent reality. Power and politics determine which constructed view of the world reigns at any particular moment.

However, the constructivist thesis that social factors completely *determine*, as opposed to influence, our perception and representation of reality is fraught with difficulties. Alister McGrath notes that it's almost embarrassingly self-referential. If postmodernism and social constructivism are to be proved, then a case must be made from the available evidence, which would include various case studies. But since all knowledge is relative and wholly constructed, then this perspective *itself* is incapable of supporting the grand claim that everything is relative. That all things are relative assumes

---

[32] Alister E. McGrath, *A Scientific Theology*, vol. 2, 181ff. See also Philip Pettit, "The Strong Sociology of Knowledge Without Relativism" in *Relativism and Realism in Science*, ed. Robert Nola (Dordrecht, 1988), 81-91.

a "God's eye" view capable of at least making the relativity claim. In other words, in order to demonstrate that truths are relative, it has to assume at least *enough* objectivity to support the social constructivist claim. But that's precisely what it cannot do, since it claims that no objectivity exists. As with all forms of relativism, its truth simultaneously implies its negation, with the consequence that it falls on its own axe.

Beyond this, there's the practical reality that the postmodernist and constructivist thesis is unlivable. When barreling down the road at 65 miles per hour while approaching a stop light, we have to assume (in order to continue to live) a realist position that there are other cars that pose a danger once the light goes red. When going to the pharmacy to get aspirin, we implicitly assume there *is* a reality outside of our language and that when we ask for aspirin, it actually makes a difference if we're given arsenic instead.[33] Finally, postmodernism and social constructivism fail to explain why the natural sciences have been so successful and useful. McGrath puts it as follows:

> Why do the laws of physics prove resilient to issues of gender, race, or social class—to name only the three most obvious factors in a constructivist account? And why can these laws be represented by mathematics, when mathematics must also be regarded as social construction, reflecting the power play of interest groups? ... Postmodernity has defeated itself, by deploying weapons that could be used more effectively against it than in its support.[34]

In the end, such forms of relativism seem to be hopelessly inadequate accounts of knowledge. With that said, let's explore a more nuanced approach.

Maximizing Advantages: Critical Realism

Unlike the relativist, critical realism argues that there's no reason to conclude that, because our senses deceive some of the time, they deceive all the time. In fact, it's only on the assumption that they don't deceive all the time that we can identify our perceptions of the bent stick and mirage as illusory. What such examples show is that it's difficult to say that the physical world

---

[33] Alister E. McGrath, *A Scientific Theology*, vol. 2, 180, 191-2.
[34] Alister E. McGrath, *A Scientific Theology*, vol. 2, 191-2.

exactly corresponds to our perceptions of it. At most, we can say that the world is like some, or even the majority, of our perceptions.

Critical realism is a way of describing the process of knowing that acknowledges the reality of the thing known and that it's something other than the knower (thus, "realism")—while also acknowledging that the knower is involved in the knowing process (thus, "critical").[35] So while accepting the fact that we know a reality that's "out there" and separate from the knower, critical realism affirms the need for a critical reflection on what we say about reality and sees it as provisional. There's always a possibility that our judgments might fail to represent the world as it is. According to this account (against postmodernism and constructivism) knowledge concerns realities that are independent of the knower. Nevertheless, critical realism accepts (against commonsense realism) that knowledge is never completely independent and is in some ways modified by the knower. The attainment of knowledge is always an approximation of the truth, not absolute truth.

While we'll devote a chapter to critical realism in the sciences (particularly on the work of Roy Bhaskar), for now it's enough to point out that critical realism enables us to solve some of the puzzles about perception that cause problems for commonsense realism. It explains the fact that alterations in a perceiver result in certain changes in the person's perception: for instance, that what's perceived to be hot or cold at one time may be perceived to be warm at another, without itself changing—or simultaneously, if one hand is warm and the other cold.[36] Colors too can appear different to different people depending on whether they're color blind or wearing colored glasses. Some people can hear high-pitched signals that are inaudible to others, which is easily explained by the critical realist by recognizing that sound is modified by the hearing apparatus of the perceiver. The same can be said for the differences in what people taste and smell.

Connecting Philosophy and Science

We'll conclude our survey with a position known as naturalistic epistemology, which has gained considerable attention due to its claim to deal more effectively with the problems of traditional epistemology. Difficult to

---

[35] Alister E. McGrath, *A Scientific Theology*, vol. 2, 196-7, 206.
[36] William H. Halverson, *A Concise Introduction to Philosophy*, 111-13.

characterize easily, naturalism should be seen more as a general approach than a specific thesis. Broadly, proponents of naturalistic epistemology argue that there should be a close connection between philosophical investigation (such as knowledge, justification, rationality) and empirical or natural science—a connection which they charge is weakly defined in the traditional approach.[37]

To begin, it will be helpful to look at four assumptions that traditional epistemology adopts, from which naturalism takes its departure. Patrick Ryslew summarizes them as follows: First, much of the discussion over the centuries about the ideas of knowledge, justification, and evidence has been carried out *a priori*; in other words, through reflection rather than empirical investigation. Second, epistemology has traditionally been considered autonomous and independent of the sciences, such that science can't tell us anything about what could inform our answers to those philosophical questions. Epistemology, in other words, has enjoyed priority over science. Third, due to its priority, epistemology was seen as concerning itself with normative matters, meaning it has a *prescriptive* function, i.e., an ability to tell us how we *should* form our beliefs and offering useful advice. Fourth, one of the primary tasks of traditional epistemologists was to articulate a response to skepticism. That is, they sought to establish not only that we do have some justified beliefs but also how best to avoid error. Though naturalists vary, they all reject one or more of these features of the traditional approach.

While epistemology, traditionally conceived, attempted to provide an analysis of the *concept* of knowledge (usually its necessary and sufficient conditions), naturalists (for example, Hilary Kornblith) argue that epistemology should provide an account of certain natural phenomena, namely, knowledge itself. It should investigate knowledge as a phenomenon in the world, and this distinguishes naturalism from traditional approaches. It should proceed by looking at clear cases of knowledge and then finding what they have in common. Emerging from this is a picture of the true nature of knowledge, fitting a reliabilist framework: knowledge consists in true beliefs that are reliably produced. Through an empirical investigation of the mechanisms of belief formation and retention, we can determine where we're most in need of guidance and what steps can be

---

[37] Patrick Rysiew, "Naturalism in Epistemology," The Stanford Encyclopedia of Philosophy (Fall 2020 Edition), ed. Edward N. Zalta, https://plato.stanford.edu /archives/fall2020/entries/epistemology-naturalized/>.

taken to overcome our shortcomings. Truth is the epistemic goal, as we should care about having a cognitive system that produces true beliefs reliably. That is, we should care about evaluating not just individual beliefs, but our various systems and methods for producing them (in terms of their reliability).

In a slightly different fashion, David Papineau argues that epistemology should aim at telling us how to get the right beliefs and avoid doxastic error. An epistemological theory should specify a certain type of technique for acquiring beliefs, and then make recommendations about how to avoid error. When a belief derives from such a technique, the theory is *justified*, and when a justified belief is also true, then it is said to be *knowledge* (provided its truth isn't an accident).

According to Papineau, we embody a set of perceptual belief-forming habits which generate beliefs in response to non-conscious stimuli (perception being defined as the *non-inferential adoption of beliefs* via the operation of our sense organs). We should consider our dispositions to form beliefs in various circumstances, and then evaluate the reliability of those habits for truth.[38] That is, we can consider what belief-forming habits we actually engage in and then consider whether or not those habits are reliable for discovering truth. And if we determine that the process is unreliable, we should reconstruct ourselves as belief-formers. Thus, a correct technique for acquiring beliefs is simply to be a reliable belief-former, i.e., to have belief-forming processes that generally produce true beliefs. This means that an actual belief is justified if it arises from a reliable process. (Note that a naturalized notion of justification doesn't necessarily involve conscious inference, because, whereas our perceptual and memory processes deliver beliefs into consciousness, the processes leading up to those beliefs are outside consciousness.)

Papineau puts it as follows:

> You want to be a reliable belief-former? Well then, you'd better do what has to be done to bring this about. In particular, you'd better investigate what belief-forming processes you embody, and you'd better consider what alternative such habits you might adopt. And then you'd better investigate which of those habits, actual and possible, are reliable for generating truths. And having done all that, you should take steps to rid yourself of any bad,

---

[38] David Papineau, *Reality and Representation* (Oxford, 1987), 124, 129-32. Papineau takes habits to involve perceptual, memory, inductive, and deductive dispositions.

unreliable habits you already have, and take steps to instill any good, reliable ones that are open to you.[39]

Take Galileo as an example. When critiquing the "tower argument"— the observation that a stone dropped from a tower falls straight down— leveled against Copernican heliocentrism, Galileo argued that, despite appearances, a stone isn't falling straight down in an inertial reference frame. In other words, since the earth itself is moving, people are misled into thinking that slanting stones are falling straight. Papineau suggests that Galileo's critique shouldn't be seen as new theoretical conclusions *within* a current belief system, but rather as a *reconstruction* of himself as a belief-former. The practical implications for all knowers, from a naturalized point of view, is that we should do what we can to make sure we're suitably constructed for coming to the right beliefs in the first place—not be more careful about the theoretical inferences we make within our existing system of beliefs.

So you should think of yourself as a system for generating true beliefs. Since you want to be as reliable as possible, you should consider ways of redesigning the system and then implement those promising improvements. Insofar as you succeed in reliability, you won't need to ask further questions about the soundness of your mental moves. This is because a reliable belief-former is already someone whose initial beliefs are generally true and whose further inferences are generally truth-preserving.

As attractive as naturalism has proven to be, Hillel Einhorn (in completely unrelated literature on heuristics) hints at some possible problems.[40] Naturalist proponents argue, as does Papineau, that our belief-forming processes (or habits) are vindicated by whether they generate truth—and that the feedback from actual results should spur us on to redesign ourselves to be better at generating truth. But it can often be that positive (or negative) feedback can mislead us into thinking either that our habits are reliable or not. Einhorn asks us to imagine that we've judged the probability of some event to be .70, and that the event doesn't happen. What does the outcome tell us about the quality of the rules used to generate the

---

[39] David Papineau, *Reality and Representation*, 126, 135-6, 138-9.

[40] Hillel J. Einhorn, "Learning from Experience and Suboptimal Rules in Decision Making," in *Judgment Under Uncertainty: Heuristics and Biases*, eds. Danial Kahneman, Paul Slovic, and Amos Tversky (New York, 1982), 275-6.

judgment? Because small samples are often misleading[41]—since they can artificially skew results—relying on any *single* result can cause us to draw the wrong conclusion about our belief-forming processes. In an important sense, immediate outcome information is irrelevant for correcting our belief-forming processes.

It seems then that the only way to make it work would be to keep a history of the relative frequency of outcomes when we judge events with a certain probability that we can check against actual outcomes. But how practical is this? We'd first have to determine how much history is sufficient to decide whether our habits are or aren't calibrated to truth. We'd also need to decide how close is close enough to say that the habits are truth-producing. Even if we can come up with good answers, it's important to note that this way of evaluating outcomes is delayed for long periods, meaning that it's unclear how helpful it really is. So it's not certain that such feedback will necessarily be self-correcting, as the naturalist seems to think. Further, in order to learn about the goodness of our belief-forming processes, our history must include not only our estimates and outcomes, but also an articulation of the processes used for deriving those estimates. Since it's likely that many different belief-forming processes could have been used to estimate probabilities in different situations, the outcome information is irrelevant unless we're aware of—and have recorded *at the time*—the processes we used. Lastly, because much of what goes into our belief-forming processes lies outside consciousness, it's hard to understand what the naturalist is recommending we do to correct habits over which we have no direct control.

None of this is to suggest that this would be impossible to do, but simply acknowledges the reality of what may be involved. Even if we could do it in one or two areas of our lives, how much energy can a person reasonably exert? No matter what answers are offered, we can say that naturalism—while having problems of its own—at least attempts to connect philosophical analysis with empirical results. And despite its hurdles, it's considered by many philosophers to be a move in the right direction.

---

[41] Charles Wheelan, *Naked Statistics: Stripping the Dread From the Data* (New York, 2013), 113, 138.

Conclusion

Having surveyed some of the key components of knowledge from a philosophical perspective, we can see how easy answers to such issues aren't quickly forthcoming, unless we are willing to settle for simplistic ones. Many of the greatest minds in history have devoted themselves to these problems, and we still lack consensus. Some see human knowledge as possessing inherent constraints and stricter limitations, while others see certain truths as deducible from other truths known solely by the mind of the knower. No matter what position one takes on the questions we've discussed, it's clear that, depending on how we view the capabilities of the mind and from whence it gets its ideas, our optimism about what—and to what degree—we can know can change dramatically. At the very least, exploring even these limited debates should give ample reason as to why it would be foolhardy to treat any purported knowledge of the world as certain and beyond dispute. Legitimate questions about the very nature of knowledge remain and will continue long after we're gone. But it's also apparent that, such questions notwithstanding, most philosophers concede that we do have some justified knowledge of the world, meaning that most would reject the various forms of relativism we've discussed.

One thing that stands out regarding how we've discussed epistemology so far is that it focuses on the individual—on how the knowing agent can use his or her personal cognitive abilities to investigate various questions. While this is important, much of what we claim to know is mediated through social interactions and is therefore acquired from others. In fact, a little reflection reveals that a fairly significant proportion of what we know comes through some sort of testimony, whether from news sources, the groups with which we most identify, religious leaders, and so on. To be sure, we have to use our individual resources (such as our senses and language) and should have already determined that there *are* such people and groups—and, in this sense, any talk of a *social* epistemology rests on individual epistemology—but an independent examination of how people and groups influence our judgments is critical to our understanding of knowledge. Because of that, it's to this social component that we now turn.

Chapter 2
The Social Side of Knowledge

Traditionally conceived, epistemology has been marked by two characteristics. The first is that its focus has been heavily individualistic, since it
sought to define what justified knowledge might look like for an individual
knower. Second, it tended to consider knowledge acquisition in ideal situations, in which knowers have unlimited logical competence and no significant limits in their investigational resources.[1] One of the consequences
was that it examined the knower as an abstraction from his or her social
environment. Rationality (as summed up in Kant's maxim "think for yourself") was understood as sticking to one's own independent judgment. But
recent philosophers have begun to question this as a more romantic ideal
than what actually occurs in the real world. As they correctly point out, a
great deal of what we claim to know comes from some sort of authority or
testimony—experts, news sources, peers, and so on. While we may be able
to escape our dependence on some of these by becoming talented enough
in an area or two, attempting to do so in all fields leaves us uninformed and
irrational in other ways. It seems that if we're to be rational, we can never
avoid dependence on others, owing to the fact that we believe more than
we can become fully informed about.[2]

In this chapter, we'll try to redress the balance by exploring the relatively new field of social epistemology, which studies the effects of social
interactions and social systems on our claims to know. Offering an important

---

[1] Alvin I. Goldman, "Experts: Which Ones Should You Trust?" *Social Epistemology:
Essential Readings*, eds. Alvin I. Goldman and Dennis Whitcomb (New York, 2011), 109.

[2] John Hardwig, "Epistemic Dependence," *The Journal of Philosophy*, vol. 82, no. 7
(Jul., 1985), 340.

counterbalance to the traditional approach, it focuses on knowers with epis-temic constraints and asks what they can attain with those constraints. In a sense, social epistemology proceeds on the commonsensical notion that infor-mation is often transmitted by others, and asks when our beliefs that are social evidence-based are justified. Such issues have surfaced to the foreground because, in a complex society like ours, information is vast and oftentimes spread in a fragmentary way across multiple institutions and groups. Given these conditions, how can the non-expert know whom to trust, and how can even experts who rely on other experts distinguish the wheat from the chaff? These are the sorts of questions we'll attempt to answer here.

Before we dive in, though, a few words need to be said about an anal-ogous movement that was launched by sociologists and deconstructionists, in which the very idea of objectivity was challenged. Because it's important that we distinguish between this movement and what philosophers consider in social epistemology, we'll start by highlighting a few of the more radical thinkers.

Challenging the Very Idea of Objectivity

Though philosophers sometimes seem to agree on very little, they gener-ally concede that we can know at least some objective truths. Whether those involve purely rational or empirical truths, a measure of objectivity is granted by a strong percentage of practitioners. Still, there have been those who dis-agree both within and without philosophical circles. Alvin Goldman and Cailin O'Connor point out that members of the so-called "strong program" in the sociology of science challenged the very possibility of truth, rationality, and factuality of mainstream epistemology.[3] Bruno Latour and Steve Wooglar took issue with the idea of objective truth when they claimed that facts aren't discovered by science, but rather constructed. Readily admitting the contro-versial character of their claim, they argued that it "will not have escaped the reader's notice ... that a major problem arises from our contention that scien-tific activity comprises the construction and sustenance of fictional accounts which are sometimes transformed into stabilised objects."[4]

---

[3] Alvin Goldman and Cailin O'Connor, "Social Epistemology," The Stanford Encyclopedia of Philosophy (Spring 2021 Edition), ed. Edward N. Zalta, https://plato .stanford.edu/archives/spr2021/entries/epistemology-social/.

[4] Bruno Latour and Steve Wooglar, *Laboratory Life: The Construction of Scientific Facts* (Princeton, 1986), 177, 235. For a critique of Latour and Wooglar, see Philip

In a slightly different way, the postmodernist/constructivist Richard
Rorty rejected the traditional idea of knowledge and claimed that there's
no such thing as objective truth. The real point of philosophy (what he
called edifying philosophy) "is to keep the conversation going rather than
to find objective truth."[5] Thus, in a dispute such as what occurred between
Galileo (who argued for the truth of Copernicanism) and Bellarmine (who
offered an alternate account), there is no fact that could have shown one of
them to be correct. Having now adopted Galileo's system, we simply call
Bellarmine's view "unscientific," but all we're really doing, according to
Rorty, is expressing our preference for Galileo. We can only claim that our
beliefs are justified relative to the particular epistemic system we've come
to accept, but not justified by any objective evidence.[6]

There were, however, other deconstructionist approaches inspired
by social factors that were less extreme. Thomas Kuhn held that purely
objective considerations would never settle disputes between competing
scientific paradigms, which meant that scientific beliefs must be influenced
by social factors. For him, the history of science consists of (1) periods of
normal science in which a paradigm is universally accepted; (2) crisis which
begins with a blurring of a paradigm and sees the rise of challenges—usually
by those who are new to the field and less committed to old ways of thinking—caused by anomalies within the reigning paradigm; which ultimately
leads to (3) scientific revolution in which a new paradigm defeats the old,
ushering in a new period of normal science. More often than not, Kuhn
argued, these paradigm switches occur all at once, not gradually. But once
the switch occurs, the scientist is completely reoriented and sees the data
before him in a new system of relations, given that they're now viewed from
a different framework.

Though Kuhn mildly criticizes using the gestalt switch (e.g., where a
drawing on a piece of paper can either be seen as a bird or antelope, and
vice versa) as a prototype for his thinking, he concedes that it's a useful way
of looking at what actually happens. In essence, competing paradigms are
two different ways of seeing the world, made incompatible by the different
paradigms through which data is seen. When an argument between the two

---

Kitcher, *The Advancement of Science: Science Without Legend, Objectivity Without
Illusions* (New York, 1993), 160-9.
[5] Richard Rorty, *Philosophy and the Mirror of Nature* (Princeton, 1979), 377-8.
[6] See Paul Boghossian, "Epistemic Relativism Defended," *Social Epistemology:
Essential Readings*, eds. Alvin I. Goldman and Dennis Whitcomb (New York, 2011), 40-1.

ensues, it can only proceed in a circular fashion because each group will use its own paradigm to mount its defense. This means that a case can't be made logically or probabilistically (or experimentally), but only through persuasion of how the world would look through a particular paradigm. Kuhn suggests that "there is no standard higher than the assent of the relevant community."[7] In such a way of looking at things, the ultimate criterion of truth is social.

As you can see, all of these approaches challenge the idea of objectivity in their own way, regardless of how extreme each may be. The reason we highlight them here is because the views they represent have been generally rejected as too radical within the mainstream of philosophy and science, and they need to be distinguished from what follows. This isn't to say that the debates didn't provide important insights into the role of cultural beliefs and biases in the production of knowledge. They did, in fact, and this chapter will explore a new area within mainstream epistemology tasked to deal with the complexities of social influence on the knower.

Three Areas of Social Epistemology

Goldman notes that there are three areas of social epistemology, with the first counterintuitively involving the individual. While it's normally the task of classical epistemology to deal with the individual, evidence used by a knower can be social in nature if it involves communication by others, whether that's by communicating personal beliefs or through traces of such acts (e.g., printed messages, etc.).[8] Questions that are addressed in the first area of social epistemology include: under what conditions are social evidence-based beliefs justified; and under what conditions are they rational, and when do they qualify as knowledge?

Testimony is one of the prime sources for investigation and can be seen from a few perspectives. One concerns the case of the layperson hearing testimony from an expert. How much deference should he accord to the expert? Also, what are we to do when we hear testimony from different people—including experts—who disagree with one another? How can the non-expert justifiably determine which one has the best expertise and

---

[7] Thomas S. Kuhn, *The Structure of Scientific Revolutions* (Chicago, 2012). 84-5, 90, 92, 94.

[8] Alvin I. Goldman, "A Guide to Social Epistemology," *Social Epistemology: Essential Readings*, eds. Alvin I. Goldman and Dennis Whitcomb (New York, 2011), 14-9.

deserves greater credence? Another problem concerns peer disagreement. Is it reasonable for two peers, who see each other as peers, to disagree with one another about something for which they both have equal competence? Should each recognize the other as equally likely to be right and continually adjust in the peer's direction?

The second area of social epistemology involves collective agents composed of members who make judgments—whether those are collective or aggregate judgments—about the truth of certain propositions. In such cases, these collective judgments are presumably determined by the judgments of their individual members—and, in many circumstances, something like beliefs are ascribed to collective entities. For example, we talk of governments, courts, juries, corporations, and political campaigns as thinking, endorsing, or denying the truth of certain propositions. One of the problems philosophers have tackled is that inconsistency (irrationality) arises more easily for collectives than individuals.

The third area of social epistemology concerns epistemic systems, which are institutions with publicly specified aims, rules, and procedures. Examples include science, education, and journalism. Each of these systems attempts to heighten its community's possession of truth, knowledge, and justified belief. In each, social epistemology looks at the system to see whether its mode of operation is conducive to its goal—and it identifies alternative organizational structures that might be epistemically better than the existing systems.

With this quick survey of the major areas, let's look more closely at each, beginning with testimony.

Testimony

Virtually everything we know depends in one way or another on the testimony of others. We don't perceive firsthand our family histories, how ingredients in many of our meals are prepared, the methods of constructing the devices we use to navigate the world, or even the circumstances of our own births.[9] These are all things we're told, and if we were to subtract everything we have via testimony, our lives would be indecipherable. History, scientific discoveries, wars, traditions from

---

[9] Jennifer Lackey, "Testimony: Acquiring Knowledge from Others," *Social Epistemology: Essential Readings*, eds. Alvin I. Goldman and Dennis Whitcomb (New York, 2011), 71, 73.

distant lands—all of these would be nonexistent to us without some sort of testimony. Given this, it's easy to see why the importance of testimony is universally accepted.

The philosophical issue with testimony is similar to what we saw in the last chapter and is framed in terms of what constitutes justified belief: under what circumstances is a hearer justified in trusting statements made by others?[10] Jennifer Lackey notes that answers have traditionally fallen into two camps. The first is called nonreductionism (traced back to Thomas Reid), which says that testimony is a *basic* source of justification on an epistemic par with perception and memory. Unless there are stronger reasons not to (so long as, as philosophers say, there are no undefeated defeaters), nonreductionists say that a person is entitled to accept as true something that's presented as true and intelligible to him. In other words, hearers are justified in accepting what they're told *merely* on the basis of the speaker's testimony unless there's positive evidence against doing so.

On the other hand, reductionists (traced back to David Hume) maintain that—in addition to the absence of undefeated defeaters—hearers must also have *nontestimonially based positive reasons* for accepting the testimony of others in order to be justified. Such reasons are usually based in induction. For instance, hearers observe conformity between reports and corresponding facts and, with memory and reason, inductively infer that certain speakers or types of reports are reliable. In this way, the justification of testimony is *reduced* to the justification for sense perception, memory, and induction. However, there are two versions of reductionism: global and local reductionism. The former submits that justification of testimony as a source of belief reduces to the justification of sense perception, memory, and induction.[11] So, to be justified in accepting the testimony of others, hearers must have nontestimonially based positive reasons for believing that testimony is *generally* reliable. The latter says that the justification of *each instance* of testimony reduces to the justification of instances of sense perception, memory, and induction. On this account, to be justified in accepting the testimony of others, hearers must

---

[10] Alvin Goldman and Cailin O'Connor, "Social Epistemology," The Stanford Encyclopedia of Philosophy (Spring 2021 Edition), ed. Edward N. Zalta, https://plato.stanford.edu/archives/spr2021/entries/epistemology-social/.

[11] Jennifer Lackey, "Testimony: Acquiring Knowledge from Others," *Social Epistemology: Essential Readings*, 74-8.

have nontestimonially based positive reasons for accepting the *particular* report in question.

Both positions have garnered objections. Against nonreductionism, some argue that it sanctions gullibility, irrationality, and intellectual irresponsibility. If hearers can acquire testimonially justified beliefs in the absence of any relevant positive reasons, then random speakers—arbitrary internet postings, unidentified telemarketers, and so on—ought to be trusted, so long as there's no negative evidence against them. But, it's insisted, accepting testimony of these kinds fits the definition of gullibility. Against reductionism, critics point out that young children acquire a great deal of knowledge from parents and teachers—and yet it's doubtful that they have nontestimonially based positive reasons for accepting what they're told. Reductionists may be unable to explain how young children could gain all the testimonial knowledge they seem to possess. Further, the observational base of ordinary people is far too small to justify the requisite induction about the general reliability that global reductionists seem to require. Many of us have never seen a baby being born, examined the circulation of the blood, or explored the actual geography of the world. Not to mention the issues involved with complex scientific or economic theories, which require conceptual machinery most of us don't have in order to check reports against the facts! And against local reductionism, are we justified in believing S only if we have positive evidence for S's reliability? If at the airport, do we need to have prior evidence of the announcer's reliability to justify his or her claim that our flight is leaving in ten minutes? This seems like an unnatural requirement, and most would agree that we're justified in trusting such announcements.

Lackey suggests that a more promising strategy would include a necessary condition requiring nontestimonially grounded positive reasons for testimonial justification, which would avoid the charge of gullibility leveled against nonreductionism. But the demands of such a condition should be weakened so that *some* positive reasons are required, e.g., factors such as the type of speaker, the kind of report, or the context. This avoids the objection against reductionism about young children. However, she also recommends an additional condition concerning the reliability of the speaker's statement, which she sets forth in her statement view (SV), as follows:

SV: For every speaker, A, and hearer, B, B knows that p on the basis of A's testimony that p only if (1) A's statement that p is reliable or otherwise truth-conducive, (2) B comes to truly believe that p on the basis of the content of A's statement that p, and (3) B has no undefeated defeaters for believing that p.[12]

However one attempts to deal with testimony, it's clear that we have to consider such issues to avoid gullibility on the one hand and requirements that are too stringent for a real-world environment on the other. One thing we can say is that, because testimony plays a significant role in our claims to knowledge, it's not an issue we can afford to sidestep if we're going to maintain that our beliefs are justified.

"But I've Never Heard That!"

So far we've discussed the reliability of the testimony that's offered to a hearer, but haven't raised the question about its completeness. To do so, consider you're with your friend Susie, who reports on a new drug that treats a virus that's been spreading through the community. You respond by saying that such treatment seems unlikely because, if what Susie is saying is true, you would have heard it by now. Events like this are rather common and can be stated more technically as follows: the fact that a person has never come across a piece of testimony to the effect that p is used as support for his or her belief in not-p.[13] The questions we'll want to ask about these cases are: under what conditions is there justification for a belief formed on this type of reasoning? And under what conditions does this type of reasoning justify the repudiation of a piece of testimony to the contrary?

Sanford Goldberg notes that usually when a hearer reasons this way—using the silence of a standard source—he does so only if he believes the following: he believes that the statement in question concerns a subject about which there is some subgroup of his community (the standard sources) who regularly reports about such matters; that such sources are likely to be reliable in covering truths about such matters; that such sources have had sufficient time to discover the facts and report on them; that he (the hearer)

[12] Jennifer Lackey, "Testimony: Acquiring Knowledge from Others," *Social Epistemology: Essential Readings*, 85.

[13] Sanford C. Goldberg, "If That Were True I Would Have Heard about It by Now," *Social Epistemology: Essential Readings*, eds. Alvin I. Goldman and Dennis Whitcomb (New York, 2011), 92-6.

would likely have heard about such a report if it had been made; and that he hasn't seen such a report.

Goldberg calls these coverage-supported beliefs, and he puts it as follows:

1. S testified that p.
2. If S testified that p, then p.
Therefore,
3. p.

This formulation is referred to as the testimony-to-truth transition. On the flip side, a person could disbelieve a statement and justify it solely on the basis of coverage considerations. Goldberg characterizes this case as follows:

1. None among the trusted sources X testified that p.
2. If p, then one among the trusted sources X would have testified that p.
Therefore,
3. It's not the case that p.

At the heart of this argument is the claim that all relevant truths have been reported. And at the heart of this is the fact that we want trustworthy testimony so that we can know something about the world through accepting another's statement. This requires that, if our source says that p, then p. We want to say that a piece of testimony is trustworthy such that it *wouldn't* be offered it if it *were* false—and we want testimony to have this property because we want it to be warranted (or justified). Goldberg suggests that all of this rests on five conditions on the fruitfulness of coverage-supported belief: (1) the source-existence condition, i.e., there must be a source that regularly reports on the facts in the domain in question; (2) the coverage-reliance condition, i.e., the relied-on source is likely to be timely and reliable in uncovering truths about the domain in question; (3) the reception condition, i.e., the person (hearer) must be likely to have come across the relevant reports from the source on which he relies; (4) the silence condition, i.e., the person hasn't encountered any report on the truth of the domain in question; and (5) the sufficient time condition, i.e., time was sufficient for the source to discover and publicize the relevant information.[14]

---

[14] Sanford C. Goldberg, "If That Were True I Would Have Heard about It by Now," *Social Epistemology: Essential Readings*, 97, 99.

In any information-rich community where there are groups dedi-cated to the reporting of facts in some domain, community members can come to rely on one or more of these groups for what they know in that domain. Here, these groups may be the primary, and maybe the only, source(s) the person relies on for the domain in question. Given the need to be able to separate the wheat from the chaff, Goldberg cites three dan-gers in such a policy. First, the coverage-relying person risks committing the fallacy of ignorance: believing not-p simply because he hasn't heard evidence (testimony) that p. Second, those who rely on particular sources risk forming beliefs in a way that reflects the vested—and often powerful—interests of their sources, and these may not be driven by a disinterested concern for truth. Third, someone who has a coverage-reliance toward a particular source can be blind to new or unrecognized sources of infor-mation when these go beyond what the relied-on sources have said about some matter. "In this respect, the individual is both persisting in retaining false belief in the face of what is in fact a reliable indication to the contrary and losing out on an opportunity to acquire reliable information."[15]

Must I Be an Expert to Choose an Expert?

How should a layperson evaluate the testimony of experts to decide which of two or more rival experts is most credible? In a complex society where there are highly specialized experts in many fields, people are constantly having to turn to them for intellectual guidance. No matter how intelli-gent a person is in any particular domain, he can't be competent in all of them, which means that everyone has to rely on other experts for some information. Having said this, there's a difference between the novice/expert and expert/expert problem. The latter appraises the credibility of other experts while the former involves the novice who isn't in a posi-tion to evaluate experts via his own opinion. He may think of a domain as requiring expertise but doesn't view himself as having it, so he can't use his own opinions to arbitrate between conflicting expert judgments or reports.

Before we look at this more closely, let's define what is meant by the term "expert." Goldman suggests that an expert in a particular domain is someone who possesses an extensive fund of knowledge (true belief) and

---

[15] Sanford C. Goldberg, "If That Were True I Would Have Heard about It by Now," *Social Epistemology: Essential Readings*, 105.

a set of skills or methods for successful deployment of this knowledge to new questions in the domain.[16] For the layperson, the task is to decide who has superior expertise or who has better deployed his expertise to the question at hand. The novice/expert problem is whether the layperson can *justifiably* choose one expert as more trustworthy than another.

At least one problem for the novice is that he's commonly unable to assess the truth of the expert's propositions. But he can also be incapable of assessing the support relations between the evidence that's cited and the conclusion the expert offers. While the expert will, of course, claim that the evidence supports his conclusion, another expert might dispute it. And the novice usually won't know which is correct. To resolve the issue, he may see what proportion of experts agree with the one in question, i.e., consult the numbers or degree of consensus among the relevant experts. But if an expert is part of a consensus of other experts, how much warrant does that give a hearer for trusting the original opinion? There are several issues with using numbers as a guide. First is the case of a guru with followers who will agree with him no matter what. Or there could be a small group of elites who have followers that will agree based solely on their say so. Many religious beliefs fall in this category, whose followers argue on the basis of their sheer numbers that they're justified in their belief. Rumors and false reports can also spread through large populations and gain a life of their own, which then adds to their apparent credibility.

Second, if two or more opinion-holders are *non-independent* of one another and the novice is justified in believing so, then his opinion shouldn't be swayed whatsoever by more than one of them. As with the guru, a follower's opinion doesn't provide any more grounds for accepting the guru's view (and so on), even if the followers are as reliable as the guru. Goldman points out that Y may be a non-discriminating reflector of X, or vice versa, or both may be non-discriminating reflectors of some third party.[17] This applies no matter how many additional experts share an initial expert's opinion—they add no more weight to the novice's evidence. The novice would be justified, however, in believing some statement of an expert if he has reason to believe that even if one expert failed

---

[16] Alvin I. Goldman, "Experts: Which Ones Should You Trust?" *Social Epistemology: Essential Readings*, eds. Alvin I. Goldman and Dennis Whitcomb (New York, 2011), 113, 115-7.

[17] Alvin I. Goldman, "Experts: Which Ones Should You Trust?" *Social Epistemology: Essential Readings*, 121-5.

to see the falsity in H, another expert wouldn't, i.e., if the latter expert's route to belief was independent of the former's. Examples of this might be cases in which X and Y are causally independent eyewitnesses or cases in which X and Y base their beliefs on independent experiments that bear on the issue.

In addition to independence, the novice's belief should depend on how reliable the members of each opposing view are. Of two sets, if the members of the smaller group are more reliable and more independent of one another than the members of the larger one, then the evidential weight of the smaller group may exceed the larger one. And it will depend on what the novice is justified in believing about these matters. Since his own belief justifications may be weak, there will be many times he has no warrant for siding with large numbers of like-minded opinion-holders.

Aside from non-independence and unreliability, there are other ways the trustworthiness of experts can be diminished. While outright deception is one of the more obvious, interests and biases can reduce an expert's credibility, with each having been shown to exert a subtle and distorting influence in more cases than we might wish to admit. Perhaps more significant is a bias that might infect a whole discipline. If all or most members of a field are infected with the same bias, the novice will have a tough time distinguishing the worth of corroborating testimony from other experts and meta-experts; which makes the numbers game even trickier. Another type of community-wide bias arises from the economics or politics of a discipline. In order to secure funding, practitioners might habitually exaggerate evidence that allegedly supports their findings. Given the competitive nature of science, where researchers compete for sparse resources and recognition, a team might apply comparatively lax standards in reporting its results, which will make it difficult for the novice to weigh the merit of such allegations by rivals outside the field.[18]

Goldman notes that one possible solution to the novice/expert problem might be that the novice can look at the past track records of experts and judge which is better at dealing with the issue at hand. If these experts have trained others in their methods, he may be able to expand his pool of reliable experts. However, there's no denying that the situation facing the novice in determining which of two experts to

---

[18] Alvin I. Goldman, "Experts: Which Ones Should You Trust?" *Social Epistemology: Essential Readings*, 125-6, 128-9.

believe can be daunting. On top of this is a point made by Adam Elga: that not even a perfect advisor deserves absolute trust since we can't be certain of our own ability to identify such a person.[19] Thus, we should never completely defer to any expert for our own judgments. Finally, we should note that the issue with expert testimony is muddied by the fact that today's focus on hyper specialization can create excessive in-the-box thinking on the part of those in a given field.[20] This can lead them to narrow-frame a problem and cause them to miss crucial details lying outside their specified domain.

Weighing Opinions

Let's now consider a case in which two peers who are equal in understanding and competence have reached opposite conclusions about an event. Imagine that Tom and Sue, both law enforcement officials, read in the newspaper about a police shooting. Tom believes the officer was at fault in the incident, while Sue believes he wasn't. Suppose further that Tom and Sue have deep respect for each other and that when they've disagreed in the past, each has been right about 50% of the time. How, if at all, should each adjust his or her initial belief about the event after learning that the other disagrees? Should they modify their beliefs in the direction of their peer, or is it rational to hold steadfastly to their original convictions?

As you might imagine, different opinions about how to navigate situations like these have emerged.[21] The equal-weight view says that if you count someone as an epistemic peer—someone who has the same relevant information, competencies, and so on—then, in a disagreement, you should give his or her assessment equal weight to your own; i.e., that you should give yourself a 50% chance that you're correct.[22] But it also implies that if you have many peers who disagree on an issue, they should have proportionally

[19] Adam Elga, "Reflection and Disagreement," *Social Epistemology: Essential Readings*, eds. Alvin I. Goldman and Dennis Whitcomb (New York, 2011), 162-3.

[20] David Epstein, *Range: Why Generalists Triumph in a Specialized World* (New York, 2020), 177, 179.

[21] Alvin Goldman and Cailin O'Connor, "Social Epistemology," The Stanford Encyclopedia of Philosophy (Spring 2021 Edition), ed. Edward N. Zalta, https://plato.stanford.edu/archives/spr2021/entries/epistemology-social/.

[22] Adam Elga, "Reflection and Disagreement," *Social Epistemology: Essential Readings*, 166-9, 172-7.

greater weight. So, if you have 99 peers who have independently assessed a question, then the equal-weight view implies that your own should be swamped by theirs. To illustrate, Elga asks us to consider a mathematical case. If you get one answer to an arithmetic problem and 99 people you count as peers get another, then you should be confident in the answer of the majority.

Having said that, the equal-weight view allows for some caveats. Suppose that, as you're evaluating some claim with a single peer, you get information about the circumstances of the disagreement. For instance, suppose the weather turns frigid and you know your peer doesn't think well when it's cold. In that case, when the two of you disagree, you can be relatively confident that he's the mistaken one. What this implies is that you shouldn't be guided by your prior assessment of your peer's *overall* judging ability, but by your prior assessment of his judging ability *conditional* on what you later learn about the judging conditions (this would also apply in cases of disagreements with superiors).

There's an additional caveat some have made in the distinction between clean and messy real-world cases. In the former, we're able to count our associates as peers based on reasoning that's independent of the disputed issue; in the latter, we're rarely able to do so because, in messy cases, one's reasoning about disputed issues is tangled up with his reasoning about many other things. Thus, in real-world cases, we tend not to count the dissenting opinions of associates as epistemic peers. And it's precisely in these scenarios that the equal-weight view doesn't require you to give their conclusions the same weight as your own. In other words, in messy real-world cases—such as hotly disputed political or religious matters—the equal-weight view allows one's independent thinking to have significant weight. But it also requires our opinions to be swamped by the majority when we count many of our advisors as peers (as odd as the two together may seem).

One of the factors that Elga notes as favoring the equal-weight view is the argument against bootstrapping, which has the same form as a well-known objection to reliabilism. According to Elga, reliabilism says that you can gain knowledge by a reliable method, even if you don't know the method is reliable. For instance, imagine that your vision is reliable. According to reliabilism, you can come to know that the wall is red by looking at a red wall, even if you don't know that your vision is reliable. Those who object say that this seems to imply that you can get evidence that your vision is reliable merely by looking at the wall. In other words, you can come to know your vision is reliable simply by checking that the outputs of your visual system agree with the outputs of your visual system. Elga finds this sort of bootstrapping illegitimate.

Against this, Thomas Kelly argues for the total-evidence view and suggests that there are some cases in which bootstrapping is permissible. This view argues that what it's reasonable to believe depends on both the first-order evidence (the direct evidence that peers evaluate to form their judgments) as well as the higher-order evidence (the judgments of other peers and of the circumstances surrounding your own and others' judgments). As more and more peers weigh in on an issue, the proportion of the total evidence consisting of higher-order evidence increases, while the proportion of first-order evidence decreases—in which case it's more or less equivalent to the equal-weight view. However, Kelly notes that it would be a mistake to be impressed by sheer numbers on any issue because they mean little in the absence of independence.[23] But even if we assume that peers have arrived at their opinions independently, we run the risk of overestimating the importance of other people's opinions and underestimating the first-order evidence. In such a case, we'll be too quick to conclude that agnosticism is the reasonable position to take when opinion is sharply divided, and too quick to conclude that deference to the majority is the reasonable course when opinion isn't sharply divided.[24]

What Do WE Know?

Having discussed some of the issues related to the first area of social epistemology, it's time to shift our focus to the second and third areas, i.e., those involving collective agents and systems, or institutions. We'll begin by exploring some of the issues pertaining to collective agents and how they might combine the different judgments of individuals to form an aggregate judgment. The first thing to note is that different institutional structures can lead to different outcomes, with some leading to more rational outcomes than others. Institutional design can be a significant

---

[23] This point has also been recently made by Daniel Kahneman, Oliver Sibony, and Cass R. Sunstein, in their book *Noise: A Flaw in Human Judgement* (New York, 2021), 99.

[24] Thomas Kelly, "Peer Disagreement and Higher Order Evidence," *Social Epistemology: Essential Readings*, eds. Alvin I. Goldman and Dennis Whitcomb (New York, 2011), 201, 203, 207.

factor because many epistemic tasks are performed not by individuals, but by members of a group, such as expert panels and committees. For instance, it's been argued that the failure of the U.S. intelligence agencies to draw particular conclusions from the available information before the terrorist attacks on 9/11 was due to flaws in their institutional structures. Some structures may facilitate information integration, while others may not, and the consequences can be serious. Christian List has suggested that aggregation procedures can affect a group's epistemic performance, which is defined as mechanisms a multi-member group can use to combine the individual judgments held by group members into collective judgments endorsed by the group as a whole;[25] a process that often culminates in ascribing actions, intentions, and beliefs to collections or groups of people.

One of the necessary conditions for epistemic agency in a group is an institutional structure that allows it to endorse certain judgments as a collective, and its performance depends on the details of the institutional structure or, more specifically, on its aggregation procedure. List asks us to consider a case where experts have to make judgments on three complex propositions about which they may disagree:[26]

p: The average particle pollution level exceeds 50 μgm $^{-3}$
            (micrograms per cubic meter air).

p→q: If the average particle pollution level exceeds 50 μgm $^{-3}$,
            then residents have a significantly increased risk of respiratory disease.

q: Residents have a significantly increased risk of respiratory disease.

Now consider the individual expert judgments and results of the majority:

---

[25] Christian List, "Group Knowledge and Group Rationality: A Judgement Aggregation Perspective," *Social Epistemology: Essential Readings*, eds. Alvin I. Goldman and Dennis Whitcomb (New York, 2011), 221-3. List sets aside the question of whether groups can be fully fledged agents, focusing only on how they perform as epistemic agents.

[26] Christian List, "Group Knowledge and Group Rationality: A Judgement Aggregation Perspective," *Social Epistemology: Essential Readings*, 225-6, 229.

	p	p→q	q
Individual 1	True	True	True
Individual 2	True	False	False
Individual 3	False	True	False
Majority	True	True	False

Notice how a majority of experts judges p to be true, a majority judges p→q to be true, and yet a majority judges q false, leading to an inconsistent set (called the discursive dilemma). In other words, the committee doesn't meet the rationality criteria (the requirement to endorse consistent judgments). This illustrates that, under an initially plausible aggregation procedure of majority voting, a group might not have consistent collective judgments, even when every member has consistent judgments. Philip Pettit notes that it would be crazy to take your testimonial cue from the majority in a case like this. "Being responsive to majoritarian testimony within any group of people, even a group you regard as suitably intelligent, informed and impartial, will be a hazardous policy. Majorities are not persons and, not being responsive to the demands of consistency and the like, they may make for rotten advisors."[27]

List argues that the only way for a group to meet the rationality challenge is to find an aggregation procedure that can relax what he refers to as (1) universal domain (accepts any logically possible combinations of complete individual judgments on the propositions), (2) anonymity (judgments of all individuals have equal weight in determining the collective judgments), and (3) systematicity (collective judgment on each proposition depends only on the individual judgments on that proposition). Alternatively, the group could permit the incomplete collective judgments, which allows it to make no collective judgment on disputed propositions (while propositions judged true or false by all members are collectively judged as such). The difficult choice a group has is whether to let the views of the collective be fully responsive to the individual views of the members, thereby risking collective inconsistency, or to ensure that the views of the group are collectively rational, even when that means compromising

---

[27] Philip Pettit, "When to Defer to Majority Testimony - And When Not," *Analysis*, July 2006, 183, 185.

the views of individual members and endorsing a conclusion the majority rejects.[28]

In the end, Pettit suggests that a policy of deference to a majority might work well with beliefs like the perceptual belief that a car ran a red light and thereby caused an accident. However, with beliefs that are deeply embedded in one's credal web, such as belief in intelligent design or the wrongness of some action, it's not advisable to espouse a policy of testimonial deference to a majority. You shouldn't need to shift just because a majority of those you regard as equally competent and informed take a different view. Regardless of the position one adopts, we can see how appraising majority views in these circumstances should always be done with caution.

Networks

One way of understanding the social aspects of knowledge is by considering epistemic networks, which represent social or informational ties where beliefs, evidence, and testimony are shared. The most popular approach takes a contagion view of beliefs, in which a belief or idea is transmitted from person to person across network connections, much like a virus can be transmitted. For example, imagine you live in a suburb and believe someone who poses a danger to children lives close by. You'll likely tell your neighbor friends what you've learned, they'll tell their friends and neighbors, and so on.[29] The idea starts with a particular individual and spreads, virally, through the community.

According to the contagion model, individuals don't gather evidence (and share it) or form beliefs in a rational way. Because of this, philosophers of science have opted to use the network epistemology framework instead. To illustrate, imagine again our example above but with the one difference that the person who believes there's a child predator in the neighborhood

---

[28] Philip Pettit, "Groups with Minds of Their Own," *Social Epistemology: Essential Readings*, eds. Alvin I. Goldman and Dennis Whitcomb (New York, 2011), 249-50, 262. Pettit argues that collectives should be regarded as persons of a bounded, robotic variety that form judgments on a restricted range of matters.

[29] Alvin Goldman and Cailin O'Connor, "Social Epistemology," The Stanford Encyclopedia of Philosophy (Spring 2021 Edition), ed. Edward N. Zalta, https://plato .stanford.edu/archives/spr2021/entries/epistemology-social/. In his recent book, Gad Saad uses something to this effect to explore trends in beliefs among higher education faculty members. See *The Parasitic Mind: How Infectious Ideas Are Killing Common Sense* (Washington DC, 2020), xiff.

THE SOCIAL SIDE OF KNOWLEDGE

forms evidence-based beliefs. He becomes suspicious that the neighbor poses a danger to children and obtains credible evidence that it's true. He shares the evidence with neighbors, who in turn do the same with other neighbors and friends, and so on. Beliefs still spread through a network, but they do so on a semi-rational belief-forming basis. In science, actionable theories would be involved that can yield differing levels of scientific success. Here, knowing agents have beliefs about which option is preferable and change their beliefs in light of evidence they gather through their actions (via experiments, etc.).

While communication seems vital to such network knowledge, Kevin Zollman has highlighted the counterintuitive fact that it's sometimes worse for communities to communicate more. Groups with more network connections can be less likely to arrive at a correct consensus. In tightly connected networks, misleading evidence is widely disseminated and may cause the community to settle on a bad theory prematurely.[30] This can be exacerbated by the fact that people have various cognitive and social biases that influence how they absorb information from peers. Among these is conformity bias, which causes someone to espouse the views of group members even when he disagrees.[31] This can prevent coming to true beliefs because agents are often unwilling to pass on good information if it goes against the group narrative. Confirmation bias is also common; this occurs when a person seeks out evidence that confirms his point of view, while discounting disconfirming evidence (more on this in a later chapter).

---

[30] Kevin J. S. Zollman, "The Communication Structure of Epistemic Communities," *Philosophy of Science*, 74(5): 574-587. See also the observations of James Owen Weatherall, Cailin O'Connor, and Justin P. Bruner, "How to Beat Science and Influence People: Policy Makers and Propaganda in Epistemic Networks," *British Journal for the Philosophy of Science*, https://www.journals.uchicago.edu/doi/full/10.1093/bjps/axy062. Here, the authors argue that selective sharing of evidence in which theory A is favored over rivals can be used by a "propagandist" to influence policy makers, even while not influencing the scientific community. To do so, he or she endeavors to bias the total body of evidence that policy makers see.

[31] Geoffrey L. Cohen, "Party Over Policy: The Dominating Impact of Group Influence on Political Beliefs" in *Journal of Personality and Social Psychology*, 2003, vol. 85, no. 5, 808-810. Robert M. Sapolsky, *Behave: The Biology of Humans at Our Best and Worst* (New York, 2017), 246-48, 443-4, 458-69.

Institutionalized Knowledge

Science has long since passed the period when it was performed by individual and small-scale university research. We've now entered a time when it's appropriate to talk of Big Science in which large numbers of scientists bring different expertises to a common problem (e.g., the Manhattan Project). Given its current institutional structure, various concerns have been raised that need to be considered as one explores the social nature of the discipline. One concern is the dependence on central funding and private foundations or commercial organizations, which has prompted questions about the degree of independence of science from its social and economic context.[32] Another concern, and the one on which we'll focus here, is the fact that scientists and researchers often stand on each other's shoulders and rely on work done by others in key areas. As you'll see, this reliance on prior authority or testimony raises the same types of questions we posed above regarding the novice and the expert.

To illustrate the problem, John Hardwig asks us to imagine that person A has good reasons (evidence) for believing that p, but a second person B doesn't. It seems that B in this case lacks sufficient reasons to believe that p. But suppose that B has good reasons to believe that A has good reasons to believe that p. Does B then have good reasons to believe that p?[33] Such a scenario highlights an odd kind of good reason for belief, one that doesn't constitute evidence for the truth of p. Hardwig notes two reasons for this. First, though A's evidence counts toward the truth of p, the case for p isn't stronger after B discovers that A has this evidence than it was before B found out about A and A's reasons. Second, to be sound, the chain of appeals to expert authority has to end somewhere, i.e., with someone who has the necessary evidence for p. The only thing that can be said here is that B may have good reasons to believe that A has the necessary evidence for believing that p.

But here's where some important problems arise. Oftentimes, extensive training and special competence may be necessary before a person can assess—or even understand—the expert's reasons for believing that p. He may also be unable to determine whether the person really is an expert.

[32] Helen Longino, "The Social Dimensions of Scientific Knowledge," The Stanford Encyclopedia of Philosophy (Summer 2019 Edition), ed. Edward N. Zalta, https://plato.stanford.edu/archives/sum2019/entries/scientific-knowledge-social/.

[33] John Hardwig, "Epistemic Dependence," The Journal of Philosophy, vol. 82, no. 7 (Jul., 1985), 336-7, 339-41, 345-6.

Thus, we have to acknowledge the fact that laymen don't fully understand what constitutes good reasons in the domain of expert opinion. Given these facts, can we say that B can (1) know that p by knowing that A knows that p, and (2) know this without first knowing that p? And can we say this even if it means that B can know that p without having evidence for p and without even understanding p?

This question relates to science in that scientists and researchers often stand on each other's shoulders. Hardwig notes that for reasons of time and competence, they couldn't do their work without presupposing many conclusions that they can't validate themselves. Scientists don't repeat the experiments of other scientists except in cases where something seems amiss. It would be impossible for a researcher in physics or psychology to rely only on the evidence of his own inquiry and dismiss accepted beliefs in his field. This means that the expert is such partially because he so often takes the role of the layman within his own field. Further, research is increasingly done by teams rather than individuals. In many published studies, authors won't know how a particular number in the article was arrived at. Moreover, it's inevitable that better techniques will become available and render the present study obsolete.

The bottom line is that dependence on other experts pervades any complex field of research, as most footnotes citing references are appeals to authority. These, in turn, are often used to establish the premises for the study, which means that they involve the author in a layman/expert relationship even within his own field of knowledge. Given the extent of the dependence, cases in which a fraudulent researcher is uncovered can (and should) cause unease. And biases—including confirmation bias—along gender, language, nationality, prestige, and content have been documented by researchers.[34] Thus, there's clearly a complex network involved which appeals to the prior authority of various experts, with the resulting knowledge incapable of having been achieved by any one person. Hardwig illustrates this with the following:

A knows that m.
B knows that n.
C knows (1) that A knows that m, and (2) that if m, then o.

---

[34] Helen Longino, "The Social Dimensions of Scientific Knowledge," The Stanford Encyclopedia of Philosophy (Summer 2019 Edition), ed. Edward N. Zalta, https://plato.stanford.edu/archives/sum2019/entries/scientific-knowledge-social/.

D knows (1) that B knows that n, (2) that C knows that o, and
(3) that if n and o, then p.
E knows that D knows that p.[35]

He asks us to suppose that this is the only way to know that p, and that no
one who "knows" that p knows that m, n, and o except by knowing that
others know them. The question is, does D or E know that p? Or even more,
does anyone know that p? He suggests that unless we're going to admit that
most of our scientific research could never result in knowledge, we must
say that p is known in such cases. But if we grant that D and E know that p,
we must also say that someone can know vicariously, i.e., without having
evidence for the truth of what he knows or perhaps even fully understands.

If this seems troubling, Hardwig proposes another possibility. Perhaps
p isn't known by any one person, but by the community composed of A, B,
C, D, and E. In other words, it might be that the community of inquirers is
the primary knower from which individual knowledge is derivative. At any
rate, such problems reveal the potentially disturbing extent to which our
rationality rests on trust of authority. If we can't say that such beliefs are
rationally justified, then we're forced to conclude that a large percentage of
beliefs in any complex culture are irrational or nonrational.

The Price of Knowledge

We'll end this chapter by noting some often overlooked factors in socially
generated knowledge. While so far we've discussed how knowledge and
judgments can be justified in various scenarios, we have not yet noted that
we tend to harness both when making decisions. Rarely is knowledge produced for its own sake, at least when it comes to institutions, but rather is
valued for its utility in real-world circumstances. For this, we turn to the
Stanford economist Thomas Sowell, who notes three factors that deserve
consideration in any discussion of social epistemology.

First, he points out that the impetus for the production of knowledge
(and the decisions that follow) comes from the internal and external incentives facing those who form judgments. Incentives can involve rewards or
penalties, with how much of each likely to follow from various judgments
and decisions. This is different from how we've described it so far, in terms
of explaining the production of knowledge and the resulting judgments by

---

[35] John Hardwig, "Epistemic Dependence," 348-9.

way of an organization's purpose (as with a jury or expert panel). After all, an organization may make decisions that fail to serve its purpose, especially when it's responding to the actual structural incentives confronting it, rather than the rhetoric surrounding its original mandate. An example of this might occur with government regulators whose purpose is to control a particular industry. Due to the messy reality that regulators make less money than those whom they regulate, and that they're often hired by the firms they're suppose to control, they're incented—despite their intended mandate—to side with the companies who are their future employers.[36] So, given the realities of real-world environments, we can't overlook who forms the judgments, under what constraints and incentives they occur, and the nature of the feedback mechanisms to which they are subject.

Second, judgments and decisions differ when they're instantaneous or sequential. Instantaneous decisions happen all at once (even if a long period preceded it), while sequential decisions occur at various points in time as reactions to previous parts of decisions require adjustments or reinforcements. With the latter, all the knowledge that's finally available wasn't there when the decision-making process began, and the course of action followed may be completely different from what it would have been if all the knowledge had been available at the start. Piecemeal decisions can often acquire a momentum of their own, which can add a level of complexity for both the novice and expert relying on the testimony of other experts to arbitrate the truth of a given proposition.

Third, there are costs associated with the acquisition of any form of knowledge, which go well beyond the salaries of those producing it. These can involve disaster if the wrong course of action is taken, opportunity costs from foregoing other potential lines of research, process costs, and so on. Thus, the cost of any knowledge and decision-making process must be assessed in light of the consequences entailed by the alternatives. Generally, things cost what they do because other things could have been produced with the same time, effort, and material. We have to weigh the potential benefits of acquiring a piece of knowledge against the costs of doing without it, and we have to beware of the assumption that knowledge is economically free or accessible to all. "In reality," Sowell points out, "knowledge can be enormously costly, and is often widely scattered in uneven fragments, too small to be individually usable in decision-making. The communication and coordination of these scattered fragments of knowledge is one of the

---

[36] Thomas Sowell, *Knowledge and Decisions* (New York, 1996), 14-5.

basic problems—perhaps *the* basic problem—of any society, as well as of its constituent institutions and relationships."[37]

In sum, we can say that all institutions must be recognized as operating under certain constraints and incentives. Failure to do so results in a naive and unwarranted view of the nature of these institutions and the knowledge and judgments they produce. The effectiveness with which knowledge is transmitted and coordinated through these social processes depends on the actual characteristics of those processes. We saw how this can be especially true within networks. To the extent that biases and agendas play a role, the transmission of knowledge is distorted to represent the views of those reporting the results. Again, all of this can make it difficult for those relying on the authority of others—which, as we've shown, is universal—to separate the wheat from the chaff.

Conclusion

If anything has become clear, it's that human knowledge involves inherent constraints. We saw in the last chapter how this is true for the individual, but it should also be evident that the limiting factors surrounding how knowledge is both spread and acquired in social contexts poses additional constraints. Exactly how a person can be justified in testimonial knowledge is far from settled, and while we can (and must, if we're to avoid saying nothing at all) say we're justified some of the time, the discussion above demonstrates that we aren't justified in every circumstance. Clearly, there must be some basic parameters around testimony to shield it from charges of gullibility and irrationality. Similarly, acquiring knowledge from experts—which is a necessity in a complex society—can be fraught with problems. In many cases, it's difficult to spell out how the novice (whether the layman or expert relying on other authorities) can know, and be justified, in his or her dependence on various experts; a scenario that's further complicated by peer disagreement. Since information can spread through networks like a virus, both true and untrue, the epistemic uncertainty of certain propositions becomes all the more heightened.

We also saw that in real-world situations, we have to account for the fact that the costs associated with the acquisition of knowledge can be substantial. Taking one line of research always involves forgoing others,

---

[37] Thomas Sowell, *Knowledge and Decisions*, 17-20, 26, 80, 114, 152.

which may in fact have been more fruitful. Further, the incentive structures of particular disciplines can distort the knowledge that is broadcast among those consuming it. Not only those with expertise but also an unsuspecting populace can be completely unaware that any such underlying incentives are present, as is so often the case in things like governmental decisions. At any rate, we can say that at least some (healthy) skepticism should attend most claims to knowledge, with more emphasis placed on independence and the open debate of important questions. Because of phenomena like the viral spread of fashionable ideas, it's possible that critical debate could be shut down in favor of majority opinion which may not be warranted.

Having examined some of the issues philosophers explore within social epistemology, it's time to turn our attention to the field often lavished with the most trust and praise: namely, the sciences.

Chapter 3

Science and Scientific Realism

Throughout the COVID-19 pandemic, we heard the term "science" loosely thrown around by public policy makers, medical experts, politicians, and the media with an intensity most of us have never experienced before. So pervasive was the drumbeat of the slogan "follow the science," that even if one disconnected from the news, it was nearly impossible to avoid hearing the prevailing narrative from friends and colleagues. Though there continues to be legitimate disagreement over aspects of COVID's scientific and political dimensions (particularly how the two should relate), one thing the pandemic has highlighted is the need for a more nuanced view of the nature of science itself.

Perhaps with good reason, science is considered by most thinkers to be one of humankind's greatest achievements. Having demonstrated stunning success in explaining and predicting phenomena, it has also given rise to innumerable technological innovations that have impacted our everyday lives. On the face of it, it seems only proper to lavish it with praise and respect. Deserved as that might be, it's also imperative that we step back and ask more fundamental questions about its working methods, its claims to truth, and its history. Specifically, we'll want to ask such questions as: What is science, and what separates its claims from those we consider non-scientific? What is its aim? Do its theories give us truth about the inner workings of nature, or should we think of them more as fictions that allow us to make useful predictions? What lessons might its history provide, and how certain can we be about current scientific theories? These are the types of questions with which philosophers and historians of science have grappled for centuries, offering and debating many different viewpoints.

While the term "science" might be defined as our knowledge of the world, based on unbiased observations and experimentations and a search for fundamental laws, what we'll see is that such definitions aren't as simple as they sound. How do we know, for instance, that the theoretical entities of which we speak (such as electrons) really exist outside of the theories which postulate them? How deep can we really say that our knowledge of nature is? And what even distinguishes between non-scientific and scientific knowledge? Due to its potentially controversial nature, it's to this last question that we turn first.

What Makes Something Scientific?

Ours is a society that places a great deal of emphasis on the knowledge imparted by the sciences. Everything from popular publications to cable news commentaries use the term "science" to signal a type of pronouncement that's seemingly final and uncontroversial on any subject about which it speaks. But few, if any, of these sources ask the more basic question of what separates scientific knowledge from other types. What makes science different than other forms of knowledge? If scientists tell us the universe is 14 billion years old or that the continents move, we believe them. We also generally go along with what they tell us not to believe, such as in UFOs or the biblical creation story. In the latter cases, many of us often adopt the scientist's contempt as our own.

As Larry Laudan has pointed out, much of our intellectual life (social, political, and spiritual) rests on the assumption that we can tell the difference between science and non-science.[1] But how? Since the nineteenth century, philosophers and scientists have insisted that the difference between science and everything else is its methodology, that there was something called the "scientific method." Though thinkers saw the method as fallible, it was typically thought to be self-correcting. Still, there was no agreement about what the scientific method was, and absent that, those who wanted to provide a clear demarcation between it and non-science faltered. To make matters worse, what philosophers of science proposed as the scientific method bore little resemblance to the methods actually used by working scientists. Thus, even as science gained influence over the lives and institutions

---

[1] Larry Laudan, "The Demise of the Demarcation Problem," in *Physics, Philosophy and Psychoanalysis*, eds. R. S. Cohen and L. Laudan (Dordrecht, 1983), 111, 115-6, 119-21, 123-5.

of Western people, and as "scientism" (the belief that only science has the answers to all our answerable questions) was gaining acceptance, scientists and philosophers were coming up empty-handed in their attempts to provide a clear demarcation.

In the 1920s and 1930s, logical positivists argued that perhaps the theory of meaning would do the job. As they suggested, a statement was only scientific if it had a determinate meaning, and meaningful statements were those that could be exhaustively verified. Despite the simplicity of this approach, it wasn't long before critics pointed out that many statements in the sciences aren't open to exhaustive verification (for instance, all universal laws). Further, the majority of non-scientific and pseudo-scientific beliefs have verifiable constituents, and because they're verifiable (in the sense that we can specify some possible observations that would verify them), they're both meaningful and scientific. A second approach was Karl Popper's falsification criterion, which suggested that for a theory to be considered scientific it needs to be capable of being proven false. This fared no better since it had the consequence of considering any belief scientific as long as adherents could indicate some observation (no matter how improbable) that would (if it happened) make them change their minds.

Another approach attempted to separate science from non-science by saying that scientific theories are well tested, whereas non-scientific ones are not. However, we have no account that tells us when we know a claim should be regarded as well-tested (how much testing does it take to meet the threshold of well-tested?). Even if we did, does it make sense to say that all the claims in scientific texts have been well tested and that none of the claims of non-scientific areas such as literary theory, software development, or basketball have been? And what about emerging scientific claims, ones that we're not yet sure of what would count as a test? Do those cease to be scientific because they're not well tested already? If so, then how could science move forward with new ideas? The fact is, as Laudan points out, that much of science is highly speculative, and its history suggests that many of our most cherished theories turned out to be false. So how reasonable is it to say that science is the repository of all and only well-confirmed theories? Some scientific theories are well tested and some are not.

Others have proposed demarcation criteria such as cognitive progress or cumulative theory transitions. But many disciplines (literary theory, philosophy, military strategy) can claim that they know more now than they did a century ago. On top of that, there are several sciences that, during certain periods, exhibited little or no progress. Nor will cumulative theory transitions do the job, since many scientific theories fail to retain their predecessors. But if those all fail the test, what about predictions? Doesn't anything worth the name "scientific" make predictions? Sadly, no. While some theories have made useful predictions of surprising phenomena, others have made few, if any. Stephen Meyer notes that the difficulty comes when one tries to equate science with a particular systematic method of studying nature to the exclusion of other methods.[2] And as Laudan and others have shown, methods vary widely across the scientific spectrum.

Given the failures to predetermine what counts as science and what doesn't, Laudan suggests that we drop terms like "unscientific" and "pseudo-science," as they tend to be hollow phrases that do only emotive work. Worse, attempts to demarcate science from non-science have often been associated with hidden agendas, i.e., polemical ways of discrediting rival camps. As such, they're more suited to the rhetoric of politicians than to empirical researchers. Our focus, Laudan argues, should be squarely on the empirical and conceptual credentials for claims about the world—with the "scientific" status of those claims being completely irrelevant. Nicholas Rescher agrees, adding that the "contention that this or that explanatory resource is inherently unscientific should always be met with instant scorn."[3] For him, the unscientific can only lie on the side of process and not that of product. Thus, it can be argued with considerable force that the line between science and pseudoscience can't be defined in terms of what sorts of theories are maintained, but only in terms of how these theories are substantiated.

If it's not as easy to demarcate science from non-science as it might first seem, it may be more productive to turn our focus to the central questions philosophers of science have raised about the very nature of scientific knowledge.[4] These questions, as we'll see, tend to get more traction. To do so, we'll begin with a position known as scientific realism, which presents one of the more positive attitudes towards the outputs of our best theories and recommends belief in both the observable and unobservable aspects of the world described by the sciences.

---

[2] Stephen C. Meyer, *Signature in the Cell: DNA and the Evidence for Intelligent Design* (New York, 2009), 402.

[3] Nicholas Rescher, *The Limits of Science* (Pittsburgh, 1999), 107.

[4] Anjan Chakravartty, "Scientific Realism," The Stanford Encyclopedia of Philosophy (Summer 2017 Edition), ed. Edward N. Zalta, https://plato.stanford.edu /archives/sum2017/entries/scientific-realism/.

Scientific Realism

Although we touched on realism in a previous chapter, it will help to refine its definition for our present purposes. David Papineau notes that realism involves two theses:[5] (1) an independence thesis, which says that our judgments answer for their truth to a world that exists independently of our awareness of it (e.g., when we say there is a moon that's independent of us, the realist means that it's non-mental, exists outside of us, we didn't create it, and it continues to exist when we're not looking at it[6]) and (2) a knowledge thesis, which says that, for the most part, we can know which of these judgments are true. In line with these, scientific realists (generally) argue that the aim of science is, in its theories, to give a true picture of what the world is like, and the acceptance of a scientific theory involves the belief that it's true (antirealists reject this for various reasons that we'll highlight in the next chapter).[7] (Note: whatever position one takes—realist or antirealist—what the aim of science is determines what counts as success.)

Realism is presented differently by its various proponents, but there exists a common core of ideas underlying the vast majority of them. For its succinctness, we'll use Laudan's definition as follows:[8]

R1) Scientific theories (at least in the mature sciences) are typically approximately true, and more recent theories are closer to the truth than older theories in the same domain.

R2) The observational and theoretical terms within the theories of a mature science genuinely refer (roughly, there are substances in the world, such as electrons, which correspond to the ontologies presumed by our best theories).[9]

---

[5] David Papineau, "Introduction," in *The Philosophy of Science* (New York, 1996), ed. David Papineau, 2.

[6] Alan Musgrave, "NOA's Ark - Fine for Realism," in *The Philosophy of Science* (New York, 1996), ed. David Papineau, 55.

[7] Bas C. van Fraassen, *The Scientific Image* (New York, 1980), 8.

[8] Larry Laudan, *Science and Values: The Aims of Science and Their Role in Scientific Debate* (Berkeley, 1984), 106-8.

[9] Ian Hacking makes a distinction between realism about theories (in which we try to form true theories about the world) and realism about entities (which asserts the existence of at least some of the entities that are the stock and trade of physics). The former is about what we might achieve, or about an ideal at which we aim. The latter is about aiming a beam at electrons using present electrons. His point is that realism about theories involves the principles of faith and charity, whereas realism about entities needs no such virtues because it arises from what we can do at present.

R3) Successive theories in any mature science preserve the theoretical relations and the apparent referents of earlier theories (i.e., earlier theories are
limiting cases of later theories, the latter of which are not wholesale replacements but refinements).

R4) Acceptable new theories do and should explain why their predecessors
were successful, insofar as they were successful.

R5) Theses R1-R4 entail that (mature) scientific theories should be successful;
indeed, these theses constitute the best, if not the only, explanation for the
success of science. The empirical success of science (in the sense of giving
detailed explanations and accurate predictions) accordingly provides striking
empirical confirmation for realism.[10]

Laudan refers to this as convergent epistemological realism. Many of its
proponents maintain that R1-R4 are empirical hypotheses which, via the
link of R5, can be tested by an investigation of science itself. In this aim,
they propose two abductive arguments (i.e., the type of reasoning, different
from that of induction and deduction, that infers *past* conditions or causes
from *present* clues or evidence[11]). The first is as follows (relevant to R1-R2):

1. If scientific theories are approximately true, they'll typically be empirically
    successful (e.g., make accurate predictions).
2. If the central terms in scientific theories genuinely refer, those theories
    will generally be empirically successful.
3. Scientific theories are empirically successful.
4. (Probably) Theories are approximately true and their terms genuinely
    refer.

The second is as follows (and relevant to R3):

1. If the earlier theories in a mature science are approximately true and if
    their central terms genuinely refer, then later, more successful theories
    in the same science will preserve the earlier theories as limiting cases.

See "Experimentation and Scientific Realism," in *Scientific Realism* (Berkeley, 1984),
ed. Jarrett Leplin, 154-157.

[10] See also Ernan McMullin, "A Case for Scientific Realism" in *Scientific Realism*
(Berkeley, 1984), ed. Jarrett Leplin, 26; Richard N. Boyd, "The Current Status of
Scientific Realism," in *Scientific Realism* (Berkeley, 1984), ed. Jarrett Leplin, 41-2.

[11] Stephen C. Meyer, *Return of the God Hypothesis: Three Scientific Discoveries That
Reveal The Mind Behind The Universe* (New York, 2021), 223. This type of reasoning
is also referred to as retroduction.

2. Scientists seek to preserve earlier theories as limiting cases and generally succeed.
3. (Probably) Earlier theories in a mature science are approximately true and genuinely referential.

Realists argue that scientists construct theories that explain the observational features of the world by postulating models of the hidden structure of the entities being studied. This structure is then taken to account causally for the observable phenomena. The only scientifically plausible explanation for the reliability of science is that its methodology is reliable at producing further knowledge, precisely because currently accepted theories are approximately true. Further, it's not possible to explain even the instrumental reliability (their ability to make predictions) of scientific practice without adopting the realist conception of scientific knowledge it entails.[12]

To the realist, it seems undeniable that, in its account of nature, science continually makes progress vis-a-vis predecessor theories. This progress seems to require realism for an explanation. Specifically, science exhibits not just an accumulation of knowledge at the pragmatic/empirical level, but theory transitions produce a marked increase of predictive success; this seems only explicable by the superiority of the newer theories over their predecessors.[13] But how are we to understand the notion of progress? Jarrett Leplin suggests that it involves an increasing explanatory, problem-solving, and question-answering power as science develops. It can also consist in an extension of the scope of observation, or in our ability to observe newly postulated entities. Observation doesn't mean "direct" observation, as it's understood in the normal sense in which we're free of theoretical presuppositions, but in its scientific sense of achieving the best possible access to the entities that the theory postulates.

Ernan McMullin points to some key areas where we can see growth in our knowledge of these structures, beginning with geology, where the length of the periods and dominant forms of life were gradually established

---

[12] Richard Boyd, "Realism, Approximate Truth, and Philosophical Method" in *The Philosophy of Science* (New York, 1996), ed. David Papineau, 223.

[13] Jarrett Leplin, "Truth and Scientific Progress" in *Scientific Realism* (Berkeley, 1984), ed. Jarrett Leplin, 205-6. See also Richard Boyd, "Realism, Approximate Truth, and Philosophical Method" in *The Philosophy of Science* (New York, 1996), ed. David Papineau, 244-46.

with increasing accuracy.[14] He also notes that the notion of geological period, such as the Devonian, as well as the long-vanished species of the Devonian, are theoretical entities, which are—in principle—inaccessible to our direct observation. But the many theory changes that have occurred over the years haven't altered the fact that the growth in our knowledge of the life forms inhabiting the earth aeons ago have been mostly cumulative. The realist would say that the success of the synthesis of geological, physical, and biological theories gives us good reason to believe that species of these kinds did exist at the times and under the conditions the theory proposes.

Another example of progress comes from cell biology, where the techniques of microscopy have intertwined with genetics to produce an ever more detailed picture of what goes on inside the cell. It was only gradually that the theoretical unit of hereditary transmission, the gene, became linked to the chromosome. The discovery of the structure of DNA by Watson and Crick made it possible to understand how the gene (and many other components) operate in the development of an organism.

What these examples show, according to the realist, is that the discontinuous replacement of one theory by another—favored by antirealists (discussed later)—is one-sided. Second, scientists seem to have confidence in these structural models and operate as if they provide an analysis of complex real structure. Third, the history of science seems to show that there's a single form of abductive (or retroductive) inference throughout, and the degree of success of such abductive hypotheses warrants the degree of their acceptance as truth. Abduction, in other words, works in the world we inhabit and with the senses we have for investigating that world. In a word, scientific realism purports to explain why certain ways of proceeding in science have worked as well as they have.

Hilary Putnam insists that if this (realist) picture of science is false, then the success of science would be miraculous and without explanation.[15] And because, realists (generally) argue, it explains the fact that science is successful, the theses above are confirmed by the success of science;[16] non-realist epistemologies are refuted by their inability to explain the success

[14] Ernan McMullin, "A Case for Scientific Realism" in *Scientific Realism* (Berkeley, 1984), ed. Jarrett Leplin, 26-30.

[15] Hilary Putnam, "What is Realism?" in *Scientific Realism* (Berkeley, 1984), ed. Jarrett Leplin, 140.

[16] Jarrett Leplin, "Introduction" in *Scientific Realism* (Berkeley, 1984), ed. Jarrett Leplin, 1-2. See also Jarrett Leplin's "Truth and Scientific Progress" in *Scientific Realism* (Berkeley, 1984), ed. Jarrett Leplin, 204.

of current theories and the progress science historically exhibits. Thus, the most natural account of the way scientific theories succeed one another (for instance, the way Einstein's Relativity succeeded Newton's Universal Gravitation) is that a partially correct account of a theoretical object (the gravitational field or the structure of space-time) is replaced by a better account of the same object. As Putnam puts it, "if these objects do not really exist at all, then it is a *miracle* that a theory which speaks of gravitational action at a distance successfully predicts phenomena; it is a *miracle* that a theory which speaks of curved space-time successfully predicts phenomena."[17]

Do Theories Themselves Have To Be True?

While most realists are concerned to show that our mature theories are true, Ian Hacking and Nancy Cartwright propose a mid position between realism and antirealism by drawing a distinction between "entity realism" (which they favor) and "theory realism" (which most realists favor).[18] The former recognizes that the physical sciences produce a number of notable physical effects, such as lasers and electron microscopes. What it denies is that such physical effects give decisive support for a fundamental physical theory. Cartwright builds her case, for instance, by noting that we look at little bits of nature under a very limited range of circumstances. Doing so, we can get precise outcomes, but to accomplish this we need tight control over our inputs and most often use some form of shielding. The trouble comes when we think that the same laws apply both inside and outside the shield, and there's an important difference between the two. Inside, we know how to calculate what the laws will produce, while outside, things become too complicated. For example, take solitons, which are a feature of nature but of nature under very special circumstances. "Clearly," she argues, "it would be a mistake to suppose that they were a general characteristic of low-loss optical fibres."[19] Yet how many of the scientific phenomena we prize are like solitons which are local to the environments we construct for experimental purposes? If nature is more holistic than we believe, then our hopes of exporting the laws of the laboratory to the far reaches of the world

---

[17] Hilary Putnam, "What is Realism?" in *Scientific Realism*, 141.

[18] David Papineau, "Introduction," in *The Philosophy of Science*, 18-9.

[19] Nancy Cartwright, "Fundamentalism vs The Patchwork of Laws" in *The Philosophy of Science* (New York, 1996), ed. David Papineau, 320-1, 324-5.

are misplaced. We have no grounds, she insists, to take our laws—even the most fundamental laws of physics—as universal. This is because we have virtually no inductive reason for counting these laws as true outside the laboratory setting. Reality may be just a patchwork of laws.

Cartwright isn't denying the existence of sub-atomic particles and other unobservable entities proposed as causing physical effects. She argues rather for a kind of antirealism that accepts the phenomenological and rejects the theoretical. She notes that in modern physics, phenomenological laws are meant to describe and they often succeed reasonably well. But fundamental laws (equations) are meant to explain, yet the cost of explanatory power ends up being descriptive adequacy. She takes from this that powerful explanatory laws don't state the truth; i.e., the falsehood of fundamental laws is a consequence of their great explanatory power. Assuming we have a number of highly confirmed phenomenological laws—e.g., laws that give us devices like lasers that are continuously tested—how do the fundamental laws of quantum mechanics (which are supposed to explain the detailed behavior of lasers) get their confirmation? Answer: only indirectly, by their ability to give true accounts of lasers, or of electron diffraction patterns, or of benzene rings. But these accounts are generally not true. While we have expertise for testing the claims of physics in concrete situations, fundamental laws don't meet these ordinary standards. "Realists are inclined to believe that if theoretical laws are false and inaccurate, then phenomenological laws are more so. I urge just the reverse. When it comes to the test, fundamental laws are far worse off than the phenomenological laws they are supposed to explain."[20]

She suggests, in other words, that we can reject theoretical laws without rejecting theoretical entities. This is because causal reasoning gives us good grounds for our beliefs in theoretical entities. Given our knowledge about what kinds of things are possible given the circumstances, we reason backwards from the effects to what characteristics the causes must have in order to bring them about (though we need to have reason to think that this cause, and no other, is the only practical possibility). This is why controlled experiments are important for discovering entities and processes we can't observe. So much so that it's rare that, outside of controlled conditions of an experiment, a cause can be inferred legitimately. Thus, in contrast to van Fraassen—who, as we'll see in the next chapter, insists that observation with the naked eye is the test of existence—Cartwright says that experiment

---

[20] Nancy Cartwright, *How the Laws of Physics Lie* (Oxford, 1983), 2-8, 11-3.

serves as the test of existence. But the entities and processes we infer here are detailed causal principles and concrete phenomenological laws that are specific to the situation and not the abstract equations of a fundamental theory. Fundamental laws are thoroughly abstract formulae that describe no particular circumstances. If they're true, then they should tell us accurately what happens in specific circumstances, but they don't. It's the physicist who makes it right by his corrections.

The problem is that laws seldomly act independently of one another, meaning that they interact with one another. For instance, the law of gravity is supposed to explain the forces that objects experience in complex circumstances. But the law can explain in only very simple/ideal circumstances.[21] It accounts for why the force is as it is when just gravity is at work but is of no help when both gravity and electricity are involved. The law of gravity becomes irrelevant to the more complex and interesting situations. In other words, fundamental laws are powerful only on the assumption that the explanatory laws act in combination just as they would separately. Yet this doesn't describe the actual behavior of objects, which is the result of simple laws in combination. The effect that occurs isn't an effect dictated by any one of the laws separately. There's a trade-off then between truth and explanatory power.

For Cartwright, this means that these fundamental laws can't literally be true, because the consequences that occur if they acted alone aren't the consequences that actually occur when they act in combination. Taken individually, we can say they're true descriptions of what happens, but taken in combination, we can't. This is what she means by saying that "the truth doesn't explain much." "The laws of physics, I concluded, to the extent that they are true, do not explain much. We could know all the true laws of nature, and still not know how to explain composite cases."[22] Yet for both Hacking and Cartwright, our success in manipulating entities is ample testimony to their existence; if they weren't real, then we couldn't use them to produce physical effects. As Hacking famously quipped (referring to theoretical entities), "If you can spray them, they exist." His point is that we can use theoretical entities in the way we want to produce certain effects, which means not only that they exist but also that we understand their behavior well enough to do so. For Cartwright, this is a good argument for the truth of some very concrete, context-constrained claims (i.e., the claims we use to describe their behavior and control them).

---

[21] Nancy Cartwright, *How the Laws of Physics Lie*, 58-9, 72-3.
[22] Nancy Cartwright, *How the Laws of Physics Lie*, 72-3.

Having said all this, the distinction between entity and theory realism has been challenged, i.e., that we can separate commitment to entities from theories. This is because we think about unobservable entities as playing certain theoretical roles, which makes it difficult (for many philosophers) to see how we can accept entities without accepting at least some of the surrounding theory.

Conclusion

We began with the basic question of how we can separate science from non-science. Though there seems to be a great deal of confusion over our ability to provide clear demarcation criteria, particularly among the popular media and even some scientists, we noted the failure of the various attempts to do so. Instead of pre-defining what can be considered scientific, we suggested it would be more constructive to focus on the empirical and conceptual credentials for claims about the world, or how theories are substantiated.

Next, we explored scientific realism and noted that it's one of the more positive attitudes about our best theories, recommending, as it does, belief in both observable and unobservable aspects of the world described by the sciences. Recognizing that there's a good deal of variation among realists, we've seen that they generally argue that the success of science speaks to its referential accuracy and that later theories refine (but do not completely replace) their predecessor theories. Thus, knowledge imparted by our theories is generally thought to be cumulative and not the product of endless fits and starts. Finally, suspended between realism and antirealism, Ian Hacking and Nancy Cartwright were seen to affirm the existence of theoretical entities—given that we can *do* something with them—and question the validity of fundamental physical theories.

As will become clear in the chapters that follow, we started with realism not only because it appears to be the majority opinion of philosophers and scientists, but also because it serves as the foil for subsequent critiques. In the next chapter, we'll examine antirealist criticisms of the realist theses above that have provided (for many thinkers) sufficient grounds for rejecting scientific realism.

Chapter 4

Antirealism and the Limits of Science

As we saw in the previous chapter, scientific realism appears to be the majority view of philosophers and scientists. Presenting one of the more positive attitudes towards the outputs of our best theories, we've observed that it recommends belief in both the observable and unobservable aspects of the world described by the sciences—and generally argues that success implies the truth of its theoretical components. Even so, scientific realism has garnered sustained criticisms over the years from both social constructivists (who say that social factors determine human perception and representation of reality) and antirealists (who simply reject the realist theses in the last chapter). While we've already noted the inadequacy and absurdities inherent in the social constructivist thesis, we have yet to spell out the reasons antirealists push back against the realist program. Far from rejecting any notion of objectivity in our knowledge of nature (as constructivists do), antirealists offer some serious critiques to realism that have to be dealt with if a realist outlook is to be sustained.

It's important to note that antirealists often come from an empiricist point of view, which insists that we have no source of knowledge other than sense experience. Given this, they want to ask how we can claim to have knowledge about things like unobservables, or entities to which we have no access apart from the theories that postulate them. As such, antirealists tend to emphasize inherent human limitations concerning what can justifiably be known. Moreover, though realists would concede the basic point, antirealists want to put the fallibility of our theories (and our knowledge in general) front and center. But if human knowledge is limited (and therefore fallible), what exactly are the limitations? Is there an upper limit to the certainty we can place on a given scientific proposition? Could we theoretically reach the end goal of definitely explaining all natural phenomena and removing all unknowns? Further, can we justifiably claim that science progresses and that later theories contain the central theoretical terms of predecessors? It's these questions we will seek to answer in this chapter.

The Problem With Unobservables

To begin our analysis of antirealism, let's recap the realist position as formulated in the last chapter. Recall that realism involves two theses:[1] (1) an independence thesis, which says that our judgments answer for their truth to a world that exists independently of our awareness of it (e.g., when we say there is a moon that's independent of us, the realist means that it's non-mental, exists outside of us, we didn't create it, and it continues to exist when we're not looking at it[2]) and (2) a knowledge thesis, which says that for the most part we can know which of these judgments are true. We saw that scientific realists (generally) argue that the aim of scientific theories is to give a literally true picture of what the world is like; and the acceptance of a scientific theory involves the belief that it's true.[3] In contrast, antirealism rejects any scientific claims to knowledge about the unobservable world, and they do because they accept (per our two-part definition of realism) that such claims answer to a world beyond us. Thus while they accept the independence thesis, they reject the knowledge thesis. The reason is because it's not at all obvious that we know the entities postulated by our scientific theories, such as gravitational waves or neutrinos.[4] We don't have any direct sensory evidence for these entities, and many antirealists point out that the track record of past theories that postulate similar unobservables isn't good. It might be one thing to accept claims about rocks and birds, but it's entirely different to accept unobservable entities like electrons. In keeping with this, antirealism rejects the realist theses R1-R5 in our last chapter.

Bas van Fraassen, for example, argues that the aims of science can be served without giving a literally true picture of the world, and our

---

[1] David Papineau, "Introduction," in *The Philosophy of Science* (New York, 1996), ed. David Papineau, 2.

[2] Alan Musgrave, "NOA's Ark - Fine for Realism," in *The Philosophy of Science* (New York, 1996), ed. David Papineau, 55.

[3] Bas C. van Fraassen, *The Scientific Image* (New York, 1980), 8.

[4] David Papineau, "Introduction," in *The Philosophy of Science*, 3-5.

acceptance of a theory may involve something less than belief that it's true.[5] This means that the entities a theory postulates need not exist for the theory to be empirically adequate. Arguing for an empiricist approach, he says that we should accept a scientific theory only as it "saves the phenomena," or as it correctly describes what is observable (i.e., has at least one model that all the phenomena fit inside)—a position he calls constructive empiricism.[6] "Constructive" indicates that scientific activity is one of construction rather than discovery, as it aims to construct models that are adequate to the phenomena and not the discovery of truth concerning unobservables.

As such, van Fraassen is prepared to accept only those parts of a theory as correct that rely on things observable with the unaided human eye. That doesn't necessarily imply that conditions are right for observing some present object. The principle he articulates simply says: X is observable if there are circumstances which are such that, if X is present to us under those circumstances, then we observe it. This means that looking through a telescope at the moons of Jupiter provides a clear case of observation because astronauts will at some point be able to see them from close up. The observation of micro-particles in a cloud chamber, however, is entirely different and isn't a case of the particles' being observed.

Being agnostic about unobservables, van Fraassen insists that constructive empiricism makes better sense of science than realism, and it does so without inflationary metaphysics (i.e., without a proliferation of unobservable entities). He asks, for instance, what explains the fact that all observable planetary phenomena fit Copernicus' theory (if they do)? Appealing to the nominalist tradition—which affirms that only particular objects exist, and that universals or general ideas are mere names without any corresponding reality—he answers that the fact that observable phenomena exhibit these regularities (because of which they fit the theory) is merely a brute fact which may or may not have an explanation in terms of unobservables behind the phenomena. His point is that unobservables behind the phenomena really don't matter to the goodness of the theory or to our understanding of the world; this is in stark contrast to the realist who insists that regularities in observable phenomena must be explained in terms of deeper structure. Otherwise (so the realist contends), we're left with a belief in lucky accidents and coincidences on a cosmic scale. But

---

[5] Bas C. van Fraassen, "To Save the Phenomena," in *Scientific Realism* (Berkeley, 1984), ed. Jarrett Leplin, 250, 258.

[6] Bas C. van Fraassen, *The Scientific Image*, 4-5, 12, 16-7, 24-5, 73.

van Fraassen retorts that there shouldn't be a requirement for science to eliminate coincidences or accidental correlations.

Against Abduction

Antirealists often raise objections to realism on the basis that it rests on abductive inference (which again infers unseen facts, events, or causes in the past from clues or facts in the present). Though the systematization and coherence brought about by scientific explanations should be valued, Arthur Fine notes that what antirealists question is whether acceptable explanations need to be true and whether the entities used in them need to exist.[7] If not, then the usual abductive methods that lead us to good explanations can't be counted on to get us theories that are approximately true. For Laudan, the realist reliance on abductive reasoning commits the fallacy of affirming the consequent[8] (the error of ignoring other possible causes with the power to produce the same effect[9]). But the arguments for realism are usually based on this very sort of abductive inference. This would mean that the inference of realism as the best explanation would be of no significance. In other words, we can't beg the question about the significance of explanatory power by assuming that it carries truth as well as explanatory power. Just because a theory has some true consequences doesn't entail that the theory is true; false theories as well as true ones could have true consequences. To argue that realism is true because it has true consequences is a monumental case of begging the question. Explanatory success, for the antirealist, doesn't entail truth.

Another way of saying this is to note that the issue over realism is precisely whether we should believe in the reality of those entities, properties, and the like that are used in well-supported explanatory hypotheses. The abductive inference of realism as an explanation of scientific practice is that our accepted scientific theories are approximately true; i.e., there's an extra theoretical relation between theories and the world. "Thus, to address doubts over the reality of relations posited by explanatory hypotheses," Fine

---

[7] Arthur Fine, "The Natural Ontological Attitude," in *Scientific Realism* (Berkeley, 1984), ed. Jarrett Leplin, 85-6.

[8] Larry Laudan, "A Confutation of Convergent Realism," in *The Philosophy of Science* (New York, 1996), ed. David Papineau, 134, 136.

[9] Stephen C. Meyer, *Signature in the Cell: DNA and the Evidence for Intelligent Design* (New York, 2009), 153, 161.

argues, "the realist proceeds to introduce a further explanatory hypothesis (realism), itself positing such a relation (approximate truth)."[10] For Fine, such a move is unsatisfactory, as it provides no support for realism by showing that realism is a good hypothesis for explaining scientific practice. It merely begs the question (even if successful) of whether we should consider good explanatory hypotheses to be true.

Further, antirealists have argued that the underdetermination of theory by evidence weakens any link between explanatory goodness (simplicity, unificatory power, elegance) and truth. Underdetermination says that we'll always be left with empirically equivalent theories, no matter how much evidence we gather. Two proposals have been offered for this.[11] According to the Duhem-Quine thesis, any theory can retain its central assumptions in the face of anomalous evidence by making adjustments to the less central assumptions. The other proposal notes that we can always gerrymander T_1 and create a different version, T_2, which has the exact same predictions. In such a case, T_2 will assert all the observable claims made by T_1 but deny the existence of any of the unobservable mechanisms postulated by T_1. Since we have no independent access to the unobservable realm, and if there are always alternative theories consistent with the evidence, how could we know that the most explanatory theory will generally be true? As Nancy Cartwright characterizes the objection, for any set of phenomena, there will in principle always be more than one equally satisfactory explanation, and some of these will be incompatible. Since they can't all be true, it's clear that truth is independent of satisfactoriness for explanation (at least so far as we can ever tell).[12]

Miracle Argument

Closely related to the realist's abductive inference to truth, the miracle argument appeals to the reliability of empirical success as a test for truth and insists that it would be a miracle if a highly successful theory were false. However, Peter Lipton has cited a poignant objection to such an argument. He notes that once we take underdetermined competitors into account, a miracle no longer seems required for a successful theory to be false. In fact, it would be a miracle if the truth didn't lie somewhere among the many

---

[10] Arthur Fine, "The Natural Ontological Attitude," in *Scientific Realism*, 85-6.

[11] David Papineau, "Introduction," in *The Philosophy of Science*, 7, 10.

[12] Nancy Cartwright, *How the Laws of Physics Lie* (Oxford, 1983), 90.

underdetermined competitors. The case for this objection rests on the work of Daniel Kahneman and his colleagues on base rates. The classic case, which we'll encounter again later, is this. A test for a disease has a false negative rate of nil, meaning that no one who has the disease will test negative. The false positive rate is 5 percent: five out of a hundred of the people who don't have the disease will still test positive, and one in a thousand people have the disease. A patient is given the test and the result is positive, so what is the probability the patient has the disease?

When staff and students at Harvard Medical School were asked, most said 0.95. The correct answer is just under 0.02. If we give the test to a thousand people, about fifty will test positive even though they don't have the disease, compared to the one person who has the disease. Those who guessed the probability at 0.95 were wildly incorrect because they ignored the base rate, which would have told them that results for healthy people are swamping results of the ill. The medics act as if the test makes the prior probability irrelevant. The miracle argument for realism seems to work the same way, with realists in the role of the probabilistically challenged medics. Lipton explains:

> On this analogy, being true is the disease and making lots of true and precise predictions is testing positive for it. The false negative rate is nil: no true theory makes false predictions. The false positive rate is low, since relatively very few false theories are so empirically successful. So we are inclined to infer that highly successful theories are likely to be true. What we ignore is the base rate that, to put it crudely, the vast majority of theories are false, so even a very small probability that a false theory should make such successful predictions leaves it the case that the great majority of successful theories are false. Most false theories are unsuccessful, but alas what counts is that most successful theories are false. Beware false positives, even if unlikely, because the truth is rare.[13]

As we'll see later, most of us are prone to commit the base rate fallacy, but why here? Because we tend to focus on the comparison between the relatively few false theories that are successful and the many false ones that aren't, and ignore the comparison between the very few true theories and

---

[13] Peter Lipton, *Inference to the Best Explanation* (London, 2004), 196-8. It should be noted that Lipton has given a detailed defense of abductive reasoning, some of which we'll explore in the next chapter.

the many more false theories that are successful. When Putnam said that it would take a miracle for a false theory to make so many true predictions, our attention (because of the way the issue is phrased) is focused on the low proportion of successful theories among false theories, but this diverts our attention from the low proportion of true theories among successful theories.

Another way of putting this is that the miracle argument encourages us to look at the reliability of empirical success as a test for truth by estimating its false positive rate (the chance that a false theory is successful), which we judge (correctly) to be low. We ignore the unlikelihood that, prior to testing, a particular theory should be true—and this hides from view all those other theories that would be just as successful even though they're false. But underdetermination arguments force us to keep in mind those false but successful theories. Underdetermination serves in this case as the adverse base rate and can be the source of a great deal of trouble to the realist.

Nothing Succeeds Like Success?

Laudan has been particularly vocal about the fact that there's ample evidence that theories whose central terms genuinely refer (according to realists) are often unsuccessful.[14] The chemical atomic theory in the eighteenth century was abandoned for a more phenomenological, elective affinity chemistry. The Proutian theory that the atoms of heavy elements are composed of hydrogen atoms had a markedly unsuccessful run throughout the nineteenth century. The Wegenerian theory that the continents are carried by large subterranean objects moving laterally across the earth's surface was (for thirty years in the recent history of geology) unsuccessful until major modifications made it geological orthodoxy in the 1960s and 1970s. Yet, according to Putnam's principle of charity—or the principle of benefit of the doubt (discussed in the next chapter)—these theories all postulated entities that genuinely exist. For Laudan, this shows that the realist claim that referring theories should be empirically successful is false.

On the other hand, there are many once-successful, yet by current standards non-referring, theories. Consider the subtle fluids and ethers of eighteenth- and nineteenth-century physics and chemistry. The etherial

---

[14] Larry Laudan, "A Confutation of Convergent Realism," in *The Philosophy of Science*, 112.

theories of the 1830s and 1840s proposed electrical fluid that was used to explain many phenomena of current electricity. Within chemistry and heat theory, the caloric ether had been widely used to explain everything from heat in chemical reactions to the conduction and radiation of heat, along with several problems of thermometry. Within the theory of light, the optical ether played a central role in explanations of reflection, refraction, and polarization. In fact, optical ether theories made some successful predictions. Laudan comments as follows: "It would be difficult to find a family of theories in this period as successful as ether theories; compared with them, nineteenth-century atomism (for instance), a genuinely referring theory (on realist accounts), was a dismal failure. Indeed, on any account of empirical success ... non-referring nineteenth-century ether theories were more successful than contemporary, referring atomic theories."[15] To this list, Laudan adds the following:

- the crystalline spheres of ancient and medieval astronomy;
- the humoral theory of medicine;
- the effluvial theory of static electricity;
- "catastrophic" geology with its commitment to a universal deluge;
- the phlogiston theory of chemistry;
- the vital forces theory of physiology;
- theories of spontaneous generation.

What this suggests is that the realist claim that he can explain why science is successful rings false, because part of the historical success of science has been that of theories whose central terms didn't refer. Further, there were many theories that were both genuinely referring and empirically successful which we're still loath to regard as approximately true. For instance, virtually all the geological theories before the 1960s denied lateral motion of the continents. These were, by all standards, highly successful, but would anyone today say that their theoretical claims (laterally stable continents) are approximately true? And what about the chemical theories of the 1920s that assumed that the atomic nucleus was structurally homogeneous; or the chemical theories of the late nineteenth century that assumed that matter was neither created nor destroyed? None of these could now be regarded as truth-like. Further, it's unclear what it means for a statement or theory to be

---

[15] Larry Laudan, "A Confutation of Convergent Realism," in *The Philosophy of Science*, 115-24.

"approximately true." Even so, it doesn't follow that an approximately true theory will be explanatorily successful. "The realist who would demystify the 'miraculousness' (Putnam) ... of the success of science needs more than a promissory note that somehow, someday, someone will show that approximately true theories must be successful theories."[16]

Do Theories Retain Older Theories?

As we've seen, realists argue that any viable successor to an older theory must retain the laws of its predecessor as a limiting case. But do scientists follow the realist prescription in actual practice? The historical record seems to say no. No one criticized the wave theory of light because it didn't preserve the theoretical mechanisms of the earlier corpuscular theory;[17] no one faulted Lyell's uniformitarian geology because it dispensed with some of the causal processes in catastrophic geology; most geologists failed to criticize Darwin for not retaining many of the Lamarckian evolutionary mechanisms; relativistic physics didn't retain the ether or the mechanisms associated with it; modern genetics doesn't have Darwinian pangenesis as a limiting case. It seems, if there's any widespread strategy, it's that we should accept an empirically successful theory regardless of whether it contains the theoretical laws and mechanisms of its predecessor.

   Laudan contends that loss from older to newer theories happens at virtually every level. Confirmed predictions of earlier theories are at times not explained by later ones; observable laws explained by earlier theories aren't always retained; and theoretical processes and mechanisms of earlier theories are often treated as scrap. Yet any genuine realist must insist that the underlying ontology of an earlier theory T_1 be preserved in a successor T_2, because it's that ontology he alleges to be approximately true. Classical ether physics had many postulated mechanisms for dealing with the transmission of light through the ether. But these mechanisms obviously couldn't be in a successor theory like the special theory of relativity that denies the very existence of an etherial medium. This is all to say that when the mechanisms of an earlier theory involve entities that the later one denies, scientists shouldn't worry about repudiating those earlier mechanisms.

---

[16] Larry Laudan, *Science and Values: The Aims of Science and Their Role in Scientific Debate* (Berkeley, 1984), 119.
[17] Larry Laudan, "A Confutation of Convergent Realism," in *The Philosophy of Science* (New York, 1996), ed. David Papineau, 126-30.

If scientists accepted such a realist constraint on theory development, then neither relativity nor statistical mechanics would have been viable theories. Thus, for Laudan, the realist generalization that we see theory succession in all the advanced sciences is false. If we take seriously the realist contention that any new theory must capture the mechanisms and entities of its predecessor, then any ontological changes would be barred at the outset. "Equally outlawed," Laudan notes, "would be any significant repudiation of our theoretical models. In spite of his commitment to the growth of knowledge, the realist would unwittingly freeze science in its present state by forcing all future theories to accommodate the ontology of contemporary (mature) science and by foreclosing the possibility that some future generation may come to the conclusion that some (or even most) of the central terms in our best theories are no more referential than was 'natural place', 'phlogiston', 'ether', or 'caloric'."[18]

Nicholas Rescher adds another point worth considering. The notion that science successively leads ever closer to the truth itself lies completely outside the possibility of confirmation. Given that we don't have any science-independent way for determining the truth about nature, we have no prospect of verifying that our scientific claims are drawing nearer to "the real truth." It might be countered that later theories are localized readjustments and that the old theories continue to hold good if we restrict their domains of validity. For instance, we could say that Einstein's theory doesn't replace Newton's, but rather sets limits to the phenomena (large-scale slow-moving objects) where Newton's theory is adequate. But, Rescher insists, this is like saying that "All swans are white" is true as long as we restrict it from being valid in Australia. What this would come down to is the unhelpful truism that a theory works where it works, but in science we're not looking for theories that are correct within limited ranges; we're looking for theories that are global in application and can take special forms within limited ranges. And this, to echo the concerns of Nancy Cartwright, is what makes scientific theories vulnerable.

Hubris and The Fragility of Science

Notwithstanding historical concerns, there have been (and will continue to be) those who are confident in the human ability to bring science to

---

[18] Larry Laudan, "A Confutation of Convergent Realism," in *The Philosophy of Science*, 131.

completion, in which there remain no major outstanding questions about the inner workings of nature. As an example, Rescher asks us to consider attitudes in the last quarter of the nineteenth century. Lord Kelvin believed that the basic structure of physics was pretty well complete and that no major questions remained unanswered. In 1885, Berthelot announced that the world is now without mysteries, and in 1887 T. C. Mendenhall said that it's safe to say what's possible and what's not. "No one would claim for a moment that during the next five hundred years the accumulated stock of knowledge of geography will increase as it has during the last five hundred."[19] It seemed that the course of scientific knowledge showed it to be nearing its final and completed stage, with all that's left being to alter a decimal or two in some physical constant. Beginning in the first years of the twentieth century, however, things had changed dramatically. With the onslaught of new discoveries and technological advances, those previous attitudes receded back to the shadows; that is, until the pendulum began to swing back in the other direction. Physicist Richard Feynman (who was an American 1965 Nobel laureate) wrote that we're lucky to be living in an age when discoveries are still being made, because that will end at some point. Presumably, for Feynman, science as it's practiced now will come to an end—after which there will be a degeneration of ideas, just like the degeneration great explorers feel when tourists move in on some territory.

But are such attitudes realistic or simply another manifestation of human hubris? How confident, at any point in time, can we really be in our current science? To this, Nicholas Rescher insists that even our best theories will one day prove to have been merely provisional. Scientific "knowledge" at the level of deep theory is always going to be purported knowledge, that is, knowledge as we see it today. This means that we know we may see things differently tomorrow and need to be ready to acknowledge the fragility of our scientific theorizing.[20] All we can do is select the optimal answer to the questions we formulate among the alternatives by means of the conceptual machinery of the day. But we have no reason to doubt that this conceptual machinery will at some point be abandoned as inadequate. We have little alternative. We need to look upon our knowledge as real knowledge, yet we shouldn't have the arrogance to think our science has got it right. All we can do is conceive of our knowledge as estimation, but our truth in scientific theorizing may never be the real truth. Our present knowledge (at any

---

[19] Nicholas Rescher, *The Limits of Science* (Pittsburgh, 1999), 23-6.
[20] Nicholas Rescher, *The Limits of Science*, 29-30, 35-6.

time) can only provide us with tentative and provisional knowledge, and it's always open to outright rejection at some later state. Thus, for Rescher, we're wrong to view the science of our day—or of any day—as affording the final truth of the matter. All attempts to equate the real truth with apparent truth (the truth as we now see it) are doomed to failure.

For Rescher, however, none of this necessitates skepticism that our science means nothing, but only that our scientific knowledge of how things work in the real world is flawed. There's simply nothing epistemologically privileged about the present, or any present, which means we have to reject the egocentric claim that we ourselves occupy a special position not occupied by those before us. "A kind of intellectual humility is in order—a diffidence that abstains from the hubris of pretensions to cognitive finality or centrality."[21] Just as we think our predecessors had an inadequate grasp on the furniture of the world, so our successors will likely take the same view of our purported knowledge. Again, this fallibilism shouldn't be taken as an invitation to a full-blown skepticism. The ideal of doing the best we can under current circumstances is a worthy one, despite the fact that we must recognize its full attainment lies beyond our grasp.

Four Constraints

From the perspective of the antirealist, realism tends to equate current science with what actually exists, but there's a distinction that needs to be made between the intent of science—which may in fact be to provide a true account of nature—and its actual achievement. It's here that the antirealist argues that both the nature of science as well as inherent human limitations push back against the idea that our mature (successful) theories are true. To illustrate, Rescher highlights four significant constraints.

The first is that conceptual innovation involves the formulation of issues that couldn't have been contemplated at an earlier point, and the history of science is replete with such examples. In many cases, today's scientific problems couldn't have been contemplated one or two generations ago, as their presuppositions were cognitively unavailable. This is to say that inexpressible questions are unaskable in that they can't be posed by the current state of knowledge. Here, we're not even able to formulate such a question because it lies beyond the reach of the prevailing state of

---

[21] Nicholas Rescher, *The Limits of Science*, 37.

science. For instance, Newton couldn't have wondered whether plutonium is radioactive. It's not that he didn't know the correct answer, but rather that the very question couldn't have occurred to him given that the current scientific knowledge didn't provide the cognitive framework within which this question could be posed. Yet every discipline has its own conceptions that set limits precluding certain matters from even arising, which also means that it limits the range of questions we can ask.[22] There's an inescapable amount of ignorance that's built-in, as it were. The fact that current ideas went unrealized in earlier periods implies the possibility that some legitimate ideas may go unrealized in all historical periods. It's perfectly possible that some facts will never be recognized as such, and that some questions can never be appropriately posed.

The second constraint is Kant's principle of question propagation, which shows that new answers change the presuppositions available for new questions; that is, as we deepen our understanding of the world, new problems and new issues come to the fore. For example, once we discovered that atoms aren't really "atomic" but have a deeper internal complexity, questions about a subatomic domain became available for investigation. Kant's insight was that, no matter what answer we have, we can dig deeper by raising further questions about these answers themselves. And as we get new and different answers, our interest is deflected to the issues they pose. Thus, the apparent completeness of a state of knowledge S need not imply its comprehensiveness or sufficiency, but might simply reflect the paucity of the range of explanatory questions it's in the position to contemplate. The fact that an array of issues can stand outside the purview of a given science makes its capabilities within its range distinctly less impressive. Completeness ends up being completeness of a narrow kind, in that our body of scientific knowledge could be complete yet fundamentally inadequate because it's too myopic. Matters that are outside the boundaries of one era (for instance, action at a distance) can become the orthodoxy of a later generation.

In forming our questions, we always have and always will operate within the conceptual framework of the day—and our inadequacy is rooted in precisely this. Even so, getting our questions answered may not mean all that much because the important innovations are always conceptual ones, and those that lie in the future are by definition beyond our present horizons. Therefore, apparent completeness in a given field may well indicate poverty rather than wealth. Further, we may have reasons to regard

---

[22] Nicholas Rescher, *The Limits of Science*, 9-10, 104.

completeness as the hallmark of a pseudoscience, which derives such a designation only by contriving the exact questions the machinery is in a position to resolve. As Rescher puts it, science "emerges as a project of self-transcendence. It embodies an inner drive that always presses beyond the capacity limits of the historical presence."[23]

The third constraint is that, as Max Planck observed, with each scientific advance, the difficulty is increased as ever larger demands are made on the achievements of researchers. Nature imposes increasing resistance to intellectual and physical penetration. Rescher asks us to consider the analogy of extracting air for creating a vacuum. The first 90 percent comes out relatively easily, but the next 9 percent is virtually as difficult to extract as all that went before. The next 0.9 percent is just as difficult, and so on. Each successive step involves a massive cost for lesser progress, meaning that each successive investment of effort yields a substantially diminished return. Intellectual progress is exactly the same. When we extract knowledge from mere information (knowledge should be distinguished from mere information by its significance), the same sort of quantity/quality relationship exists. Initially, a sizable amount is of high value, but as we press on this, the proportion of what is significant gets smaller. To double knowledge we have to quadruple information.

The fourth constraint is the limitlessness of what may be discovered. Consider the fact that even though some mechanism in nature has a finite structure, one can still have rearrangements of items, and rearrangements of rearrangements (and so on ad infinitum), with lawful characteristics arising at every stage. The workings of a structurally finite, simple system can exhibit an infinite intricacy in operational and functional complexity—a limitless complexity it demonstrates in its workings. While the number of constituents of nature may be small, the ways they can be combined are infinite. To illustrate, Rescher offers the example of letters/syllables/words/ sentences/paragraphs/books/book families/libraries/library systems, which in theory has no ceiling to its integrative complexity. The emergence of new concept concatenations and laws can be expected at each stage, with each level exhibiting an order of its own. New laws and phenomena can arise at every new level of integrative order. "The different facets of nature can generate new strata of laws that yield a potentially unending sequence of levels, each giving rise to its own characteristic principles of organization,

---

[23] Nicholas Rescher, *The Limits of Science*, 13-8, 58-9, 68-9.

themselves quite unpredictable from the standpoint of the other levels."[24] This fact is enough, for Rescher, to underwrite the potential limitlessness of science. Any system could always be shown in the future to be part of yet a more comprehensive system, which is precisely what we've seen in biological studies since the 1950s.

There's also the role that our own cognitive limitations play. Science progresses by the interaction of the human mind with nature, of the mind's exploitation of the data to which it has access in order to penetrate nature's secrets. Scientific progress doesn't just depend on the structure of nature itself but also on the structure of the information-acquiring processes by which we investigate it. The endless levels referred to above aren't physical levels but ones inherent in the activities of inquiring beings, meaning the complexity of which we speak lies less in objects than in the eyes of their beholder. As Herschel once commented, particles moving in mutual gravitational interaction are forever solving differential equations that, if written in full, could circle the earth.

A potential conceptual limitlessness thus emerges as a feature of our conceptions about real things. When claiming knowledge about them, we should understand that the objects transcend our knowledge of them. It's always the case that further facts can be discovered and that what we *say* about them doesn't exhaust what *can* be said. The furnishings of the world are opaque, and we shouldn't assume we can always see to the bottom of them. "Knowledge can become more extensive without thereby becoming more complete."[25] We can never get away from the distinction between things as we think them to be and things as they actually are.

To be a real thing is to be something about which we can always acquire more information. We should never have unwavering confidence in either the definitiveness of our data or our theories explaining them. We simply can't estimate the amount of knowledge yet to be discovered because we have no way of relating what we know to what we don't. To base this on the science that we have is circular, which implies that there's no adequate way to maintain the completeness of science in a rationally satisfactory way. Unfortunately, to see if a given state of knowledge or technology meets the criterion of "finished," we must already have a perfected science in hand to tell us in advance what is indeed possible. We thus have no alternative but to see our present-day science as deficient, regardless of what the question

---

[24] Nicholas Rescher, *The Limits of Science*, 80-4.
[25] Nicholas Rescher, *The Limits of Science*, 148-52, 160-1.

is or the date on the calendar. It isn't simply that perfection is unrealizable, but that we could never recognize its attainment; i.e., even if we arrived at it, we could never know that we did. Rescher comments as follows:

> We cannot ever expect to reach a position of definitive finality in this imperfect dispensation: we do have "knowledge" of sorts, but it is manifestly imperfect. Expelled from the garden of Eden, we are deprived of access to the God's-eye point of view. Definitive and comprehensive adequacy is denied us: we have no basis for claiming to know the truth, the whole truth, and nothing but the truth in scientific matters. We yearn for absolutes but have to settle for plausibilities; we desire what is definitively correct but have to settle for conjectures and estimates.[26]

Having stressed the limits of science, Rescher is equally right to point out that we can operate perfectly well in the realization that perfection is unattainable. Improvement and progress is possible, which is stimulated by the dissatisfaction with the deficiencies of the current positions. Still, Rescher thinks that the claims of the scientific realist are implausible on these grounds. The incompleteness of our current knowledge about the world entails its potential incorrectness. Realism equates the current state of natural science with the domain of what actually exists, but this only works if science—as it stands—has actually got things right. And it's precisely this that (for Rescher) we're not entitled to claim. At best, we can claim that our present theories provide an estimate of nature, an estimate that will probably need revision and whose theoretical entities may be deemed eventually as non-existent.

This isn't to denigrate the fact that the intent of science is to answer our questions about the world correctly and to describe it as it actually is. Such a quest is built into the nature of the discipline, but there still remains a distinction between its intent and its achievement. Realism prevails with regard to the language of science but should be abandoned with regard to the status of science. In other words, no matter what its goal may be, the tone of its practitioners should always be provisional or tentative. In this, Rescher proposes a realism of his own: a realism about human capabilities and one that, while imperfect, still allows us to do the best we can under the circumstances. And while this realism recognizes a mind-independent reality of which we have some understanding, it acknowledges that human understanding will always be imperfect or deficient.

---

[26] Nicholas Rescher, *The Limits of Science*, 157-8, 163-5.

Is Science Self-Correcting?

Part of the idea of scientific progress for many thinkers—such as Charles Sanders Pierce—involves an accretional view (or convergentism) which says that the magnitude of the issues to be solved tend to be smaller and smaller as science progresses. Later questions are smaller questions, so that later science is always lesser science, yielding advances of ever smaller importance. The advance of science leads, step by diminished step, toward a fixed and final view. For Pierce, this ultimate convergence is bound up with his belief that the scientific method is self-corrective, an idea with roots going back to the eighteenth century. According to this thesis, even if science has erroneous theories, if it persists in following the scientific method, it will eventually correct those mistakes and get closer to the truth. Felipe Romero formulates this as follows: in the long run, the scientific method will refute false theories and find closer approximation to true theories.[27] Thus, it's easy to see that if truth is the goal of scientists (as it is for the realist), then the self-corrective thesis is essential.

Against this, Rescher argues that the conception of science as automatically self-corrective can't be sustained for the simple fact that when an accepted hypothesis becomes untenable, the scientific method (or any other cognitive resource people have) provides no automatic mechanism for producing a new one that can replace it. Romero adds that, from his estimation, the self-corrective thesis is only true in a scientific utopia in which three conditions must be met: (1) scientists have enough time, participants, and funds to run all the experiments and direct replications they want—along with sample sizes that are large enough to yield statistical power; (2) individual and social bias[28] are absent, and scientists report results regardless of whether they're consistent or not with previous theoretical expectations; and (3) negative results are published—i.e., the "file drawer problem," in which negative (non statistically significant) results aren't reported, doesn't

---

[27] Felipe Romero, "Can the Behavioral Sciences Self-Correct? A Social Epistemic Study," *Studies in History and Philosophy of Science*, Part A (2016), 60, 55-69. It should be noted that Romero isn't necessarily pessimistic about the idea of self-correction, but rather that we can't examine the question in isolation from the actual social and institutional context within which scientists work.

[28] For an overview of potential biases, see John P. A. Ioannidis, Marcus R. Munafo, Paolo Fusar-Poli, Brian A. Nosek, and Sean P. David, "Publication and Other Reporting Biases in Cognitive Sciences: Detection, Prevalence, and Prevention," *Trends in Cognitive Sciences*, May 2014, vol. 18, no. 5, 236.

exist. As we'll see below, the non-publication of negative results introduces bias for significant results in the literature.

Rescher and Romero aren't alone in their concerns. In an article entitled "Why Science Is Not Necessarily Self-Correcting," John Ioannidis of the Stanford University School of Medicine has also given caution to the assumption that science is necessarily self-correcting. He does so by making several observations. First, when science is at a low ebb, the production of wrong evidence or the distortion of evidence abounds.[29] Historically, we've seen examples in areas such as phrenology (feeling the bumps in the skull to determine one's psychological attributes), eugenics in Nazi Germany (aimed at preserving the Aryan race) and America (aimed at reducing the numbers of those seen as unfit for society), and the massively funded research of the tobacco industry in the twentieth century aimed at evaluating the consequences of smoking. In these periods, it's possible that the scientific environment becomes perverted to the point that people don't see what's happening and that they're deluded into believing their current science is delivering the truth.

Second, Ioannidis has shown that efforts to reproduce published results are dismal. (It's interesting, as he notes, that even hedge funds don't put much trust in published scientific results.) For instance, it's unlikely that replication efforts exceed 5% of current psychological literature with original data, and it may even be closer to 1%. Of the 1.07% identified by researchers, only 18% included direct rather than simply conceptual replications, and only 47% were done by investigators entirely different from the original authors. Unfortunately, the claimed findings with no published replication attempts make up the majority of psychological science. It's been estimated that 56% of the original research findings may be false positives, and (in the absence of replication) the vast majority remain unchallenged fantasies. However, Ioannidis notes that this figure doesn't account for potential biases, and, if there is even a modest amount, the prevalence of unchallenged fallacies may represent up to 95% of the significant findings in some areas.

Third, scientific findings are often shown to be the result of overestimation of result, random error, bias, or a combination, and can persist in the literature despite being contradicted. It can be shown that most claimed research findings are false and that the high rate of nonreplication

---

[29] John P. A. Ioannidis, "Why Science Is Not Necessarily Self-Correcting," *Perspectives on Psychological Science*, 7(6) 646ff.

of discoveries is a consequence of claiming conclusive findings on the basis of a single study—and typically with a p-value less than 0.05 (a p-value estimates how likely it is that data could come out the way they did if a "null hypothesis" were true—e.g., in a comparison of two drugs, that there is no difference between the effects of drugs A and B). This is on top of the fact that research isn't best summarized by p-values, despite the widespread belief that it is.[30] P-values, which are increasingly and incorrectly being reported as indicating true findings, are potentially misleading and selectively reported in favor of more significant results. (For an actual estimate of how likely a result is to be true or false, it has been argued that researchers should instead use false-discovery rates or Bayes factor calculations.)[31] Further, empirical evaluations have shown that small studies consistently give more favorable results than larger studies, with study quality being inversely related to effect size.[32]

As far as bias goes, Ioannidis notes that it doesn't usually arise from poor design and conduct but rather through picking in advance the research questions in such a way that the desired results are obtained. For academic investigators, these can involve things like confirmation and allegiance biases (which shouldn't be confused with chance variability). Bias can involve the manipulation in the analysis or reporting of findings, of which selective or distorted reporting can be typical forms.[33] He points out that even in the most stringent research designs, bias appears to be a major problem. There's strong evidence that selective outcome reporting—with manipulation of the outcomes and analyses reported—is a common problem even for randomized trials. In addition, the pressure to publish has influenced the publication system. For instance, after a journal has published a series

---

[30] John P. A. Ioannidis, "Why Most Published Research Findings Are False," *PLoS Medicine* 2 (8) 0696ff. It should be noted that Ioannidis proposes several ways to improve the process of scientific research and the reporting of results (0700-1).

[31] Jennie Dusheck, "Misleading P-Values Showing Up More Often in Biomedical Journal Articles," Stanford Medicine News Center, https://med.stanford.edu/news/all-news/2016/03/misleading-p-values-showing-up-more-often-in-journals.html.

[32] John P. A. Ioannidis, Marcus R. Munafo, Paolo Fusar-Poli, Brian A. Nosek, and Sean P. David, "Publication and Other Reporting Biases in Cognitive Sciences: Detection, Prevalence, and Prevention," *Trends in Cognitive Sciences*, May 2014, vol. 18, no. 5, 237.

[33] See also James Owen Weatherall, Cailin O'Connor, and Justin P. Bruner, "How to Beat Science and Influence People: Policy Makers and Propaganda in Epistemic Networks," https://www.journals.uchicago.edu/doi/full/10.1093/bjps/axy062.

of articles supporting some trend, its threshold for accepting contradictory articles is higher.

Evidence of bias at the editorial and peer review levels has also been demonstrated and adds to the problem. Included here is the bias to publish findings that seem striking and have positive magnitude, since these have better odds of being published. As an example, comparisons of published results against FDA records demonstrate that, though almost half of the trials on antidepressants for depression have negative results (in FDA records), these either remain unpublished or are published with distorted reporting that shows them as positive.[34] Thus, the published literature shows larger estimates of treatment effects for antidepressants than is warranted by the FDA data (this is also true for trials on antipsychotics). While financial interests may account for some of this, allegiance bias that favors specific cognitive, behavioral, or social theories may also play a part.

In addition, two other biases deserve mention. The first occurs when financial interests, conflicts of interest, and prejudice exist. The latter two items on this list can increase bias and are common in biomedical research, though they are seldom reported. While prejudice doesn't necessarily have a financial component, scientists can still exhibit it purely because of their belief in a scientific theory or a commitment to their own findings. Investigators may suppress (through the peer review process) the appearance and dissemination of findings that refute theirs, thereby perpetuating false dogma.

The second bias occurs in hotter scientific fields in which research findings are less likely to be true because many teams are rushing to get results published in order to beat their competition. Each team may prioritize reporting their most impressive "positive" results. But each team also tends to make extreme and divergent research claims, while trying to refute the opposing teams' research findings. This is especially common in molecular genetics. Epidemiological studies perform on the whole very poorly, especially when there are underpowered studies. Yet even with well-powered epidemiological studies, there may be only a one in five chance of their being true. The claimed effects can simply be a reflection of the net bias that exists within a given scientific literature. While investigators have traditionally viewed large and significant effects with excitement, too large

---

[34] John P. A. Ioannidis, Marcus R. Munafo, Paolo Fusar-Poli, Brian A. Nosek, and Sean P. David, "Publication and Other Reporting Biases in Cognitive Sciences: Detection, Prevalence, and Prevention," 238.

and too highly significant effects may actually be more likely to be signs of large bias in most fields of modern research. All of this is compounded by the fact that there are constant pressures to secure funding for research, which has had an adverse impact on the quality of scientific output. The resource deficiencies that have resulted, and the extreme pressure to publish, force researchers to run low-power experiments.

The fourth reason why science isn't necessarily self-correcting is that, even without findings that are a result of bias or chance—i.e., the finding is indeed true (non-null)—results often inflate true effect sizes.[35] For instance, a quarter of the most-cited clinical trials and 5/6 of the most-cited epidemiological studies were either fully contradicted or found to have exaggerated results. Evidence has demonstrated across a large sample of 379 epidemiological studies that investigators selected data to show larger effects. Inflated interpretation is another source of trouble for many studies, because investigators may make an extra effort to present results in the most favorable way. Typical ways this might occur include unwarranted extrapolations and overstated generalizability, downplaying limitations and caveats, and mishandling external evidence. Ioannidis comments that the "sparse successful clinical translation of major promises made in the most high-profile basic science journals shows that this over-interpretation is common."[36] While there may sometimes be a financial component, even when investigators fervently support their research, strongly refuted associations continue to have supporters years after the refutation. Investigators may simply suppress new findings when they don't suit their beliefs.

An example here will be instructive. In a meta-analysis of published research on the effectiveness of vitamin E for decreasing cardiovascular events, the authors demonstrate how completely contradicted claims can persist in the literature.[37] They focused on two highly cited articles published in 1993 that presented data from two observational cohorts showing that vitamin E was associated with major decreases in the risk of cardiovascular

---

[35] John P. A. Ioannidis, "Why Most Discovered True Associations Are Inflated," *Epidemiology*, vol. 19, no. 5 (September 2008), 640ff. See also Felipe Romero, "Can the Behavioral Sciences Self-Correct? A Social Epistemic Study," *Studies in History and Philosophy of Science*, Part A (2016), 60, 55-69.

[36] John P. A. Ioannidis, "Why Most Discovered True Associations Are Inflated," 643.

[37] Athina Tatsioni, Nikolaos G. Bonitsis, and John P. A. Ioannidis, "Persistence of Contradicted Claims in the Literature," *JAMA*, December 5, 2007, vol. 298, no. 21, 2518ff.

events. Based on these articles, vitamin E was thought to be cardioprotec-tive for many years. Despite several studies suggesting evidence supporting this, however, a recent meta-analysis concluded that, among high-quality trials, vitamin E increases mortality regardless of dose. Currently, vitamin E supplementation isn't recommended. Yet the story of the positive benefits of vitamin E persisted in the literature. Through 2005, 101 citing articles (61.2%) were favorable, 36 (21.8%) were equivocal, and 28 (17.0%) were unfavorable. Thus, despite the accumulation of strongly refuting evidence, even in 2005, 50% of the articles citing these epidemiological studies were still favorable to the vitamin E claim. The same thing happened in the case of beta-carotene for cancer prevention, with citing articles not mentioning contradicting trials.

The authors note that, while some counter-arguments (i.e., in defense of the persisting viewpoint) may be valid, this is also consistent with a belief being defended at all costs. "Sometimes investigator beliefs in scientific circles may have similar psychological characteristics as the nonscientific beliefs observed in other areas of society. The wish bias of individuals, irre-spective of topic, can be large and may also influence the interpretation of scientific results."[38]

Fifth, even if we have an increasing number of successful (hopefully correct) scientific results, this says nothing about the proportion of scientific results that aren't correct. Beyond this, Ioannidis points out that arguments linking progress to credibility make a logical leap of attribution; i.e., even when some progress is documented, it's not certain that we know where to attribute it. As an example, longer life expectancy is modest in devel-oped countries in recent years, and it's not at all clear that the majority of improvements are due to medicine rather than other practical improve-ments (hygiene, sanitation, etc.). Developed countries have spent over $10 trillion annually on medicine in the last decade (which is accelerating), but if the return is modest, there's a chance that wrong and inefficient medicine is becoming a major problem for civilization.

An Alternative Account of Progress

As we've now seen, the realist notion of progress isn't as easily supported as it first appears. Given this, Laudan proposes another way of looking at

[38] Athina Tatsioni, Nikolaos G. Bonitsis, and John P. A. Ioannidis, "Persistence of Contradicted Claims in the Literature," 2525.

progress that doesn't make it parasitic upon rationality.[39] Recall that for realists, rationality and scientific progress is bound up with the question of truth of scientific theories. As the argument goes, rationality amounts to accepting those statements about the world that we have good reason for believing to be true. Progress is thus seen as a successive attainment of the truth by a process of approximation and self-correction. However, Laudan proposes that we turn this on its head and make rationality parasitic upon progressiveness. Rather than seeing progress only as cumulative, he argues that rationality consists in making the most progressive theory choices. This is to say that, relative to the aspirations of science—which he views as primarily a problem-solving activity—he suggests that it's cognitive progress that the history of science demonstrates. By linking rationality to progressiveness, we can have a theory of rationality without presupposing anything about the truth or approximate truth of our theories—which has its upsides since no one has been able to say what it means to be "closer to the truth," let alone offer criteria for determining how we could assess such proximity.

As a way forward, Laudan offers two theses: (1) the first test for any theory is whether it provides acceptable answers to interesting questions, i.e., whether it provides satisfactory solutions to important problems; (2) in appraising the merits of theories, it's more important to ask whether they constitute adequate solutions to significant problems than to ask whether they're "true" or "well-confirmed." Of the problems science is designed to solve, one of the primary is the empirical. But to suggest this, Laudan points out that both history and philosophical analysis have shown that the world is always perceived through the lenses of some conceptual framework that puts a tint to what we perceive. Problems of every sort (including empirical ones) arise within a particular context and are partly defined by that context. Whether something is thought of as an empirical problem will depend (in part) on the theories that propose them as such. Kuhn also (correctly) pointed out that judgments of projectibility (i.e., as worthy of serious scientific and experimental consideration) and degrees of confirmation are dependent on the very theories under consideration. Theoretical traditions, or background theories,[40] dictate the terms in which questions

---

[39] Larry Laudan, *Progress and Its Problems: Towards a Theory of Scientific Growth* (Berkeley, 1977), 5-7, 13-16, 80-93, 95, 125-6.
[40] Peter Lipton, "Is The Best Good Enough?" in *The Philosophy of Science* (New York, 1996), ed. David Papineau, 100, 106. Lipton acknowledges that, given the background objection, realists need to be thoroughgoing fallibilists, allowing for the possibility of error about theory, the data that support it, and the assessment about the support itself.

and answers are posed, as well as the standards for experimental design and assessment of experimental evidence.[41] Thus, as long as we insist on the idea that theories are designed only to explain "facts" (true statements about the world), we'll be unable to explain most of the theoretical activity that's taken place in science.

Because research traditions (or theoretical traditions, just mentioned) play such a decisive role in theory formation and development, they deserve a bit more discussion here. Laudan describes a research tradition as a set of ontological and methodological do's and don'ts. It's a set of general assumptions about the entities and processes in a domain of study, as well as the appropriate methods to be used for investigating problems and constructing theories in that domain. But research traditions are historical creatures created within a particular intellectual milieu, and they wax and wane just as other intellectual traditions do. Whereas a research tradition specifies a *general* ontology for nature and a *general* method for solving problems, a theory offers a specific ontology and specific and testable laws about nature. A successful research tradition leads to the solution of an increasing range of empirical and conceptual problems. In determining whether a research tradition is successful, we shouldn't take that to mean that the tradition has been confirmed (or disconfirmed) or that it's true (or false). This is because, while it may be successful at generating fruitful theories, it may be flawed in its ontology or methodology.

One of the important things about a research tradition is that it can strongly influence the range of empirical problems with which its component theories must grapple. It also has a decisive influence on what can count as a conceptual problem that the theories in that tradition can generate. It does so by indicating that it's appropriate to discuss certain empirical problems, while others are pseudo-problems that can be legitimately ignored. Either the methodology or ontology of the research tradition can influence what counts as a legitimate problem. If the methodology specifies certain experimental techniques that are legitimate in investigation, then only "phenomena" that can be explored by those means can count as legitimate empirical problems. Serving as a sort of

---

[41] All of this raises the question antirealists want to ask: why should such a theory-dependent methodology be reliable at producing knowledge about theory-independent observable phenomena? Richard N. Boyd, "The Current Status of Scientific Realism," in *Scientific Realism* (Berkeley, 1984), ed. Jarrett Leplin, 57.

guardrail, those who attempt what's forbidden by the metaphysics and methodology of a research tradition put themselves outside that tradition.

An example of this comes from nineteenth-century phenomenological chemistry, which insisted that the only legitimate problems involved those that concerned the observable reactions of chemical reagents. This means that to ask how atoms combine to form diatomic molecules can't count as an empirical problem to be solved. For ontology, the emergence of special relativity theory made all empirical problems about the ether moot since it denied its very existence. Thus, traditions make assumptions about causal processes and entities whose existence and operation become givens for a theory within the tradition. The upside is that a tradition frees the scientist from having to justify all his assumptions and gives him time to pursue specific problems of interest, while the downside is that the tradition may foreclose exploring alternatives that might be more productive.

For Laudan, this all boils down to the claim that the single most cognitive aim of science is problem solving and that maximization of the empirical problems we can explain and the minimization of the anomalous and conceptual problems we generate are science's reason for existence. Any research tradition that can exemplify this over time is a progressive one. Thus, the primary way of being scientifically rational is to do whatever we can to maximize the progress of scientific research traditions. Rationality, in turn, consists in accepting the best available research tradition.[42] Because this isn't tied to the notion of truth, we may endorse theories that are progressive and rational, that turn out to be false (assuming that we could definitively establish such a thing). But this shouldn't give us pause since past theories are already suspected of being false, which means that there's reason to think that current theories will suffer a similar fate. This shouldn't render scientific theories and research traditions irrational or non-progressive. Far from siding with the instrumentalist (who contends that science has no bearing on the real world or on truth), Laudan insists that his model allows the possibility for theories to be true and that science may have moved closer and closer to the truth. Yet this doesn't change the fact that we have no way of knowing for sure that science is true, probable, or that it's

---

[42] Larry Laudan, *Progress and Its Problems: Towards a Theory of Scientific Growth*, 124, 126-7, 144-5. Laudan also suggests because it's rational to discuss the problems research traditions generate, it's rational to raise philosophical and religious objections against it if it runs counter to a well-established worldview.

getting closer to the truth. Such aims are utopian, and we can never know whether they're being achieved.

None of this is to say, as Kuhn did, that we can't assess the merits of competing research traditions. In the late seventeenth century, for example, there were conflicting theories of light that addressed the problem of reflection. The various optical theories all solved the problem in their own ways, and that was possible because the problem to be solved could be characterized in a way that was independent of any of the theories that sought to solve it. In other words, the shared problems provided a basis for rational appraisal of the problem-solving effectiveness of competing research traditions. When early nineteenth-century geologists debated the idea of stratification, they could all (no matter what position they took) agree that one problem for any geological theory was to explain how uniform and distinct layers were formed. In his more radical view, Kuhn was misled by the fact that some empirical problems aren't jointly shared between different traditions (paradigms) into believing that no problems are common to them.

Nicholas Rescher has countered Laudan by noting that, if progress turns on the numerical increase in the sheer quantity of answered questions, then how are we to understand the counting process?[43] How many questions does "What causes cancer?" amount to? And how do we avoid the ambiguity that once an answer is given, we can always raise more questions about its inner details and outer relationships? In contrast, Rescher thinks that progress should be understood along practical lines, i.e., as it's manifested in its technical advances. This idea is practical in the sense that it isn't heavily theory-laden, but rather is based on the fact that our control over nature and its predictive successes have been extended in many ways that impact our everyday life. Thus, a new theory needn't explain the purported facts of an older one because these "facts" may not even remain facts. The new theory may revise them or dismiss them altogether.

Conclusion

We've now seen several serious objections to the realist program that, if unanswerable, casts doubt on the realist's ability to make his claims about scientific activity. As noted, most antirealists are empiricists who are

---

[43] Nicholas Rescher, *The Limits of Science*, 21, 39, 41.

skeptical of claims to "know" those elements of a theory that are unobservable—or those to which the only access we have is through the very theories that postulate their existence. Concerning the realist's use of abductive inference to bolster the case that success equals truth (or approximate truth), antirealists question whether acceptable explanations need to be true and whether the entities used in them need to exist. For them, we can't beg the question about the significance of explanatory power by assuming that it carries truth as well as explanatory power. Similar problems face the realist miracle argument, which may be another manifestation of a failure to consider base rates—in which we ignore the unlikelihood that, prior to testing, a particular theory should be true—which has the effect of hiding from view all those other theories that would be just as successful even though they're false.

Perhaps one of the more formidable objections against realism comes from the history of science. There seems to be ample evidence that theories whose central terms genuinely refer (according to realists) are often unsuccessful. Conversely, there are many once-successful, yet by current standards non-referring, theories. Laudan argues that the realist claim that he can explain why science is successful appears to be false, insofar as part of the historical success of science has been the success of theories whose central terms didn't refer. Further, against the realist idea that new theories typically retain central elements of predecessors, the historical record seems to indicate that scientists have accepted empirically successful theories regardless of whether they contain the theoretical laws and mechanisms of their predecessors.

It's these types of considerations that lead Rescher to the conclusion that we're wrong to view the science of our day—or of any day—as affording the final truth. Any attempts to equate the real truth with apparent truth are doomed to failure. To base such attempts on the science that we have is circular, which implies that there's no adequate way to maintain the completeness of science in a rationally satisfactory way. Add to this that meta-analyses of peer-reviewed studies are often flawed in many ways and tend to overestimate results, and we seem to have one of the critical realist assumptions put into serious jeopardy. Finally, we saw that one of the central realist theses concerning the idea of progress was attacked and reformulated. Rather than making progress parasitic upon rationality, Laudan suggests that we make rationality parasitic upon progressiveness; i.e., rather than seeing progress only as cumulative, rationality consists in making the most progressive theory choices.

Predictably, realists have launched sustained replies to antirealist objections and account for much of the back-and-forth between the two camps. So that we don't short realism of the ability to defend itself against these charges, it's to those responses we turn next.

Chapter 5
Realist Replies

Antirealists, as we've now seen, have put forth some serious objections to realism. Not only have they assaulted its philosophical foundations, but many of their objections are rooted in the actual history of science, which seems to show some of the core realist arguments to be more like wishes than facts. Taken as a whole, such criticisms have raised a conundrum for realism and have prompted some key questions about its epistemic status. To cite just a few, consider the following: If past, highly successful, theories touted unobservable entities we now regard as fictional, then how can we justify the conclusion that our current theories accurately describe the world? Also, if theoretical terms tend to change over time, then aren't we forced to say that they no longer refer to the same referent and thereby undermine a realist conception of progress?

Beyond this, haven't antirealists cast the validity of the very abductive reasoning on which the realist argument rests into doubt? How, the former want to know, is abduction not question-begging, and why does an acceptable explanation need to be true and its proposed entities need to exist? Doesn't theory underdetermination weaken the link between explanatory goodness and truth? Further, how can we justifiably say that we know much of anything about entities that fall outside of normal human perception? And since those sense-extending instruments we use to gain this knowledge are themselves theory-dependent, how do we know that we're not seeing something other than the entity we believe we are? Finally, if our scientific judgments truly are as theory-dependent as it would seem, why would we think they're reliable at producing knowledge about observable phenomena?

To be sure, in order to maintain the central theses we've discussed, the realist must provide reasonable answers or be charged with promoting a fictional account of science. It's these rejoinders that this chapter will evaluate, beginning with the idea of theory-dependency.

Theory-Dependency

In the last chapter, we discussed the fact that science depends in large part on theory-dependent judgments about the inner workings of nature. Judgments of projectibility (i.e., as worthy of serious scientific and experimental consideration) and degrees of confirmation are dependent on the very theories under consideration. Further, theoretical/research traditions dictate the terms in which questions and answers are posed, as well as the standards for experimental design and assessment of experimental evidence.[1] Thus (for the antirealist), as long as we insist on the idea that theories are designed only to explain "facts" (true statements about the world), we'll be unable to explain most of the theoretical activity that's taken place in science. All of this raises the question antirealists want to ask: why should such a theory-dependent methodology be reliable at producing knowledge about theory-independent observable phenomena?

In response, Richard Boyd goes on the offensive and insists that only a realist conception of science accounts for why scientific theories are *instrumentally* reliable.[2] Against the constructivist, he insists that the reliability of theory-dependent judgments of projectibility and degrees of confirmation are best explained on the assumption that theoretical claims are approximately true. In the long run, scientific methodology produces an increasingly accurate picture of the world. And the approximate truth of current theories explains why our existing measurement procedures are reliable. This, in turn, explains why our experimental/observational investigations are successful in revealing new theoretical knowledge (which, in turn, produces improvements in measurement techniques).[3] Though we'll

---

[1] Richard N. Boyd, "The Current Status of Scientific Realism," in *Scientific Realism* (Berkeley, 1984), ed. Jarrett Leplin, 57.

[2] Richard N. Boyd, "The Current Status of Scientific Realism," in *Scientific Realism*, 59-60. Boyd argues that, like the causal or naturalistic theories of perception (discussed in a previous chapter), the realist must see epistemology as an empirical science (64-5), even if it's still considered normative.

[3] Richard Boyd, "Realism, Approximate Truth, and Philosophical Method" in *The Philosophy of Science* (New York, 1996), ed. David Papineau, 222.

have more to say about this in the next chapter, the bottom line (from Boyd's perspective) is that theory-dependent technological progress can't be explained by a simple appeal to the social construction of reality.

Abduction Revisited

Recall that antirealists question whether acceptable explanations need to be true and whether the entities used in them need to exist. For them, we can't beg the question about the significance of explanatory power by assuming that it carries truth as well as explanatory power. In short, the usual abductive methods that lead us to good explanations can't be counted on to get us theories that are approximately true. To these objections, Boyd points out (per Fine's insistence) that the issue between empiricists and realists over the legitimacy of abduction is a double-edged sword. It may highlight a sort of circularity in realism, but it's just as important to note that its prohibition would place a significant restriction on intellectual inquiry. If the fact that a theory provides the best explanation for some phenomenon isn't a justification for thinking it is approximately true, then it's difficult to see how intellectual inquiry could proceed.[4]

Further, empiricists want to allow for some types of induction as long as they're confined to observable phenomena (and exclude unobservables). But Boyd notes that the methods of science are profoundly theory-dependent, and this dependence extends to the methods scientists use when making inductive generalizations about observables. The choice, generalizations, and assessment of the evidence rest upon theoretical inferences that depend on the very abduction the empiricist rejects. Thus, theory-dependent considerations are intertwined with the confirmation or disconfirmation of inductive generalizations, which means that a commitment to (knowledge) empiricism leads to the unwelcome conclusion that even inductive inferences concerning observables are unjustified. In the end, Boyd contends that, when the theory-dependent methodological practices display the intricacy and instrumental reliability characteristic of modern physics and chemistry, only a realistic account of science gives an adequate explanation of that reliability.

Beyond Boyd's remarks, one of the more detailed defenses of abduction—or what he refers to as inference to the best explanation—comes

---

[4] Richard N. Boyd, "The Current Status of Scientific Realism," in *Scientific Realism*, 67-73, 77.

from Peter Lipton, who highlights the fact that these sorts of explanatory inferences are extremely common.[5] The tracks in the snow, for instance, are evidence for what explains them—that a person has been there in snow-shoes. The doctor infers his patient has the measles since this provides the best explanation of the symptoms. The astronomer infers the existence of Neptune since that's the best explanation of the observed perturbations of Uranus, and we even use abductive reasoning to infer Napoleon's exis-tence; that is, we infer it not by traveling back in time but from our study of present effects (artifacts and records).[6] We construct causal scenarios and think about what they would explain and how well. The use of inference to the best explanation implies that our inferential practices are governed by explanatory considerations. Given our evidence and our background beliefs, we infer what would—if true—provide the best of the competing explanations we can generate of that evidence (assuming, of course, that it's good enough to make an inference).

Lipton suggests that, in such cases, explanatory considerations are a guide to inference—and that for something to be an explanation, it must be at least approximately true. Within the sciences, researchers don't just judge a possible explanation on whether it's likely to be true, but they also consider aesthetic factors—i.e., a theory's elegance, simplicity, and unification—as a guide to inference (Lipton refers to this latter notion as an explanation's loveliness).[7] One of the points of our obsessive search for explanations, he argues, is that it's an effective way of discovering the structure of the world.

Because abduction faces the problem that there may be more than one cause which can explain the same effect (encapsulated in the problem of underdetermination), the late-nineteenth-century geologist Thomas Chamberlain devised something he called "method of multiple working hypotheses" (which contemporary philosophers of science have come to call "inference to the best explanation"). With it, scientists compare various hypotheses to see which would, if true, best explain the data. They then tentatively affirm the hypothesis that best explains the data as the most likely to be true; this, when they can infer a uniquely plausible cause (one known cause of some effect), enables them to avoid the fallacy of affirming

---

[5] Peter Lipton, *Inference to the Best Explanation* (London, 2004), 56-7, 65-6.

[6] Stephen C. Meyer, *Signature in the Cell: DNA and the Evidence for Intelligent Design* (New York, 2009), 153.

[7] For Lipton's rebuttal to the objection that the notion of loveliness/beauty is too subjective to be of value, see 142ff.

the consequent. As Stephen Meyer puts it, "These illustrations show that the process of determining the best explanation often involves generating a list of possible hypotheses, comparing their known (or theoretically plausible) causal powers against the relevant evidence, looking for additional facts if necessary, and then, like a detective, progressively eliminating potential but inadequate explanations until, finally, one causally adequate explanation for the ensemble of relevant evidence remains."[8]

To the antirealists' appeal to underdetermination as an objection to abduction, Nancy Cartwright points out that underdetermination is a general feature of our knowledge and is not found, to any peculiar extent, in cases of inference to the best explanation.[9] It's worth noting that Duhem, who attacks abduction based on underdetermination, doesn't oppose phenomenological laws that arise by inductive generalization, even though it's possible to construct different inductive rules that give rise to different generalizations from the same evidence. Here, too, there will always be more than one incompatible law that appears equally true, as far as we can tell.

In his detailed defense, Lipton refers us to a poignant example of inference to the best explanation at work. It concerns Ignaz Semmelweis' research on childbed fever from 1844-1848, the first of which occurred in 1846, when a large number of women and infants were dying during childbirth in Vienna.[10] The cause was puerperal fever. What didn't make sense was that the hospital had two maternity clinics and only one of them was experiencing the high death rate. In fact, more women and infants survived giving birth in the street than in this clinic; those deaths, incidentally, all came at the hands of doctors. Midwives delivered babies in the unaffected clinic, but the stark contrast between the two made no sense.

Vienna General happened to be a teaching hospital where doctors learned their craft by cutting up cadavers. It was common at the time for doctors to go straight from dissecting corpses to delivering babies, proudly wearing their blood-stained gowns and without washing their hands.

---

[8] Stephen C. Meyer, *Signature in the Cell: DNA and the Evidence for Intelligent Design*, 154, 161, 166. Meyer notes that it's not just historical scientists that use this method, as Watson and Crick probably used it in their investigations of DNA (170).

[9] Nancy Cartwright, *How the Laws of Physics Lie* (Oxford, 1983), 90. Ernan McMullin suggests that in cases where models are empirically equivalent, our stance should be not a rejection of realism but an admission that no decision can be made in this case to what the theory commits us to. See McMullin, "A Case for Scientific Realism" in *Scientific Realism* (Berkeley, 1984), ed. Jarrett Leplin, 11.

[10] Kevin Ashton, *How To Fly A Horse* (New York, 2015), 72-75, 91-95.

Semmelweis started to wonder if the disease was being carried from the corpses to the maternity ward, and he considered several hypotheses as explanations. One of them marked a difference between the clinics, and, when eliminating the difference, he eliminated the difference in mortality. After receiving a puncture wound during an autopsy, Kolletschka (one of Semmelweis' colleagues) died from an illness with symptoms much like childbed fever. This led Semmelweis to infer that Kolletschka's death was due to "cadaveric matter" that was introduced into his bloodstream—which then led Semmelweis to hypothesize that the same explanation may also account for the deaths in the other clinic, since the doctors in one did their examinations directly after performing autopsies and midwives didn't perform them at all. This would also explain why the women who delivered outside the hospital had a lower mortality from childbed fever. Despite his colleague's resistance, Semmelweis persuaded them to wash their hands before delivering babies and the results were immediate. The death rate plummeted from eighteen to two percent, the same as the other clinic. He'd finally found a difference between the two clinics that made a difference, and Semmelweis inferred the cadaveric hypothesis.[11]

Lipton points out that Semmelweis' case highlights many of the virtues of inference to the best explanation when the account is tied to contrastive explanation. First, it shows how considering potential contrastive explanations (e.g., the contrast between the initial presence of cadaveric matter and its subsequent absence) focuses inquiry. To do so, he focused contrastive why questions, using the midwife clinic as a foil, because it provided a case where the effect (childbed fever) was absent yet the causal histories were similar. By asking why the contrast existed, he searched for explanatory hypotheses based on the remaining differences. As we noted, this strategy is widely used. If we want to find out why some phenomenon occurs—and if we're lucky enough to find a contrast where fact and foil have similar histories—then most potential explanations (of which there will be many) will be eliminated, meaning we have a manageable way forward. This contrast will be particularly helpful if, as in Semmelweis' case, it's also a contrast that the other hypotheses don't explain. Normally, this will still leave more than one hypothesis on the table, but further observation and experimentation may yield new contrasts that leave only one explanation. "By tailoring his explanatory interests (and his observational and experimental procedures) to contrasts that would help to discriminate

---

[11] Peter Lipton, *Inference to the Best Explanation*, 74-5.

between competing hypotheses, Semmelweis was able to judge which hypotheses would provide the best overall explanation of the wide variety of contrasts (and absences of contrast) he observed, and so to judge which hypothesis he ought to infer."[12]

Semmelweis' use of contrasts and prior differences to help generate a list of possible hypotheses illustrates one of the ways inference to the best explanation illuminates the context of discovery in science (which is a central feature of our inductive practice). As we consider what sort of explanation a hypothesis would provide, if it were true, we consider not just how good an explanation it would be, but also what (as yet) unobserved contrasts it would explain; this, in turn, directs future observation and experimentation. Even so, the antirealist still wants to insist that the truth of a theory isn't the best explanation of its predictive success. Van Fraassen, for instance, gave what he thinks is a better explanation of predictive success along neo-Darwinian lines: scientific theories have observed consequences that are true because they were selected for precisely that reason.[13] The scientific method has a selection mechanism that eliminates theories whose observed consequences are false, which is why the ones that remain tend to have observed consequences that are true. But Lipton retorts that, while van Fraassen may have explained why all the theories we now accept have been observationally successful, he hasn't explained why each of them has been successful, i.e., why a particular theory that was selected for its observational success has this feature.

The miracle argument, on the other hand (again, that the success of science would be miraculous if its theories were not largely true) does explain this by appealing to an intrinsic feature of the theory rather than simply to the principle by which it was selected. It's no miracle, for instance, that all the members of the club have red hair if this was a criterion of selection. The real miracle with theories we judge to be well supported, however, is that they go on to make successful predictions. The selection mechanism doesn't explain this since it doesn't explain why our best theories aren't refuted in their next application. The abductive inference to truth as the best explanation provides an explanation to a theory's continuing predictive success. "This assumes that our criteria are generally truth-tropic, so that is not explained, but the miracle argument does explain our continuing observational success and ... an explanation may be sound

---

[12] Peter Lipton, *Inference to the Best Explanation*, 80-3.
[13] Bas C. van Fraassen, *The Scientific Image* (New York, 1980), 39-40.

and provide understanding even though what does the explaining is not itself explained."[14]

Both van Fraassen and Duhem have argued that explanation has truth added on only as an extra ingredient, making the latter unnecessary. But Cartwright contends that causal explanations have truth built into them.[15] When we infer from an effect to a cause, we're asking what made the effect occur. No explanation explains anything unless it presents a cause, and when we accept such an explanation, we're accepting that it explains in the sense of making plain, but also that it poses a cause. Consider a newly planted lemon tree that is sick, with its leaves yellowing and dropping off. We explain this by suggesting that water has accumulated in the base of the planter—the water is the cause of the disease. And indeed, we find water where we expected it, but there must be water for the explanation to be correct. An explanation of an effect by a cause has an existential component and isn't just an optional extra ingredient. The same is true when we explain the change in rate in fall of a light droplet in an electric field. By saying there are positrons or electrons on the ball we're inferring from effect to a cause, and the explanation has no sense without the implication that there are positrons or electrons on the ball. While the second case doesn't involve confirmation with our eyes, there are other effects. If the ball is negatively charged, we can spray it with a positron emitter and change the rate of fall of the ball. Here, we infer the best explanation to the most probable cause, and that cause is something specific, what we call a theoretical entity. And it's not Bohr's, Rutherford's, or Lorenz's electron; it's the electron about which we have a number of incomplete and sometimes conflicting theories.

But what about the argument that inference to the best explanation ignores base rates? Lipton responds by saying that what Kahneman's research has shown is that we need help with Bayesianism.[16] In cases where we fail to acknowledge the correctness of probabilistic considerations, we can still come to see that our reasoning was flawed. And this suggests that we do have some of the constraints, embedded somewhere in our epistemic competence, of probability theory. Having said that, Lipton notes that in many real-life situations, the calculation that Bayesianism requires isn't a recipe we can readily follow; i.e., we don't always know how to work out the required probabilities. Because of this, he suggests that explanatory

---

[14] Peter Lipton, *Inference to the Best Explanation*, 193-4.
[15] Nancy Cartwright, *How the Laws of Physics Lie*, 91-2.
[16] Peter Lipton, *Inference to the Best Explanation*, 111, 114, 119.

considerations of the sort to which inference to the best explanation appeals are often more accessible than probabilistic principles to people in general or even to professional scientists in the laboratory. This can provide an effective surrogate for certain components of the Bayesian calculation.

Consider again the case of Semmelweis, whose procedure seems defensible from a Bayesian point of view. Rather than considering whether the prior of the composite evidence is higher than the likelihoods the competitors would give it, he thought about what the various hypotheses would and wouldn't explain. His causal-explanatory approach allowed him to think about his research in concrete physical terms. For most of us, this procedure is far easier than the abstract one of calculation that Bayesianism requires. It's not that we're always more reliable in our judgments, but that we at times get the abstract principle right while failing to apply it in the concrete. Lipton's point is that we tend to think in concrete terms even when we would do better with some abstraction, and that explanation generally does a good job of performing the Bayesian calculation (or at least ends up in much the same cognitive place).

The bottom line is that the research shows that we're not great at abstract probabilistic calculation and that we need to use heuristics (rules of thumb), including explanatory heuristics. While Kahneman's work has been used to demonstrate where heuristics yield a different result than straight Bayesianism, the former can be seen as a way of approximating the Bayesian result. "Bayes's theorem provides a constraint on the rational distribution of degrees of belief, but this is compatible with the view that explanatory considerations play a crucial role in the evolution of those beliefs, and indeed a crucial role in the mechanism by which we attempt, with considerable but not complete success, to meet that constraint. That is why the Bayesian and the explanationist (a person who holds that beliefs are justified by their usefulness in explaining) should be friends."[17]

Realistic Progress

As we saw in the last chapter, one of the contentions antirealists have with realism concerns the idea of progress as being cumulative, with antirealists jumping on the apparent fact that theoretical terms tend to change over time, meaning that they no longer refer to the same referent.

---

[17] Peter Lipton, *Inference to the Best Explanation*, 120.

However, Putnam says that the correct approach should be based on the "principle of benefit of the doubt" or "principle of charity," though not an unreasonable charity.[18] It's a fact, he insists, that we can assign a referent to Mendel's gene from the standpoint of modern molecular biology; that is, surely the gene discussed in molecular biology is the gene Mendel *intended* to talk about. When speakers describe a term, and then because of their mistaken factual beliefs the description fails to refer, we should assume that they would accept reasonable reformulations of their descriptions. For instance, there's nothing in the world that *exactly* fits the Bohr-Rutherford description of an electron. But there are particles which approximately fit Bohr's description: they have the correct charge and mass, and they're responsible for key effects that Bohr-Rutherford explained with the term electron. We should stipulate that we have a different theory of the *same* entities Bohr called "electrons," and we can say this because present theory asserts the existence of entities that fill many of the *roles* Bohr's electrons were supposed to fill. Believing that the terms in theory T_1 have genuine referents will provide an important constraint on T_2—it will narrow the class of candidate theories that T_2 must retain.

In a similar vein, Philip Kitcher argues that conceptual shifts in science can be understood as progressive by recognizing them as improvements in reference potentials of key terms. He illustrates this with one of Kuhn's favorite problematic cases involving the chemical revolution of the eighteenth century, centered around the work of Priestley and Lavoisier. Recall that Kuhn insisted on the conceptual incommensurability of competing theories, or that to accept a theory is to accept a quasi-private language that no one who doesn't accept the same theory can understand[19] As the story is framed, Priestley employed language containing the terms "phlogiston" and "principle," each of which fail to refer. Since the referent of "phlogiston" is fixed through the description "the substance is emitted in combustion" and since nothing is emitted in combustion, phlogiston fails to refer. This means that statements that talk about the properties of phlogiston can't be true. Lavoisier used language containing the terms "oxygen" and "element" that refer in a way that Priestley couldn't have identified. Thus, we see between the two a conceptual advance, or the replacement of terms as we move from

---

[18] Hilary Putnam, "What is Realism?" in *Scientific Realism* (Berkeley, 1984), ed. Jarrett Leplin, 143, 145.

[19] Larry Laudan, *Progress and Its Problems: Towards a Theory of Scientific Growth* (Berkeley, 1977), 142.

Priestley's theory to Lavoisier's, i.e., terms that fail to refer in the former case to ones that do in the latter. Yet Priestley was a successful chemist and was responsible for the experiment that isolated a new gas, which Lavoisier called "oxygen." But this presents a puzzle. If Priestley's central theoretical terms don't refer, then how do we ascribe to him the achievements warranted by the historical record? And if those terms do refer, then aren't we saying that the world must contain entities we no longer recognize?

Kitcher suggests that an adequate solution to this must (1) recognize Priestley's contributions to the development of chemistry, (2) avoid populating nature with strange entities and, (3) specify the exact manner in which Lavoisier made a conceptual advance. Since Priestley wasn't engaged in fictional work, we should recognize (similar to Putnam's principle of charity) that contained within his inadequate language are some important new truths about chemical reactions that are trying to get out. Unfortunately, a false presupposition that something is emitted in combustion infects most of his terminology. Still, true doctrines are trying to escape flawed language. "Surely Priestley's token of 'dephlogisticated air,'" Kitcher insists (after citing a passage by Priestley), "refers to the substance which he and the mice breathed—namely, oxygen."[20] At least on some occasions, Priestley (and his colleagues) have as their dominant intention to refer to the type of stuff that was isolated in the experiments they are reporting, namely, oxygen. Lavoisier made a conceptual advance by revising his language so as to avoid presupposing false hypotheses.

Recall that one of Kuhn's objections to realism is that the notion that there's a match between the scientist's representation of the world and what's "really there" (a correspondence theory of truth) is illusory. Because our descriptions of what's really there are theory-dependent—in that they presuppose some language and some conceptualizations of nature—and because there is no Archimedean (completely independent) point from which both can be viewed, Kuhn concludes that there's no way we can match the two or ever know they match. But Kitcher complains

---

[20] Philip Kitcher, *The Advancement of Science: Science Without Legend, Objectivity Without Illusions* (New York, 1993), 97-100, 103, 129-33. Kitcher argues that once we liberate ourselves from the presupposition that there should be a uniform mode of reference for all tokens of a single type, we can see that a scientific term may have a heterogeneous reference potential. Because on some occasions the referents of the tokens "dephlogisticated air" are fixed differently, Priestley (and Cavendish) enunciate important new truths (101-2). See also Philip Kitcher, "Theories, Theorists and Theoretical Change," *The Philosophical Review*, vol. 87, no. 4 (Oct., 1978), 519-547.

that Kuhn's move from the theory-dependence of our *perception* of nature to the theory-dependence of *nature* is illegitimate. This is because realists insist that there is a constant fixed nature. And, as they would characterize it, Lavoisier, as a result of his interactions with this nature, underwent some changes in his understanding of it. (Laudan also criticizes Kuhn for failing to explain how, if paradigms are self-reinforcing as he claims, advocates of one paradigm might ever find reasons that would lead them to change their paradigmatic allegiances.[21]) Realism, Kitcher insists, provides us with a picture of the genesis of perceptual belief that attributes a causal role to a world beyond our own cognition. And that picture offers an explanation of the fact that some of our beliefs come to us unbidden, as well as allowing us to understand our seeming ability to achieve increased match between our representations and an independent reality.

Laudan, who, as we've seen offers an alternative view of progress, insists against Kuhn's account that scientific revolutions are not so revolutionary and normal science isn't so normal.[22] The posing and resolving of problems is continuous throughout the life of any active research tradition. Kuhn and his followers haven't been able to point to any lengthy period in the history of any major paradigm when its adherents closed their eyes to the problems the paradigm generated. Rarely does any one paradigm achieve the hegemony that Kuhn requires for normal science, as history shows that two or more research traditions in each area have been the rule rather than the exception. It's the co-existence of conflicting traditions of research that makes the obsession with revolutionary epochs misleading. These traditions are constantly evolving, with their fortunes shifting through time. For Laudan, it's the shared empirical problems that establish the connections between successive research traditions; it's these that exhibit the partially cumulative character that is so striking about much of the history of science.

Another way to see progress, from a realist view, is by saying that science makes explanatory progress when later practices introduce explanatory

---

[21] Larry Laudan, *Science and Values: The Aims of Science and Their Role in Scientific Debate* (Berkeley, 1984), 17. Laudan notes that Kuhn lacks an account of consensus formation precisely because of his view of dissensus, which requires such deep incommensurabilities between scientists that there's no common ground upon which to shape new agreement (18).

[22] Larry Laudan, *Progress and Its Problems: Towards a Theory of Scientific Growth*, 134, 136, 140.

ideas better than earlier ones.[23] But what does "better" mean? One answer is that there's an objective order of dependency in nature: for instance, chemical reactions are objectively dependent on underlying molecular properties; mountain building and earthquakes are objectively dependent on plate tectonics, and so on. Our recognition of such dependencies, and how to extend them, is an important progressive step. Another way to understand this is to connect it with an enhanced ability to understand phenomena, e.g., by proposing that some ideas offer a more unified vision of the world.

A bit more technically, Kitcher proposes that explanatory progress involves something like this. P_2 is explanatorily progressive over P_1 if the explanatory ideas of P_2 agree with those of P_1, except in one or more of the following: P_2 contains correct ideas that don't occur in P_1; P_1 contains an incorrect idea that doesn't occur in P_2; P_2 contains a more complete version of an idea that occurs in P_1; P_2 contains an idea that correctly extends an idea of P_1. Making explanatory progress in this sense advances our recognition of the structure of natural phenomena. To flesh this out, Kitcher offers an analogy that should help. Consider children building a large and complex jigsaw puzzle. Subregions of the puzzle correspond to the dependencies among particular phenomena. Identifying correct ideas is analogous to fitting a few pieces together, the correction of ideas corresponds to scrapping faulty attempt at fitting pieces together, the completion and extension of ideas consists in putting the pieces already fitted together into larger chunks of the puzzle, with the aim of completing the picture (the last of which may not ever happen in science).

History Revisited

Recall that Laudan—who offers a particularly effective critique of realism—cited many examples in the history of science in which a theory was highly successful, yet turned out to be false (thus undermining claims of truth and reference). In response, Kitcher asks us to distinguish what he calls working posits (the presumed referents of terms that occur in problem-solving ideas) and presuppositional posits (those entities that apparently have to exist if the instances of the ideas are to be true).[24]

---

[23] Philip Kitcher, *The Advancement of Science: Science Without Legend, Objectivity Without Illusions*, 106, 111-2.

[24] Philip Kitcher, *The Advancement of Science: Science Without Legend, Objectivity Without Illusions*, 140-9.

To illustrate, he uses the ether (so often touted by Laudan) as an example of a presuppositional posit, rarely employed in explanation or prediction and never subjected to empirical measurement (at least until Michelson's famous experiment). Yet, it appeared at the time to be required to exist if the claims about electromagnetic and light waves were to be true. This is because the success of the optical and electromagnetic ideas gave scientists good reason for believing that electromagnetic waves were propagated according to Maxwell's equations. From that conclusion, they derived the existence of the ether, but only by supposing that wave propagation requires a medium (ether). Thus, the confirmation of the ether, Kitcher maintains, was no better than the evidence for that supposition. On this understanding, the thrust of Laudan's analysis isn't that theoretical positing in general is untrustworthy, but that presuppositional posits may not exist.

Whether or not Kitcher adequately answers Laudan's criticism, he nevertheless insists that a finer-grained look at the history of science shows that, where we're successful, our references tend to survive changes in practice and are built upon by later scientists. And this should give us grounds to say that our successful ideas use terms that genuinely refer, that our claims are approximately true, and that they give us insight into dependencies in nature that are correct.

What We Can Observe

In the last chapter, we saw that van Fraassen disallowed being able to know much of anything about entities that fall outside of normal human perception (at least in principle). This would seem to mean that we've observed something by an optical instrument only if we (assuming we have fairly normal vision) could have seen that very thing with the naked eye. But what, Ian Hacking asks, is so great about 20-20 vision? Observation in science isn't passive seeing, it's a skill.[25] Experimenters bring into being phenomena that don't naturally exist in a pure state (in nature).[26] The experimenter is usually convinced of the reality of the entities because they can be used to test conjectures about other, more hypothetical entities. As an example, one is sure of the electrons that are used to investigate weak

---

[25] Ian Hacking, "Do We See Through a Microscope?" https://philpapers.org/archive/HACDWS.pdf.

[26] Ian Hacking, "Experimentation and Scientific Realism," in *Scientific Realism* (Berkeley, 1984), ed. Jarrett Leplin, 155, 160, 167-8, 170.

neutral currents and neutral bosons. "This should not be news," Hacking explains, "for why else are we (nonskeptics) sure of the reality of even macroscopic objects, but because of what we do with them, what we do to them, and what they do to us?" This isn't to say that there wasn't a time when it made sense to doubt that there were electrons. As luck has it, we don't have to pretend to infer the existence of electrons because of their explanatory success. Experimenters don't explain phenomena with electrons; they know how to use them.

The difference between electrons and neutral bosons, according to Hacking, is that no one can yet manipulate a bunch of neutral bosons (if there are any) and use them to investigate something else. The best evidence for the reality of a postulated entity is that we can measure it or understand its causal powers. We can build, from scratch, machines that will work reliably using this or that causal nexus—meaning that engineering, not theorizing, is the best proof of scientific realism about entities. Thus, Hacking (admitting his own skepticism) concedes that long-lived theoretical entities that don't end up being manipulated often turn out to have been wonderful mistakes.

But what about the argument that any statement about what is seen through a microscope (or any other sense-extending device) is theory-laden? In other words, these devices are loaded with the theory of optics or other radiation, so how do we know that we're not actually seeing something other than the entity we believe we are? While we need theory to make a microscope, we don't need it to use one. Theory may help us understand why objects perceived with an interference-contrast microscope have asymmetric fringes around them, but we can learn to disregard that effect empirically. Practice creates the ability (say, of the biologist) to distinguish between visible artifacts of the instrument and the real structure that's seen with the microscope. Hacking asks us to consider the grid we use for identifying dense bodies, which are tiny grids made of metal that are barely visible to the naked eye. They're made by drawing a large grid with pen and ink, with letters neatly inscribed at the corner of each square on the grid. The grid is then reduced photographically. When we look at the tiny disc through virtually any microscope, we see exactly the same shapes and letters that were drawn in the first place. It's impossible, Hacking argues, that the minute disc doesn't in fact have the structure of a labelled grid. We know it is because we made the grid to be that way. Can we legitimately entertain the possibility that the two looking identical is some gigantic coincidence?

"To be an anti-realist about that grid you would have to invoke a malign Cartesian demon of the microscope."[27]

We can take this further by pointing out that several off-the-shelf instruments that are built on entirely different principles reveal the same structure, showing that one would have to be the most ardent of skeptics to say that the structure is made by the instruments rather than inheres in the specimen. While it's not conclusive, the fact that we can see the same fundamental features of structure, using different systems, is a strong argument for saying "that's real" rather than "that's an artifact."

Ernan McMullin adds that the "observable in principle" notion is hopelessly vague. There are organisms with sense organs that are different from ours which can perceive things like ultraviolet light. Why isn't it possible that smaller organisms could exist that can perceive micro entities that are only theoretical to us, and who are also able to communicate with us?[28] Antirealists argue that theoretical entities, such as electrons—whose only warrant for existence lies in the theories built around them—are vulnerable to being either changed (via theory change) or dropped entirely. This is not so much because they're unobservable but because the reference of the term "electron" may shift with theory change.[29] He suggests that one way such objections can be dealt with is the manner in which theoretical entities can be causally connected to our measurement apparatus. For instance, an electron could be defined as the entity that's causally responsible for certain kinds of cloud tracks. Such an entity thus could be argued to exist if certain causal lines lead to it. The reason to affirm the entity's existence lies not in the theory's success (in which it plays an explanatory role), but in the operation of traceable causal lines.

Conclusion

In light of the sustained criticisms of antirealists, it's imperative that realists have responses that bolster their central claims about our knowledge of nature. To this end, we've seen various attempts to answer both the philosophical and historical objections proposed by their antirealist

---

[27] Ian Hacking, "Do We See Through a Microscope?" https://philpapers.org/archive/HACDWS.pdf.

[28] Ernan McMullin, "A Case for Scientific Realism" in *Scientific Realism* (Berkeley, 1984), ed. Jarrett Leplin, 20.

[29] Ernan McMullin, "A Case for Scientific Realism" in *Scientific Realism*, 21-3.

critics. Beginning with the charge that knowledge is theory-laden, we saw how Boyd flipped the argument on its head by insisting that only a realist conception of science accounts for why scientific theories are *instrumentally* reliable—and that the reliability of theory-dependent judgments is best explained on the assumption that theoretical claims are approximately true.

Concerning the problem of abduction, or inference to the best explanation, we explored in some detail various responses which included an actual case from the history of science. While realists concede that there may be a sort of circularity to realism, given its use of abduction, they note that its prohibition would place a significant restriction on intellectual inquiry. If a theory provides the best explanation for some phenomenon, and if that isn't a justification for thinking it approximately true, then it's difficult to see how intellectual inquiry could even proceed. The fact is that we seem to use this type of reasoning quite effectively both within and without the natural sciences. And while we might not always be great at abstract probabilistic calculation—per the base rate problem—we do use explanatory heuristics as an appropriate substitute and still function in a reasonably productive way.

To antirealist objections to progress, realists (such as Putnam) propose that the principle of charity dictates that, when past scientists described a term that fails to refer, we should assume that they would accept reasonable reformulations of their descriptions. Beyond this, Kitcher argued that conceptual shifts in science can be understood as progressive by recognizing them as improvements in reference potentials of key terms. He further asked us to distinguish between working posits and presuppositional posits, which would counter (as he sees it) Laudan's objection that theoretical positing in general is untrustworthy. Finally, realists have highlighted the fact that observation with the naked eye may not be as straightforward as it might sound. This is partly because experimenters bring into being phenomena that don't naturally exist in a pure state of nature, and partly because we can know that certain entities exist (for example, an electron) because of what we can do to and with them. On top of that, Hacking provided reasons why we can justifiably trust the instruments we use to measure such entities.

In the end, no matter how one views the back-and-forth between these rival conceptions of science, one thing should be clear. The problems and issues each explores are complex and involve nuances that can't be easily boiled down to simple slogans about science being of this or that nature. Even in the sciences, it turns out that knowledge involves a great many factors that must be adequately appreciated to avoid reducing it to some arbitrary component.

With that said, there still remains an additional line of thought that deserves consideration. It concerns the critical realism of Roy Bhaskar, who takes seriously both the fact that knowledge is a product of social activity, and that what we discover in that social activity exists and acts independently of men. Because of his willingness to explore each of these aspects of human knowledge in some detail, we'll conclude our discussion of science proper with his proposals.

Chapter 6
Critical Realism of Roy Bhaskar

The intent of this book has been to explore what we've referred to as the dual nature of knowledge. On the one hand, we have the remarkable ability to understand the world, which often occurs through the use of theoretical models that empower us to make useful predictions and technological advances. On the other hand, our knowledge is inherently fallible; it has built-in constraints which means that the productions of our imagination will often prove inadequate. In emphasizing both features, we've pushed back against various forms of reductionism that tend to confine knowledge within a single (and arbitrary) variable. One such approach has come from constructivism (as well as postmodernism), which reduces human knowledge to socially determined factors. Ultimately self-referential, we've seen that such positions end up being self-defeating and unable to account for the fact that we seem to have knowledge about a great many things—with the stunning success of the natural sciences serving as just one example. On the other end of the spectrum, recognition of this dual nature has also provided reasons for resisting the elevation of any current state of knowledge (scientific or otherwise) to an omni-competent status. It thus rejects any tendency to see current knowledge as final or in a way that overestimates human abilities, given our inherent limitations.

Certainly, one of the benefits of our approach is that it highlights the problem of viewing knowledge through any single colored pair of glasses, which inevitably obscures the fact that there are other equally central features that play a role in its output. And failure to recognize that knowledge involves the often complex interplay between the intellectual environment out of which it arises and the world itself can easily lead one to misjudge what can be justifiably known. While it might be tempting to think that science is immune from such issues, we've now seen that this is far from the truth. It too is just one of many forms of human knowledge that potentially suffers from the same production errors and biases that inflict other forms.

It's because of this that the present chapter will explore the critical realism of Roy Bhaskar, which seeks to affirm two often competing strains of thought. On the one hand, it affirms the existence of an objective and knowable world, even if that knowledge is fallible, while, on the other, it simultaneously recognizes that human knowledge is a social product. For Bhaskar, the task of science can be explained as the uncovering by experimentation of deeper layers of the causal forces operating within nature. While these forces exist independently of our scientific investigation of them, that investigation itself must be understood as a historically contingent and socially located process.[1] Part of the attractiveness of Bhaskar's critical realism—in addition to its rejection of the constructivist thesis—is that it deals with the classic issues in the philosophy of science in light of the increasing recognition of the socially conditioned character of scientific practice, and that it offers a potential way to engage with intellectual disciplines beyond the natural sciences.[2]

It's these aspects of Bhaskar's thought that will be the subject of the present chapter, beginning with his insistence that experimental activity presupposes causal laws that must persist outside our laboratory attempts to define them.

Generative Mechanisms Versus Events

For Bhaskar and critical realists, scientists attempt to discover what kinds of things there are in nature, as well as how those things behave. They capture the real essences of things in real definitions and describe the ways they act in statements of causal laws. The real essences of things are their intrinsic structures (e.g., their atomic constitutions) that constitute the real basis of their natural tendencies and causal powers. It's only if we assume the real independence of the generative mechanisms of nature from the events they generate that we are justified in thinking that they go on acting outside the experimentally closed conditions that enable us to identify them. But this

---

[1] Alister E. McGrath, *A Scientific Theology*, vol. 2, (Grand Rapids, 2002), 211-3.

[2] For this, see Andrew Collier, *Critical Realism: An Introduction to Roy Bhaskar's Philosophy* (London, 1994), 137-68.

means that there's an ontological distinction between those mechanisms (which form the basis of scientific laws) and patterns of events observable to humans (what Hume called the constant conjunction of events).[3]

Another way this distinction is brought out by Bhaskar is his insistence that the intelligibility of experimental activity presupposes the "intransitive" character (meaning that the objects we discover in the activity of science exist and act independently of men) of the objects of scientific knowledge insofar as these are causal laws. Only if causal laws are irreducible to the flux of conditions can the idea of the universality of a known law be sustained. Laws aren't simply empirical statements, but statements about the types of activity characteristic of the world. In other words, as implied above, there's a distinction between the *real* structures and mechanisms of the world and the *actual* patterns of events they generate.[4]

One of the consequences of his position is that real structures exist independently of, and are often out of phase with, the actual pattern of events. It's only under closed conditions (i.e., experimentally induced conditions) that there's a one-to-one relationship between a causal law and the sequence of events, and it's normally only in the laboratory that these enduring mechanisms of nature, whose operations are described in causal laws, become manifest and empirically accessible to men. Though they're real, it's rare that they are actually manifest and rarer that they're empirically identified by men; yet they are the intransitive objects of scientific theory which are independent of men. The task of science is to come to know the enduring and continually active mechanisms of nature that produce the phenomena of our world. What's critical for Bhaskar is that, in order for experimental activity to be intelligible, causal laws must persist in open systems, i.e., outside the closed conditions that enable us to identify them.

Having said this, Bhaskar is quick to emphasize that there's nothing mysterious about the concept of the generative mechanisms that provide the basis of causal laws, as it's nothing other than a way of acting of a thing. It

---

[3]   Roy Bhaskar, *A Realist Theory of Science* (London, 2008), 13- 17, 21-, 27, 163, 173-4. Bhaskar calls the position he's advancing Transcendental Realism, which shouldn't be misconstrued to imply anything mystical or mysterious. His position drives him to criticize the Humean (along with the positivism which followed it) concept of laws because it ties its proponents to closed systems, i.e., systems where a constant conjunction of events is observable. The consequence is that any application beyond the experimentally closed conditions of experiments can't be maintained, i.e., our knowledge can't be extended into open systems.
[4]   Roy Bhaskar, *A Realist Theory of Science*, 46-7, 49-52, 146, 228.

endures, and under the right circumstances is known by men; this is to say that laws are statements about the ways of acting of independently existing and active things. Thus, the discovery of the machinery of nature isn't the aim of metaphysics. Rather, it's the aim of all the empirical efforts of science, and it's up to actual experiments—the aim of which is to get a single mechanism going in isolation and record its effects—to tell us what the mechanisms of nature are. That some real things and generative mechanisms must exist can be established by philosophical argument (their existence is a condition of the possibility of science). Nevertheless, it's contingent and the job of science is to discover which ones actually do exist.

At any rate, a scientist can never rest content with effects but must search for causes. Charged clouds and magnetic fields can only be detected through their effects. Yet we don't deny their existence. The mechanisms underlying the natural order are rarely capable of being observed directly, and their nature must be inferred on the basis of empirical evidence. The observed regularities aren't in themselves the primary objects of inquiry, but rather the underlying causal mechanisms that generate the observed regularities.[5]

Levels of Nature

Bhaskar conceives of science as a process-in-motion, having no foreseeable end. When a new stratum (or level) of reality is discovered and described, science moves to construct and test possible explanations for what occurs at that level. This will involve relying on whatever ideas are then available and possibly the invention of new equipment that extends our perception of reality. Once the explanation is discovered, science then constructs and tests possible explanations for it, thus moving from one stratum to the next. What this means is that both our knowledge and the world itself are structured and differentiated, so that the task of science is to come to terms with the different mechanisms of nature.

Bhaskar's image of "stratum" is a telling one, suggesting a difference in depth that allows a causal explanatory link between two different strata, as well as a distinction between surface phenomena and what may be argued (and subsequently shown) to lie beneath the surface.[6] It's this impetus to go deeper and identify underlying causal mechanisms that seems to underwrite

---

[5] For example, see A. J. Ayer, *Language, Truth, and Logic* (New York, 1946).
[6] Alister E. McGrath, *A Scientific Theology*, vol. 2, (Grand Rapids, 2002), 219.

natural science. As an example, Bhaskar points to the historical development of chemistry that occurred along these lines:

Stratum I	$2Na + 2HCI = 2NaCI + H_2$	
	explained by	
Stratum II	theory of atomic number	Mechanism 1
	and valency	
	explained by	
Stratum III	theory of electrons and	Mechanism 2
	atomic structure	
	explained by	
Stratum IV	[competing theories of sub-	[Mechanism 3]
	atomic structure][7]	

Note that the historical order of the development of knowledge of the different strata is opposite of the causal order of their dependence in being. No end to the process of discovery and the description of new and deeper strata can be envisaged. When a stratum of reality has been adequately described, the next step consists in the discovery of the mechanisms responsible for behavior at that level, and so on. This involves the postulation of hypothetical entities and mechanisms whose reality can be ascertained by experimental activity. Importantly, Bhaskar regards the stratification of the world to be unbounded, as it's always possible that there are reasons at the deeper level that phenomena behave the way they do. Even so, our knowledge may be practically bounded by technical or conceptual problems or by the domain-specific assumptions of a particular field—or even by the fact that reality itself is bounded at the level of knowledge that the scientist has attained. But even if the stratification of the world has an end—if there are entities that are truly ultimate in the sense that no further discovery is possible—we could never know that *that* level is ultimate.

In order to fully appreciate Bhaskar here, we need to consider his notion of rootedness and emergence, which Andrew Collier has explained as follows: "Emergence theories are those that, while recognizing that the more complex aspects of reality (e.g., life, mind) presuppose the less complex (e.g., matter), also insist that they have features which are irreducible; i.e., they cannot be thought in concepts appropriate to the less complex levels: and not because of any subjective constraints on our thought, but

---

[7] Roy Bhaskar, *A Realist Theory of Science*, 169, 171, 187-90, 196.

because of the inherent nature of the emergent strata."[8] As an example, Collier notes that while all animals are composed of chemical substances, not all chemical substances are parts of animals (and so on). This means that animals are governed by both biological and chemical laws. Yet animals can do many things that the chemicals of which they are composed couldn't do were they obeying only chemical laws. Accordingly, anything that belongs to a higher stratum of nature will be governed by more than one kind of law.

This drives Bhaskar to oppose the perspective of what he calls the "strong actualist" (one who believes that all reality can be reduced to a single basic stratum), because we can't predict or construct an emergent stratum from the one in which it's rooted. On the contrary, only when the emergent stratum has been adequately described can it be explained in terms of a more basic one. We could never, for instance, predict consciousness—however highly developed—from neurophysiology. If we didn't already know about consciousness, we would be in the dark about what neurophysiological facts were significant. Thus, it's important to avoid believing that a mechanism that explains another explains it away, such that the higher-level mechanism drops out of the scientific account. We're simply never in a position to predict a higher-level mechanism from our knowledge of a more basic one: the former has to be discovered first, after which it becomes the phenomena to be explained in the next state of ever-deepening scientific knowledge.

The Two Sides of Knowledge

Because humans are not simply passive recipients of facts and recorders of their conjunctions, a discussion of the prior social activity of science becomes important. This is due to the fact that, as we saw in an earlier chapter, knowledge is a partly social product, produced by prior social products (its transitive nature). Yet the objects we discover in the social activity of science exist and act independently of men (its intransitive nature) and would do so in a world without men. In this, Philip Kitcher has echoed Bhaskar's distinction by pointing out that while the realist thesis is that we

---

[8] Andrew Collier, *Critical Realism: An Introduction to Roy Bhaskar's Philosophy*, 107-13. Also based on intrinsic divisions in a stratified nature, science is stratified in that it's divided into distinct sciences (physics, chemistry, biology, economics, etc.) which are ultimately irreducible (while still ordered). In this sense, physics is more basic than chemistry, which is more basic than biology, which is more basic than the human sciences.

arrive at true statements about the world, this doesn't mean we have unbiased access to nature. It only means that our biases aren't so powerful that they prevent us from working our way out of false belief.[9] David Papineau agrees (in general) as he argues for naturalism: while the sociology of science has shown that scientists are swayed by prejudice and ambition, it has done nothing to show that scientific practice isn't generally reliable for generating true theories.[10] The bottom line is that any adequate philosophy of science has to come to terms with a central paradox, what Bhaskar calls the two sides of knowledge.

The first is that men in their social activity produce knowledge that is a social product much like any other, which is no more independent of its production and the people who produce it than motor vehicles, books, or computer chips. These all have their craftsmen, engineers, publicists, standards, and skills and are no less subject to change than any other commodity. They include antecedently established facts and theories, paradigms and models, methods and techniques currently available to the worker. The fact that scientists must be trained shows that knowledge is a social product and can't be conceived as a purely individual acquisition.[11] For any cognitive act to be possible, there has to be something that precedes it, some knowledge already established or already produced. No sum of individual cognitive action can yield knowledge because the first member of the series would already presuppose it.

A recognition of the transitive dimension implies that scientific beliefs can't be distinguished simply by their content. Experiences and the facts they generate are socially produced, and what is socially produced is socially changeable (as the history of science shows). With Rescher, Bhaskar concedes that there are no privileged statements. Knowledge, viewed as a transitive process, has not so much a foundation as a structure in time. The sciences have histories which, like all histories, are characterized by continuity and change—and the theories they produce are always liable to change, as part of our social intellectual endowment. It's from this endowment that we have to draw in order to deepen our knowledge of the way things are and act in the world, and in so doing, we continually add to and

---

[9] Philip Kitcher, *The Advancement of Science: Science Without Legend, Objectivity Without Illusions* (New York, 1993), 161.

[10] David Papineau, "Does the Sociology of Science Discredit Science?" in *Relativism and Realism in Science*, ed. Robert Nola (Dordrecht, 1988), 51.

[11] See also Michael Polanyi, *Personal Knowledge: Towards a Post-Critical Philosophy* (Chicago, 1974), 53ff.

modify it. The existence of this stock of knowledge from which we draw is a necessary feature of any human cognitive endeavor. Thus, knowledge can never be seen solely as a function of individual sense experience.

One doesn't have to search far to find illustrations of Bhaskar's point. Consider, for example, the historical antecedents of Charles Darwin's idea of evolution. He was by no means the first thinker to propose the idea,[12] as the problems he was trying to answer weren't any secret to other scientists who had proposed elements that were close to what Darwin would lay out in the *Origin*. Alfred Russell Wallace independently developed some of the same ideas, which fortuitously ended up being published along with a short synopsis of Darwin's in 1858 (a year before the *Origin*).[13] Additionally, Darwin transformed the proposal of Charles Lyell (concerning the well-known problem of the sequence of different species found in the fossil records of successive geological eras) from the view of a contest among *species* into that of *individuals*. Noting the variations within members of a species, Darwin proposed that the chances of an individual's survival depend on particular variations the individual possesses (what he called "natural selection"). This transition from Lyell's interpretation was one of the keys to a new way of thinking about the world of nature.

Darwin's thinking was also precipitated by his reading from other, seemingly non-related fields. The work, for example, of Thomas Malthus—an English economist and moral philosopher—proved to be the catalyst that led Darwin (and Wallace, independently) to see the clue to the origin of species in natural selection through "a struggle for existence."[14] This enabled him to apply what he knew about the struggle at the species level to the individual level. But there are also other factors that contributed to Darwin's receptivity to Malthus in the first place, such as the principles of individualism and competition in Adam Smith's economic thinking.[15] Further, there seems to have been a feeling in the air that a divinely ordained

---

[12] I. Bernard Cohen, *Revolution in Science* (Cambridge, MA, 1985), 287-94.

[13] I. Bernard Cohen, *Revolution in Science* (Cambridge, MA, 1985), 289, 291-3. Cohen notes that there was muted reaction to their ideas, and they quickly learned that the mere publication of the idea of evolution wasn't enough to launch the scientific revolution they sought. That had to wait for Darwin's own publication of the *Origin* the following year.

[14] Anthony Flew, "Malthus, Thomas Robert" in ed. Paul Edwards, *The Encyclopedia of Philosophy* (New York, 1967) vol. 5, 145-6.

[15] Howard E. Gruber, *Darwin on Man: A Psychological Study of Scientific Creativity* (Chicago, 1981), 13.

process was continually weeding out misfits in a similar manner to the concept of "selection."[16] Howard Gruber adds that Darwin delighted in studying Paley's *Natural Theology* and Euclid's *Elements*. Ironically, it may have been Darwin's immersion in the Cambridge combination of theology and natural history that deepened his awareness of the adaptive structures he was later to explain in natural terms.[17]

Darwin's development of existing ideas leads naturally to the notion of scientific change, about which Bhaskar's concept of the transitive and intransitive process allows him to make some important insights. Given that there is no Archimedean point (or God's-eye view) from which to view scientific progress, we have to concede that it can only be shown from some theoretical standpoint or position. Knowledge changes as it grows, meaning that knowledge at a new level may lead to a revision, correction, or modification of knowledge at a previous level—for what's explained is never the "pure" phenomena or facts, but always the phenomena read in a particular way. While the scientist seeks to describe the mechanisms generating the phenomena, the results of his activity belong to the social world of science, not the intransitive world of things (here again, we see similarities with points made by Rescher). Established facts are therefore social products. This doesn't mean that it's incorrect to speak of the scientist explaining events and mechanisms, but we need to remember that what's explained is always the event known under a particular historically situated description.

Even with this social emphasis, Bhaskar insists that the ontological independence of the event is a condition of the intelligibility of its description, which brings up the second side of knowledge as he sees it and to which we've already alluded. Knowledge is *of* things that aren't produced by people at all: the specific gravity of mercury, the process of electrolysis, the mechanism of light propagation. None of these depend on human activity. If humans ceased to exist, sound would continue to travel and heavy bodies fall to the earth even though there would be no one to know it. They're the real things and structures that make our theories and observations possible. Thus, against the idealist, they're not structures imposed by men in their cognitive activity. It's precisely this dual affirmation of the social and objective that puts Bhaskar in the critical realist camp.

---

[16] I. Bernard Cohen, *Revolution in Science* (Cambridge, MA, 1985), 294.
[17] Howard E. Gruber, *Darwin on Man: A Psychological Study of Scientific Creativity* (Chicago, 1981), 74-5.

Before leaving the topic, we should note that Larry Laudan also pushes against both constructivist and realist camps; he points out that ideas like "most heavy bodies fall downwards when released" bear no straightforward relation to social circumstances. They're beliefs to which people from a wide range of cultural and social situations subscribe. Anyone who suggests that such beliefs were socially determined or conditioned betrays ignorance of the ways in which such beliefs are established. Yet there are clearly ideas and beliefs that have tangible social origins.[18] To suggest that nineteenth-century German factory workers favored socialism because of the rational well-roundedness of its doctrines suggests an enormous degree of credulity. But if all beliefs—as the social constructivist insists—are socially caused rather than rationally well-founded, then (as we've already noted) the beliefs of the social constructivist himself have no rational basis.

Epistemic Fallacy

Bhaskar complains that much thinking about science has committed what he calls the epistemic fallacy, namely, that statements about being can be reduced to statements about knowledge, i.e., that ontological questions (questions about a thing's existence) can always be transposed into epistemological terms (about our knowledge about the thing's existence). The problem, he insists, is that this collapses the fundamental distinction between our knowledge of the world and the world itself. "The idea that being can always be analysed in terms of our knowledge of being, that it is sufficient for philosophy to 'treat only of the network, and not what the network describes', results in the systematic dissolution of the idea of a world (which I shall here metaphorically characterize as an ontological realm) independent of but investigated by science."[19]

He argues this because, in a world without humans, in which there would be no knowledge of constant conjunctions, causal laws would still exist despite the fact that there are no human knowers to experience them. They would continue to operate. This helps us to see how the Humean empiricist (positivist) viewpoint depends upon a concealed anthropocentricity, a view that led to the dissolution of the concept of the ontological realm, which we need to render intelligible the transitive process of science.

---

[18] Larry Laudan, *Progress and Its Problems: Towards a Theory of Scientific Growth* (Berkeley, 1977), 199-201.

[19] Roy Bhaskar, *A Realist Theory of Science*, 34-7.

The world, which ought to be viewed as a multi-dimensional structure independent of people, under Humean empiricism, came to be flattened out and determined by a particular, historically situated concept of knowledge. And any structure, if it was allowed at all, had to be located in the human mind or scientific community. "Thus the world," says Bhaskar, "was literally turned inside out in an attempt to confine it within sentience."[20]

Conclusion

We've now seen that Bhaskar offers a critical realist position that pushes back against various forms of reductionism. For him, human knowledge has both a transitive and intransitive nature, which means that it doesn't exist in an either/or relationship. Reframed as a both/and, Bhaskar offers a way to affirm the existence of an objective—and knowable, albeit fallible—world on the one hand, while it simultaneously recognizes that human knowledge is a social product. Such an approach has the advantage of allowing us to acknowledge important sociological developments as well as appreciate the gains in knowledge that seem evident within the history of science.

More specifically, Bhaskar would affirm—against the strong constructivist program—humankind's remarkable ability to understand the workings of nature, harness its secrets for technological advance, and make predictions. At the same time, he highlights the fallibility of our historically situated knowledge of the objective world we inhabit. Knowledge, being a social product of the scientific community of which he is an undeniable member, can and will change. Along with Rescher, Bhaskar would approach any purported knowledge with an appropriate level of tentativeness and humility. This is because our knowledge can and will grow with investigations of new strata and the invention of new technical devices through which we understand the world.

Further, McGrath points out that Bhaskar distinguishes ontology (what properties does nature possess?) from epistemology (how do these properties make themselves possible objects of knowledge for us?)—meaning that existence is not dependent on observation or being observable. Generative mechanisms may exist, yet not be observed or observable, so that their powers exist unexercised or exercised without being realized. That is, there may exist variable outcomes that can't be the subject of experimental

---

[20] Roy Bhaskar, *A Realist Theory of Science*, 44-5.

closure. He thus rejects the positivist insistence on "unity of methodology," as well as certain schools of sociology that argue that "natural reality" and "social reality" can be collapsed into the latter, such that human knowledge can be reduced to social theory. In contrast to both, Bhaskar insists that methodology is determined by ontology. Each stratum must be investigated by a methodology that is determined *a posteriori* by its ontology, which provides an important bulwark against reductionism.[21] McGrath's comments are worth repeating in full:

> One of the most important aspects of Bhaskar's approach is that it demands that the different levels of reality be fully acknowledged. It is impossible to reduce reality to one ontological level, or to insist that what is 'real' is determined by whether it can be 'known'—often by the improper use of only one methodology, corresponding to the one level of reality that such a reductionism recognizes.... Perhaps more importantly, it challenges those who insist that reality is to be defined as 'what can be known through the natural sciences'—an approach which is intrinsically anti-religious and anti-metaphysical in its outlook.[22]

A few points about McGrath's observations are in order before we conclude. First, in highlighting the improper use of a single methodology, he echoes the concerns (noted in an earlier chapter) of Larry Laudan who documented the demise of the demarcation problem. As Laudan demonstrated, all attempts to reduce science to any one methodology have failed, which means that separating scientific from non-scientific knowledge based on a single method is doomed. Second, McGrath highlights two reasons Bhaskar would oppose reducing knowledge only to what can be known through science, which can be stated as follows: (1) Science is historically conditioned in that what we know through it changes over time. If reality is defined as what can be known through the natural sciences, this would mean that the nature of reality changes in accordance with our ability to know it. But this is clearly unacceptable. (2) It traps itself in the fallacy so criticized by Bhaskar that ontology is determined by epistemology, i.e., that the reality of something is determined by whether we can observe it. The bottom line is that Bhaskar provides a way to think about knowledge that preserves some of its most obvious features and prevents

---

[21] Alister E. McGrath, *A Scientific Theology*, vol. 2, 218, 223-4.
[22] Alister E. McGrath, *A Scientific Theology*, vol. 2, 225-6.

us from sliding into an unfounded reductionism that denies well-established realities.

With Bhaskar's approach now outlined, we've concluded our evaluation of science proper. What should be clear at this point is that the double-sidedness of knowledge that critical realism affirms gives it an advantage in its appreciation of the central role that various factors play in any human cognitive endeavor. This will make it especially relevant as we consider the extent of our theological knowledge. However, there remains a final area that must be addressed in any updated presentation on human knowledge: the relatively recent empirical research on judgment and decision-making. Because of its applicability to our project, it's to this that we turn next.

Chapter 7

Knowledge In Action: Judgments and Decisions

Having examined some of the relevant philosophical issues related to knowledge, it's time to turn our attention to the relatively new research field of judgment and decision-making. Although philosophical treatments have tended to ignore it, we'll see that the new research has clear implications for the main questions about human reasoning. This is because it seeks empirically, via experimental procedures, to understand how people *actually* arrive at judgments and decisions and then compares this against how they ought to make them. Especially pertinent is the fact that the research highlights some of the ways in which human knowledge, as manifested in judgments and decisions, is limited by internal constraints that aren't easily (if ever) corrected. Thus, where previous chapters have discussed competing viewpoints on our epistemic capabilities and limits, this chapter will explore how our reasoning is often derailed by completely irrelevant factors.

As we'll see, the standard material within the judgment and decision-making literature assesses how people answer various questions and then tests the processes by which the answer is produced. If the answer is incorrect, investigators elucidate the incorrect process and then try to describe the "heuristic" (a rule-of-thumb way of reasoning that can lead to error) that produced the "bias" (here understood as a probably unconscious *cognitive* bias rather than, say, a chosen leaning, like in politics) that led to the wrong answer. Because of the frequent use of these two terms, the field is often referred to as the heuristics and biases program (we'll use both designations here).

The chapter will begin by providing a high-level overview of the various positions within the heuristics and biases program and will then dive into some of the particular findings associated with its experimental research. What it will show is that there are particular errors associated with intuitive judgments that afflict both the novice as well as the expert, errors that are difficult (perhaps impossible) to completely overcome. Because such flaws in our reasoning can be detected with a little effort, this won't be to suggest that we have no grasp on an objective reality, but rather to stress that flaws are more commonplace than is often appreciated by experts in other fields.

Overview Of Positions

Before we dive into the heuristics and biases research, it will help to give some context and provide a high-level overview of the literature. To do so, we'll note some of the ways the various views within the field have been classified, starting with Kenneth Hammond's division between the correspondence and coherence metatheories of judgment and decision-making. The former, he says, attempts to describe and explain the process by which a person's judgments achieve empirical *accuracy,* while the latter attempts to describe and explain the process by which a person's judgments achieve logical, mathematical, or statistical *rationality.*[1] "Correspondence" can be roughly thought of as accuracy: did the interest rates go up as economists predicted, or did it snow as the weather forecaster predicted? "Coherence" can roughly be thought of as rationality: did the argument for that conclusion meet the test of mathematical or logical consistency? Correspondence theorists are therefore interested in the way the mind works in relation to the way the world works, while coherence theorists are interested in the way the mind works in relation to the way it ought to work.[2]

Elaborating on the distinction, Hammond notes that the correspondence theory focuses on the *empirical* accuracy of judgments, whether or

---

[1]   Kenneth R. Hammond, "Coherence and Correspondence Theories in Judgement and Decision Making," in *Judgement and Decision Making: An Interdisciplinary Reader,* Second Edition, eds. Terry Connolly, Hal R. Arkes, and Kenneth R. Hammond (Cambridge, 2000), 53-4.

[2]   Kenneth R. Hammond, "Coherence and Correspondence Theories in Judgement and Decision Making," in *Judgement and Decision Making: An Interdisciplinary Reader,* 59-60, 62-3.

not the cognitive activity the person uses can be justified. Accuracy being the main concern, researchers in this camp rarely ask whether judgments are rational, i.e., whether they conform to some normative model of how a judgment should be reached. Also, because their goal is to examine the correspondence between a person's judgments and a specific state of the world to which those judgments correspond, these theorists are committed to a Darwinian approach. This makes the ability of a species to adapt to its environment and respond appropriately central. One of their expectations is that a high degree of correspondence will be found because competence in the form of correspondence is fundamental to survival. After all, how could human beings have been so successful in their survival if they did't make accurate judgments of the world around them? Hence, they emphasize the flexibility of the organism in its adaptive efforts and its strategies to deal with its environment.[3]

Coherence theorists, on the other hand, have opposite interests. They ask if one's judgment processes meet the test of rationality/internal consistency, whether or not the judgment itself is empirically accurate. If a problem is posed to someone that can be solved by a standard statistical model, the coherence theorist first compares the answer with that produced by the statistical model, which then declares it to be correct or incorrect; tests the process by which the answer is produced; and evaluates the rationality of the cognitive processes involved. If the answer is incorrect, the theorist explains the incorrect process that demonstrates irrationality and offers a description of the irrational "heuristic" that produced the "bias" leading to the wrong answer.[4] As the coherence theorist sees them, heuristics are cognitive activities that, though generally efficient, often deceive and prevent us from achieving coherence/ rationality.

---

[3] It might be argued that a Darwinian commitment is unnecessary and that the research could stand on its own, just as easily accepted (even predicted) by the Christian theologian. Given the biblical doctrine of creation and the fall of humankind into sin, Christians should predict both a certain correspondence between the human mind and the created world, as well as a certain disconnect—due to the noetic effects of sin—between that same mind and the world. Because of this, the Christian would also see the raw notion of adaptability as important (despite the objections he may have to a Darwinian notion).

[4] Helmut Jungermann, "The Two Camps on Rationality," in *Judgement and Decision Making: An Interdisciplinary Reader,* Second Edition, eds. Terry Connolly, Hal R. Arkes, and Kenneth R. Hammond (Cambridge, 2000), 577ff.

As two of the most prominent advocates of the heuristics and biases program, Daniel Kahneman and Amos Tversky argue that there are three reasons for focusing on systematic errors and inferential biases in the study of reasoning.[5] First, they expose some of our intellectual limitations and point to ways of improving the quality of our thinking. Second, errors and biases can reveal the psychological processes governing judgment and inference. Third, our mistakes and fallacies indicate which principles of statistics or logic are non-intuitive or counterintuitive. For coherence theorists, it's important to emphasize that rationality doesn't directly imply accuracy, as the former always operates in a closed system. Given the premises, certain conclusions always follow if a rational process is followed and, when the process satisfies a logical test, the system is considered coherent (which is all it is and claims to be). Having said this, it would be a mistake to think that these theorists are dismissive of the relevance of objective reality, for one of their key assumptions is that there exists a reliable yardstick for the evaluation of judgments and decisions.

Characterizing the various camps differently than Hammond, Helmut Jungermann sees heuristic researchers as divided between those who have a more pessimistic or optimistic view of human judgment. According to his reading, researchers such as Kahneman and Tversky are more pessimistic in thinking that biases are *in* people, while another, more optimistic camp has arisen that partly questions the validity of pessimist findings and partly argues for the implicit rationality of human judgment and decision-making. Thus, optimists argue that biases aren't in human behavior but in the *analysis* of this behavior within the pessimist camp.[6] One of their key points is that strategies for judgment come at a cost in terms of cognitive effort, which is complicated by the fact that there's usually more than one strategy from which to choose. Here, violations of classical rationality (which says that the laws of human inference are the laws of probability and statistics, which Kahneman and Tversky emphasize) should be considered errors that people anticipate and tolerate. They do so because people are global maximizers of the effort required of a given task, and they sometimes decide that the costs of one method outweigh the expected benefit; hence, they often choose spontaneity instead of using a more formal method of reasoning.

---

[5] Daniel Kahneman and Amos Tversky, "On the Study of Statistical Intuitions," *Cognition*, vol. 11, issue 2 (March, 1982), 124.

[6] Helmut Jungermann, "The Two Camps on Rationality," in *Judgement and Decision Making: An Interdisciplinary Reader,* 580, 582, 589.

Still other researchers have proposed a model of "bounded rationality" instead of classical rationality.[7] Here, it's argued that information processing systems normally need to "satisfice" (a blend of sufficing and satisfying) rather than "optimize." This means that, instead of taking the time to survey all possible alternatives, estimating probabilities and utilities for the possible outcomes associated with each alternative, calculating expected utilities, and then choosing the alternative which scores the highest, people normally choose the first option that satisfies their needs. And this is because humans are limited information processors. Bounded-rationality proponents suggest that when we make choices in contexts in which inferences need to be made with limited time and knowledge, we use memory-based inference, which is an inference based solely on knowledge retrieved from memory. This occurs in things like risk assessments during driving (e.g., choosing whether to exit the highway now or stay on) and treatment decisions in emergency rooms. It also occurs when we consider questions such as the following:

Which city has a larger population?

(a) Hamburg
(b) Cologne

In these situations, it's argued, satisficing can profit from missing information. When making quick inferences about populations of German cities, for example, the fact that one of them has a professional soccer team may spring to mind as a potential cue; i.e., if one has a major league soccer team and the other doesn't, then the city with the team is likely (though not certain) to have the larger population. This works according to what these researchers call the recognition principle, by which the mere recognition of an object is a predictor of the target variable (population). In essence, the ABC program (as it's called by its proponents) sees heuristics as an essential cognitive tool for making reasonable decisions.[8] Thus, whereas the heuris-

---

[7] Gerd Gigerenzer and Daniel G. Goldstein, "Reasoning the Fast and Frugal Way: Models of Bounded Rationality," in *Judgement and Decision Making: An Interdisciplinary Reader,* Second Edition, eds. Terry Connolly, Hal R. Arkes, and Kenneth R. Hammond (Cambridge, 2000), 621-7. See also the essays in *Simple Heuristics That Make Us Smart,* eds. Gerd Gigerenzer, Peter M. Todd, and the ABC Research Group (Oxford, 1999).

[8] Gerd Gegerenzer and Peter M. Todd, "Fast and Frugal Heuristics: The Adaptive Toolbox," in *Simple Heuristics That Make Us Smart,* eds. Gerd Gigerenzer, Peter M. Todd, and the ABC Research Group (Oxford, 1999), 29.

tics and biases program sees heuristics as a frequent hindrance to sound reasoning, this school of thought sees fast and frugal heuristics as enabling us to make reasonable decisions and adapt to our environment—meaning that humans would be lost without them.

However, despite the fact that such researchers have made some valid points, the classical notion of rationality remains the standard for these debates. We should also note that all approaches accept that there are boundaries for rationality in situations of cognitive overload. The issue is how people form judgments and make decisions and whether they operate rationally within those constraints. As both Kahneman and Tversky (whose research has tended to dominate the field) concede, we should avoid overly strict interpretations that treat reasonable answers (under the circumstances) as errors, as well as overly charitable interpretations that try to rationalize every response.

Ideally, scientific research seeks both coherence and correspondence, but the reality is that most of its various disciplines are forced to tolerate contradictory facts and competitive theories. Thus, investigators have to live with the tension between those pursuing the reconciliation of facts and those trying to resolve the contradictions of theories. In sharp contrast, policymakers find it much harder to live with tensions because they're expected to act on the basis of information.

A Quick Note on Bayes' Theorem

Because the ideas of probability and Bayes' theorem surface frequently within the judgment and decision-making literature, a quick note about them is in order. Briefly stated, probabilities are often described as a number between 0 and 1, and they describe propositions about events; they are, in a sense, measures of uncertainty. Bayesians hold that a probability is a description of a person's uncertainty about the truth of a proposition asserting that an event will happen, or that it has happened. In other words, probabilities describe opinions about the truth or falsity of propositions about events.

Ward Edwards and Detlof von Winterfeldt illustrate the idea by asking a simple question: how likely is it, for you, that the 20th president of the United States was a Republican?[9] Like many people

---

[9] Ward Edwards and Detlof von Winterfeldt, "On Cognitive Illusions and Their Implications," in *Judgement and Decision Making: An Interdisciplinary Reader,* Second

unfamiliar with nineteenth-century presidents, you may not be sure whether he was or wasn't. At first, you might be inclined to just guess 50 percent. However, you do have some relevant information, such as that the 20th president served after Lincoln and before Theodore Roosevelt, and that the Republican Party existed and was successful during that period. While you may be unsure what number best describes your degree of uncertainty about the statement, on the basis of information you now have, you'd surely regard .5 as an underestimate. You revise upwards on the basis of the new information. The point here is that Bayes' theorem is one way of coming up with an estimate and, in fact, is considered the standard (and uncontroversial) method for making such assessments. Why? One reason is clearly because it recognizes that probabilities of an exhaustive set of mutually exclusive events must sum to 1, and this in turn dictates how much you should revise your prior opinions in the light of relevant new evidence.

We should also note that two characteristics are considered important when making probability assessments. The first is the preference for it to be extreme, meaning that an assessment close to 1 or 0 provides more useful guidance in terms of what to expect and what to do than one near .5 (which, being in the middle, is more ambiguous). The second is more subtle than extremeness and is something researchers refer to as calibration. Calibration can't be measured by any single assessment, but we can illustrate it by saying that, if we have a number of probability judgments, all of which are .6, we'd feel better if about 60% of those propositions turned out true and the other 40% turned out false than if 10% or 90% turned out true (meaning that the former is better calibrated than the latter).

Though it may not be obvious at first, calibration and extremeness pull in opposite directions. To illustrate, the weather forecaster wants to give a daily probability of rain. To make his determination, he may see what percentage of days last year it rained and then apply the same percentage (say, 60%) this year. The trouble is that this won't make any distinction between days it's more likely to rain, so in order to balance the inward pull of good calibration against the outward pull of extremeness, he'd have to use the evidence at hand (which is what forecasters generally do).

Edition, eds. Terry Connolly, Hal R. Arkes, and Kenneth R. Hammond (Cambridge, 2000), 594-5, 602-4, 609, 615.

Two Thinking Systems

Decades of experimental work have prompted psychologists to distinguish between two distinct thinking systems in human beings.[10] Though various labels have been proposed, most researchers now refer to them as System 1 and System 2, which reflects the terms originally proposed by Keith Stanovich and Richard West. Because the two systems feature so prominently in the heuristics and biases literature, a brief description of each is warranted.

System 1 is the part of our thinking that operates automatically and quickly and requires little to no effort and no sense of voluntary control. It's gullible, biased to believe, forms causal connections that aren't backed by evidence,[11] and isn't prone to doubt its quick conclusions. Not only does it fail to keep track of alternative ideas it rejects, it doesn't even acknowledge that there were alternatives. Further, because of its tendency to create causal connections, it constructs coherent stories (even when there are none) and suppresses ambiguity, meaning that it jumps to conclusions from little evidence. In other words, people have the irresistible tendency to perceive sequences of events in terms of causal relations, even when they're fully aware that the relation is incidental and that the causality is illusory.[12] This often results in predictable biases. One example concerns what researchers call the fundamental attribution error, which is the tendency for people to underestimate the impact of situational factors and to overestimate the role of dispositional factors in their causal narratives.[13] A person cuts in front of us on the road, and our causal machinery goes to work (but only in a particular direction) as we conclude that it's because the person is a jerk (dispositional factor), rather than, say, rushing to the hospital for an emergency (situational factor). Exacerbating the problem is the fact that subjective

---

[10] Daniel Kahneman, *Thinking, Fast and Slow* (New York, 2011), 19-49, 208.

[11] Daniel Kahneman and Amos Tversky, "Intuitive Prediction: Biases and Corrective Procedures." Technical Report PTR-1042-77-6, Sponsored by Defense Advanced Research Project Agency, June 1977, 4-5. https://apps.dtic.mil/dtic/tr/fulltext/u2 /a047747.pdf.

[12] Amos Tversky and Daniel Kahneman, "Causal Schemas in Judgments Under Uncertainty" in *Judgment Under Uncertainty: Heuristics and Biases,* eds. Daniel Kahneman, Paul Slovic, and Amos Tversky (New York, 1982), 117.

[13] Lee Ross and Craig A. Anderson, "Shortcomings in the Attribution Process: On the Social Origins and Maintenance of Erroneous Social Assessments" in *Judgment Under Uncertainty: Heuristics and Biases,* eds. Daniel Kahneman, Paul Slovic, and Amos Tversky (New York, 1982), 135.

confidence in our stories correlates with their coherence, and unless they're immediately challenged, the stories can spread as if they were true. Nassim Taleb points out that this propensity goes wrong when it increases our *impression* of understanding.[14] Kahneman and Tversky call such unwarranted confidence the illusion of validity, which persists even when the person is aware of factors that limit the accuracy of his predictions.[15]

System 2, on the other hand, is the part of our thinking that allocates attention to the effortful mental activities that demand it, which includes complex computations. While System 2 is in charge of doubt, research has shown that it's often lazy and avoids the investment required to check the automatic suggestions of System 1. Because of this, people tend to be overconfident and place too much faith in their intuitions, which is spurred on by the fact that cognitive effort feels unpleasant and we avoid it as much as possible.[16] Making things worse, when people believe that something is true, they're likely to believe arguments that appear to support it even when they're unsound.

The Problem of Representativeness

Much of the heuristics and biases research revolves around how people assess the probability of an uncertain event or the value of an uncertain quantity. As we mentioned earlier, the extensive experimental work of Kahneman and Tversky and their colleagues has set the standard for the various proposals on how people deal with such issues. As a possible answer, they've argued that people rely on a limited number of heuristic principles that reduce the complex tasks of assessing the likelihood of uncertain events and predicting values to simpler operations. While they acknowledge that heuristics are generally useful, their results show that they also lead us to make systematic errors.

---

[14] Nassim Nicholas Taleb, *The Black Swan: The Impact of the Highly Improbable* (New York, 2010), 64.

[15] Amos Tversky and Daniel Kahneman, "Judgement Under Uncertainty: Heuristics and Biases" in *Judgement and Decision Making: An Interdisciplinary Reader,* Second Edition, eds. Terry Connolly, Hal R. Arkes, and Kenneth R. Hammond (Cambridge, 2000), 41-3.

[16] Baruch Fischhoff, Ann Bostrom, and Marilyn Jacobs Quadrel, "Risk Perception and Communication," in *Judgement and Decision Making: An Interdisciplinary Reader,* Second Edition, eds. Terry Connolly, Hal R. Arkes, and Kenneth R. Hammond (Cambridge, 2000), 483.

More specifically, Kahneman and Tversky have pointed out that many of the probabilistic questions people are concerned about belong to one of the following types: What is the probability that object A belongs to class B? What is the probability that event A originates from process B? What is the probability that process B will generate event A? When answering, people often rely on what Kahneman and Tversky call the representativeness heuristic, in which probabilities are evaluated by the degree to which A is representative of B, i.e., by the degree to which A resembles B. As an example, they ask us to consider a person who's been described by a former neighbor as follows: "Steve is very shy and withdrawn, invariably helpful, but with little interest in people or in the world of reality. A meek and tidy soul, he has a need for order and structure and a passion for detail."[17] How do people assess the probability that Steve works in a particular occupation from a list of possibilities (farmer, salesman, pilot, librarian, or physician)? According to the representative heuristic, the probability that Steve is a librarian (for example) is assessed by the degree to which he's representative of (or similar to) the stereotype of a librarian. However, this approach leads to serious errors because similarity isn't influenced by other factors that should affect judgments of probability.[18]

One of those should be prior probability, or base rate frequency, of an outcome. In the Steve example, the fact that there are many more farmers than librarians should enter into any reasonable estimate of the probability that Steve is a librarian rather than a farmer. However, considerations of base rates don't affect the similarity of Steve to the stereotypes of librarians to farmers. If people tend to evaluate probability by representativeness, prior probabilities will be neglected, which is precisely what experiments have demonstrated. In one of them, subjects were given brief personality descriptions of several people and told that the group from which the descriptions were drawn consisted of 70 engineers and 30 lawyers. In another, subjects were told that the group consisted of 30 engineers and 70 lawyers, with the odds of any description belonging to an engineer rather than a lawyer being higher in the first (where there's a majority of engineers).

---

[17] Amos Tversky and Daniel Kahneman, "Judgement Under Uncertainty: Heuristics and Biases" in *Judgement and Decision Making: An Interdisciplinary Reader*, 35-6.

[18] See also Daniel Kahneman and Amos Tversky, "On the Psychology of Prediction" in *Judgment Under Uncertainty: Heuristics and Biases*, eds. Daniel Kahneman, Paul Slovic, and Amos Tversky (New York, 1982), 50ff. and Amos Tversky and Daniel Kahneman, "Evidential Impact of Base Rates" in *Judgment Under Uncertainty: Heuristics and Biases*, eds. Daniel Kahneman, Paul Slovic, and Amos Tversky (New York, 1982).

Violating Bayes' rule—which says that the ratio of these odds should be $(.7/.3)^2$, or 5.44, for each description—the subjects in both experiments produced essentially the same probability judgments. "Apparently, subjects evaluated the likelihood that a particular description belonged to an engineer rather than to a lawyer by the degree to which this description was representative of the two stereotypes, with little or no regard for the prior probabilities of the categories."[19] Interestingly, subjects used base rates correctly when they had no other information. When the personality sketch was absent, they judged the probability that an individual is an engineer to be .7 and .3, respectively. But prior probabilities were virtually ignored when a description was introduced, even when this description was completely uninformative. It may be that concrete, emotionally engaging information has greater power to generate inferences because it's more likely to call up schemas involving similar information—which, in turn, may be due to the fact that base rate information is remote and abstract, whereas emotionally relevant information is vivid, salient, and concrete.[20]

Another way representativeness leads us astray is our tendency to underestimate the importance of sample size when estimating a particular result in a sample drawn from a specified population.[21] As an example, Kahneman and Tversky asked subjects to consider the following question:

A certain town is served by two hospitals. In the larger hospital, about 45 babies are born each day, and in the smaller hospital, about 15 babies are born each day. As you know, about 50 percent of all babies are boys. However, the exact percentage varies from day to day. Sometimes it may be higher than 50 percent, sometimes lower.

For a period of 1 year, each hospital recorded the days on which more than 60 percent of the babies born were boys. Which hospital do you think recorded more such days? (Note: the values in parentheses are the number of subjects who chose each answer.)

[19] Amos Tversky and Daniel Kahneman, "Judgement Under Uncertainty: Heuristics and Biases" in *Judgement and Decision Making: An Interdisciplinary Reader*, 37.

[20] Richard E. Nisbett, Eugene Borgida, Rick Crandall, and Harvey Reed, "Popular Induction: Information Is Not Necessarily Informative" in *Judgment Under Uncertainty: Heuristics and Biases*, eds. Daniel Kahneman, Paul Slovic, and Amos Tversky (New York, 1982), 111-2.

[21] See also Richard E. Nisbett, David H. Krantz, Christopher Jepson, and Geoffrey T. Fong, "Improving Inductive Inference" in *Judgment Under Uncertainty: Heuristics and Biases*, eds. Daniel Kahneman, Paul Slovic, and Amos Tversky (New York, 1982), 452-5.

- The larger hospital (21)
- The smaller hospital (21)
- About the same (within 5 percent of each other) (53)

As you can see, most subjects judged the probability of obtaining more than 60 percent of boys to be the same in the small and large hospital, presumably because the events are described by the same statistic and are thus equally representative of the general population. However, sampling theory dictates that the expected number of days on which more than 60 percent are boys is much greater in the small hospital, because a large sample is less likely to stray from the 50 percent.[22] What this means is that the fundamentals of statistics don't seem to be part of people's intuitions and, as a result, they're often led astray when determining the likelihood of some event. Part of the trouble is that people expect that a sequence of events generated by a random process will represent the essential elements of that process even when the sequence is short. But locally representative sequences, or smaller sample sizes, deviate systematically from chance expectation, i.e., they contain too many alternations and too few runs.

The gambler's fallacy operates on similar mistaken beliefs. Here, chance is viewed as a self-correcting process in which a deviation in one direction induces a deviation in the opposite direction to restore the equilibrium. Thus, after seeing a long run of red at the roulette wheel, most people wrongly believe that black is now due, presumably because the occurrence of black will result in a more representative sequence than the occurrence of another red. And this isn't limited to novices. Studies have shown that experts reveal a lingering belief in the "law of small numbers," which deceives them into believing that small sample sizes are highly representative of the populations from which they're drawn. This may be because people believe that sampling is also a self-correcting process.[23] We saw exactly this effect in the underpowered studies in a previous chapter.

Echoing the findings of researchers like John Ioannidis, Kahneman and Tversky note that responses of investigators often reflect the expectation

---

[22] Daniel Kahneman and Amos Tversky, "Subjective Probability: A Judgment of Representativeness" in *Judgment Under Uncertainty: Heuristics and Biases,* eds. Daniel Kahneman, Paul Slovic, and Amos Tversky (New York,1982), 44-6.

[23] Amos Tversky and Daniel Kahneman, "Belief in the Law of Small Numbers," in *Judgment Under Uncertainty: Heuristics and Biases,* eds. Daniel Kahneman, Paul Slovic, and Amos Tversky (New York, 1982), 25-6, 29-30.

that a valid hypothesis about a population will be represented by a statistically significant result in a sample, yet with little regard for its size. "As a consequence, the researchers put too much faith in the results of small samples and grossly overestimated the replicability of such results. In the actual conduct of research, this bias leads to the selection of samples of inadequate size and to over interpretation of findings."[24] On top of the fact that there is a large proportion of invalid rejections of the null hypothesis among published results, blindness to sample size leads to other errors. First, the researcher overestimates the power of small samples. Second, he has unwarranted confidence in early trends (data from the first few subjects) and in the stability of observed patterns, meaning he overestimates significance. Third, when evaluating replications (his or others'), he has unreasonably high expectations about the replicability of significant results (something we noted appearing time and again in the literature). Fourth, he rarely attributes deviation of results from expectations to sampling variability because he can find a causal explanation for any discrepancy. Unfortunately, this means that his belief in small numbers will remain intact indefinitely and explains why such biases can survive considerable contradictory evidence.

What Comes to Mind

Studies show that people assess the probability of an event by the ease with which instances or occurrences can be brought to mind—a judgmental heuristic called availability. For instance, one could assess the risk of heart attack or the divorce rate in a particular community by recalling such occurrences among acquaintances. In some ways, this is a defensible mechanism which saves time and energy and often yields acceptable results. Experience has taught us that instances of large classes are recalled better and faster than less frequent ones, and that likely occurrences are easier to imagine than unlikely ones.[25] Yet while availability can be useful in determining frequency or probability, it can also lead to predictable biases that skew

[24] Amos Tversky and Daniel Kahneman, "Judgement Under Uncertainty: Heuristics and Biases" in *Judgement and Decision Making: An Interdisciplinary Reader,* 38-9.
[25] Amos Tversky and Daniel Kahneman, "Availability: A Heuristic for Judging Frequency and Probability" in *Judgment Under Uncertainty: Heuristics and Biases,* eds. Daniel Kahneman, Paul Slovic, and Amos Tversky (New York, 1982),163-4, 176-8.

judgment.[26] This is due to the fact that when the size of a class is judged by the availability of instances, a class whose instances are easy to retrieve will appear more numerous than a class of equal frequency whose instances are less retrievable. The effect of this was shown in a study where subjects heard a list of well-known personalities of both sexes and then asked to judge whether the list contained more names of men than women. Different lists were given to different groups, and some of the lists had more famous men than women, and vice versa. In each of the lists, subjects falsely judged that the class (sex) that had more famous personalities was the more numerous.

In addition to familiarity, there are other factors that affect retrievability of instances, such as salience.[27] For instance, seeing a house on fire or hearing of a plane crash can affect our judgment of the probability of such incidents as greater than they actually are. This isn't helped by the fact that much of the information people are exposed to gives a distorted picture of the world of hazards, with media exposure being a major source. Weatherall et al. have shown that journalists often select scientific studies to feature in articles—but few journalists are experts in the relevant literature and often have as their true motive the sharing of only the most striking (or sensational) studies.[28]

Consider a study of two newspapers on opposite coasts showing that many of the statistically frequent causes of death (e.g., diabetes, emphysema, cancer) were rarely reported by either paper during the period of

---

[26] Shelley E. Taylor, "The Availability Bias in Social Perception and Interaction" in *Judgment Under Uncertainty: Heuristics and Biases*, eds. Daniel Kahneman, Paul Slovic, and Amos Tversky (New York, 1982),192, 196.

[27] In terms of public policy makers and risk assessments, Slovic et al. comment that: "The effects of memorability and imaginability are capable both of enhancing public fears and obscuring experts' awareness of ways that a system could fail. Insofar as the actual risks may never be known with great precision and new information tends to be interpreted in a manner consistent with one's prior beliefs, the perception gap may be with us for a long time....For experts and policy makers, these findings pose what may be a more difficult challenge: to recognize and admit one's own cognitive limitations, to attempt to educate without propagandizing, to acknowledge the legitimacy of public concerns, and somehow to develop ways in which these concerns can find expression in societal decisions without, in the process, creating more heat than light." Paul Slovic, Baruch Fischhoff, and Sarah Lichtenstein, "Facts Versus Fears: Understanding Perceived Risk" in *Judgment Under Uncertainty: Heuristics and Biases*, eds. Daniel Kahneman, Paul Slovic, and Amos Tversky (New York, 1982), 488-9.

[28] James Owen Weatherall, Cailin O'Connor, and Justin P. Bruner, "How to Beat Science and Influence People: Policy Makers and Propaganda in Epistemic Networks," https://www.journals.uchicago.edu/doi/full/10.1093/bjps/axy062.

the study.[29] Yet dramatic occurrences such as tornadoes, fires, drownings, homicides, and car accidents were reported much more frequently than less dramatic causes of death having similar or greater statistical frequencies. For instance, homicides were the most reported category in proportion to actual frequency. Though diseases claim almost 100 times as many lives as homicides, there were about three times as many articles about homicides as about disease deaths. Further, homicide articles tended to be more than twice the length of articles about disease and accident deaths. What's perhaps more important is that there's a high correlation between judged frequency of death and the number of deaths reported in newspapers (as high as .89). (The correlation likely goes both ways: media coverage biases perception of risk and consumers' opinions about what is important influences the media. Either way, such studies illustrate the extent to which people are drawn to the sensational.)

The result is that a low-probability hazard may increase its memorability and imaginability—and therefore its perceived riskiness—regardless of what the evidence indicates.[30] Consider again the case of a clinician who heard one of his patients say he's tired of life. Since attempted suicide is a dramatic and salient event, suicidal patients are likely to be more memorable and easier to recall than depressive ones who didn't attempt suicide. As a result, the clinician may recall suicidal patients he's counseled and judge the likelihood of an attempted suicide by the degree of resemblance between these cases and his current patient. But such an approach leads to serious biases. Noting that nearly all suicidal patients he can think of were severely depressed, he may conclude that a person is likely to commit suicide if he shows signs of severe depression. He may also conclude that suicide is unlikely if a particular patient doesn't look like any suicide case he's encountered. However, such reasoning ignores the fact that only a minority of depressed patients attempt suicide, as well as the possibility that the current patient may be unlike any other person he's ever counseled. Further, recent occurrences are likely to be more available than earlier ones, and a person's mere visibility can cause people to assign disproportionate

---

[29] Paul Slovic, Baruch Fischhoff, and Sarah Lichtenstein, "Facts Versus Fears: Understanding Perceived Risk" in *Judgment Under Uncertainty: Heuristics and Biases,* eds. Daniel Kahneman, Paul Slovic, and Amos Tversky (New York, 1982), 468.

[30] Paul Slovic, Baruch Fischhoff, and Sarah Lichtenstein, "Facts Versus Fears: Understanding Perceived Risk" in *Judgment Under Uncertainty: Heuristics and Biases,* 465.

responsibility for outcomes to which he or she contributes.[31] This effect has been demonstrated with CEO's, who can be praised or vilified for organizational results even when there are large segments of the business that remain completely outside of C-suite control.[32]

Part of the problem is that many of the events whose likelihood people want to evaluate depend on several interrelated factors, and it's difficult for the human mind to comprehend multiple sequences of variations. Because of this, Kahneman and Tversky propose that when evaluating the probability of complex events, only the simplest and most available scenarios are likely to be considered—meaning that only the most obvious variations are considered. It's the simplified nature of imagined scenarios that makes the outcomes of artificial intelligence simulations of interacting processes counterintuitive to most of us.[33] Beyond this, there's a lot of evidence that, once an uncertain situation has been perceived or interpreted in a particular way, it's difficult to view it in any other way. And this means that the production of a compelling scenario is likely to constrain both future thinking and the generation of alternative scenarios with different outcomes. At any rate, most of us have experienced the temporary rise in the subjective probability of an incident after seeing a car overturned by the side of the road or some other vivid event. The trouble is that continued preoccupation with an outcome may increase its availability, and thus its perceived likelihood, which means it will appear more likely to occur than it actually is.

It remains to be investigated whether things like availability effects and failure to consider base rates influenced how individuals and governments dealt with the COVID-19 pandemic. Closer consideration of the base rate data for death rates, especially for those not already in the high-risk pool, may have helped people develop a better risk assessment, which in turn could have altered individual and government response. That is, the failure to assess actual risk, combined with the availability of 24/7 news coverage chock-full of salient stories of death, may have dramatically

[31] Lee Ross and Craig A. Anderson, "Shortcomings in the Attribution Process: On the Social Origins and Maintenance of Erroneous Social Assessments" in *Judgment Under Uncertainty: Heuristics and Biases*, eds. Daniel Kahneman, Paul Slovic, and Amos Tversky (New York, 1982), 139, 140-3.

[32] See Phil Rosenzweig, *The Halo Effect...and the Eight Other Business Delusions That Deceive Managers* (New York, 2007), 56-61.

[33] See, for example, Ajay Agrawal, Joshua Gans, and Avi Goldfarb, *Prediction Machines: The Simple Economics of Artificial Intelligence* (Boston, 2018), 53ff.

caused a subjective overestimation of the likelihood of death in any given population. More sober analysis could reveal important lessons for similar future events.

Egocentricity and Anchoring

The egocentricity bias occurs when people see their own behavioral choices and judgments as common and appropriate, while viewing alternative responses as deviant or inappropriate. Spurred on by the fact that people have greater access to their own internal states, it can affect our ability to recall. In any situation, the behaviors we've chosen or would choose are likely to be more readily retrievable from memory and more easily imagined than opposite behaviors, i.e., the behavioral choices we favor are more cognitively available. This explains why the allocation of responsibility for a joint endeavor is usually recalled in an egocentric way by those involved. That is, when recalling how much a person contributed to a project, individuals tend to give themselves a greater proportion of the credit (the effect has been shown to exist at the group level as well).[34]

Anchoring is another one of those commonly used heuristics that can distort a person's judgment. This occurs when people consider a particular value for an unknown quantity before they estimate that quantity.[35] If, for instance, you were asked whether Ghandi was more than 114 years old when he died, you'll likely end up with a much higher estimate of his age at death than you would if the anchoring question had the number 35 instead. Considering how much to pay for a house, you'll be influenced by the asking price which will appear more valuable if its listing is high. In one experiment, real-estate agents were asked to assess the value of a house that was actually on the market. To do so, they visited the house and looked at a comprehensive booklet of information that included the asking price. Half of them saw an asking price that was substantially higher than the listed price, with the other half seeing an asking price that was substantially lower. Each agent gave an opinion about a reasonable buying price for the house and the lowest price at which he'd agree to sell it if he owned it. The agents were then asked about what factors had affected their

---

[34] Michael Ross and Fiore Sicoly, "Egocentric Biases in Availability and Attribution" in *Judgment Under Uncertainty: Heuristics and Biases,* eds. Daniel Kahneman, Paul Slovic, and Amos Tversky (New York, 1982), 180-1, 187.

[35] Daniel Kahneman, *Thinking, Fast and Slow* (New York, 2011), 119-20, 124.

judgment. Interestingly, the asking price wasn't one of them as they took pride in their ability to ignore it. Although each agent insisted that the listing price had no effect, the anchoring index actually proved to be 41%. In fact, the professionals were almost as susceptible to anchoring as business school students with no real-estate expertise (whose anchoring index was 48%). It turned out that the only difference between the two groups was that the students recognized they were influenced by the anchor and the professionals denied it.

Belief Perseverance

Experiments have shown that unfounded impressions, once in place, can survive a variety of completely disconfirming evidence. One of the mechanisms underlying this phenomenon probably comes from biased search, recollection, and assimilation of information.[36] It's generally agreed that our beliefs influence the way we seek out, store, and interpret information. Much of this is necessary because, without prior knowledge and preconceptions, our understanding of everyday experience would demand considerably more time and effort—meaning it would be diminished. However, a consequence is that we tend to perceive more support for those beliefs than actually exists. Such confirmation biases cause people to see potentially confirmatory evidence at face value and potentially disconfirmatory evidence as suspect. Thus, even evidence that's random tends to bolster and sustain the initial belief when it's subjected to new empirical disconfirmation. We've already seen this effect in a previous chapter within the scholarly literature. As Lee Ross and Craig Anderson put it:

> Once again, such biased searching, recollection, and assimilation not only bolster one's initial belief, they also produce a pattern of biased evidence that remains highly available to sustain the belief in question when its initial basis is attacked or even destroyed. The critical assumption here is that people do not constantly update or reevaluate the evidence relevant to their beliefs.[37]

---

[36] Lee Ross and Craig A. Anderson, "Shortcomings in the Attribution Process: On the Social Origins and Maintenance of Erroneous Social Assessments" in *Judgment Under Uncertainty: Heuristics and Biases*, 148-9.

[37] Lee Ross and Craig A. Anderson, "Shortcomings in the Attribution Process: On the Social Origins and Maintenance of Erroneous Social Assessments" in *Judgment Under Uncertainty: Heuristics and Biases*, 150-2.

Granting this, beliefs do change, even if by brute force. While logical and empirical challenges might have less impact than we'd want, they may still get the job done. And this means that formal methods of theory testing have a protective value, even if in some of these cases the change comes about without sufficient evidence.

Framing Effects and Noise

Different ways of presenting the same information can evoke different emotions and thus different decisions. The statement that "the odds of survival one month after surgery are 90%" has been shown to be more reassuring than the logically equivalent statement that "mortality within one month of surgery is 10%."[38] In the same way, meats that are described as "90% fat free" are more attractive than when they're described as "10% fat." One experiment showing this effect was carried out with Tversky's colleagues at Harvard Medical School. Physicians were given statistics about the outcomes of two treatments for lung cancer: surgery and radiation. The five-year survival rates clearly favor surgery, but it's riskier than radiation in the short term. Half of the participants read statistics about survival rates, while the others received the same information in terms of mortality rates. Here are the descriptions of the short-term outcomes of surgery:

> The one-month survival rate is 90%.
> There is 10% mortality in the first month.

As predicted, surgery was much more popular in the former frame (84% of physicians chose it) than the latter (50% favored radiation). Because the equivalence of the two descriptions isn't hard to see, a more rational decision-maker would make the same choice regardless of how it was framed. Kahneman suggests that System 1 is rarely indifferent to emotional words, such that mortality is bad, survival is good, and 90% survival sounds encouraging whereas 10% mortality is frightening. Medical training ends up being no defense against the power of framing.

---

[38] Daniel Kahneman, *Thinking, Fast and Slow*, 88, 367. See also Daniel Kahneman and Amos Tversky, "Choices, Values, and Frames" in *Judgement and Decision Making: An Interdisciplinary Reader,* Second Edition, eds. Terry Connolly, Hal R. Arkes, and Kenneth R. Hammond (Cambridge, 2000).

While framing often works with an erroneous (emotional) appeal to System 1, researchers have identified another phenomenon they call "noise"—defined as an undesirable variability of judgments of the same problem—that manifests similarly troublesome effects. However, noise is a much broader category and manifests itself not simply because of the way statements are framed, but more generally wherever people make judgments, e.g., as Kahneman et al. put it: wherever there is judgment there is noise.[39] An example comes from a study involving 208 federal judges who were exposed to the same sixteen hypothetical cases. In only three of the sixteen cases was there unanimous agreement on sentencing, and where there was agreement that a prison term was called for, there was substantial variation in the lengths of the recommended prison terms. In one case involving fraud, the mean prison term was 8.5 years; yet, the longest term was life in prison, making the study's findings a stunning example of the real-life consequences of noise. Equally concerning, judges have been found to be more likely to grant parole at the beginning of the day or after a food break than immediately before. Temperature has even been found to influence judicial decisions. One review of 207,000 immigration court decisions over four years found a significant effect of daily temperature variations, such that when it was hot outside, people were less likely to get asylum. Further, in the U.S., asylum judges are 19% less likely to grant asylum when the previous two cases were approved. Similar effects on different outcomes have also been shown with forensic scientists, pathologists, psychiatrists, and radiologists.

Given these findings, it will come as no surprise that mood has also been shown to affect judgment. People who are in a good mood are generally more positive and find it easier to recall happy memories than sad ones, they're more approving of others, and they're more generous and helpful. Hence, mood influences what we think, what we notice in our environment, and what we retrieve from memory. But it also changes how we think. A good mood makes us more likely to accept our first impressions as true without challenge and makes us more likely to let our biases affect our thinking. Many studies have demonstrated that mood affects our propensity to agree with meaningless, pseudo-profound statements generated by randomly selected nouns and verbs, a trait know as bullshit receptivity (a phrase that has become a bit of a technical term since the work

---

[39] Daniel Kahneman, Oliver Sibony, and Cass R. Sunstein, *Noise: A Flaw in Human Judgement* (New York, 2021), 12, 16-7, 36, 40, 90, 249-53, 278-9, 283-4.

of Princeton's Harry Frankfurt). Inducing good moods makes people more receptive to nonsense and more gullible generally, which means they're less likely to detect false or misleading information. On the other hand, people who are exposed to misleading information are better able to disregard it when they're in a bad mood. If we're shown a complex judgment problem, our current mood may influence our approach and conclusions, even when we believe it has no influence.

Stress and fatigue can also alter judgment, as shown in a study of 700,000 primary care visits, demonstrating that physicians are significantly more likely to prescribe opioids at the end of a long day. Prescriptions of other pain treatments (such as nonsteroidal anti-inflammatory drugs) do not display similar patterns. "When physicians are under time pressure, they are apparently more inclined to choose a quick-fix solution, despite its serious downsides."[40] There are other studies showing that, toward the end of the day, physicians are more likely to prescribe antibiotics and less likely to prescribe flu shots.

Finally, groups can profoundly influence judgment. In an experiment by Michael Macy of Cornell University, it was shown that the visible views of other people suddenly make political positions popular among Democrats and unpopular among Republicans, and vice versa.[41] In an online group, Democrats saw that a particular point of view was gaining popularity among fellow Democrats and endorsed that position, which then led most Democrats to favor it. However, if Democrats in a different online group saw that the exact same position was gaining popularity among Republicans, they'd reject the position, ultimately leading most Democrats to reject it. This effect was also seen among Republicans.

According to the researchers, chance variations among a small number of early movers can have a major impact on large populations. Similar findings have been demonstrated in different settings. As Kahneman et al. put it, social influences are problematic because they reduce group diversity without diminishing collective error. "The irony is that while multiple independent opinions, properly aggregated, can be strikingly accurate, even a little social influence can produce a kind of herding that undermines the

---

[40] Daniel Kahneman, Oliver Sibony, and Cass R. Sunstein, *Noise: A Flaw in Human Judgement*, 86-105.
[41] See also the study by Geoffrey L. Cohen, "Party Over Policy: The Dominating Impact of Group Influence on Political Beliefs" in *Journal of Personality and Social Psychology*, 2003, vol. 85, no. 5, 808-822.

wisdom of crowds."[42] Much of this is due to informational cascades in which people are unduly influenced by early opinions. They may also bow to social pressures and silence disagreement to avoid being the contrarian. The bottom line is that groups are often detrimental to sober analysis and end up with more extreme positions than individuals would have by themselves.

Conclusion

In our previous chapters, we explored different ways of understanding the origins of human knowledge and how far it can be justifiably extended. Perhaps best seen within the philosophy of science, what these debates seem to show is that we can gain knowledge of the world, but that we have inherent constraints which place limits around the epistemic certainty we're justified to have concerning any piece of information (popular misconceptions notwithstanding, whether those come from the scientific establishment itself or the media).

What this chapter has explored adds some empirical teeth to both assertions. As we saw, human beings use heuristic principles that allow us to reason quickly and with enough efficiency that survival without them would be difficult. But the chapter also highlighted the fact that we bump up against certain limitations, and it showed that human reasoning is easily derailed by these same heuristics. That is, we appear to rely on a limited number of heuristic rules that reduce the complex tasks of assessing the likelihood of uncertain events, and we thus predict values through the use of simpler operations. While, again, these can be useful, they can also lead us into error, causing us, for example, to overestimate the frequency of rare events and underestimate the frequency of more common ones. Because most of these involve probability assessments—for which we're often intuitively unprepared—our predictions are commonly off base and swayed by completely irrelevant factors. Perhaps even more troublesome is that the same errors persistently show up in scientific literature, causing problems like the proliferation of statistically non-significant findings in published research.

Having now examined some of the more pertinent research in the heuristics and biases program, we're left with one last topic before moving on to an analysis of theological knowledge—one that, at first glance, will

---

[42] Daniel Kahneman, Oliver Sibony, and Cass R. Sunstein, *Noise: A Flaw in Human Judgement*, 97-9.

seem counterintuitive: namely, our purported knowledge of the future. Because a significant portion of what we claim to know actually comes in the form of prediction and some sort of probability assessment, the next chapter will discuss new research on the epistemic status of expert forecasts and the extent to which experts—or any of us, for that matter—can achieve accuracy.

Chapter 8
Probability Judgments In Predictions

It may not be obvious, but many of our judgments—and therefore our claims to know—come in the form of prediction, which can be not just about future events but also about the past and present.[1] Any historical work is, in a limited sense, a prediction that the proposed narrative will turn out to be accurate relative to the judgment of other experts. We make a prediction about the present when betting that a credit card transaction is legitimate or fraudulent, or whether something we see in a CT scan is malignant or benign. Current efforts in the development of artificial intelligence reflect precisely the growing recognition that predictions of this sort can be central to our assessments of uncertainty. Thus, technically, the concept of prediction shouldn't be too narrowly confined to future events. Proposing a more precise definition, Ajay Agrawal et al. suggest that prediction is simply the ability to see otherwise hidden information, whether in the past, present, or future.[2] At the very least, we can say that, whether a prediction concerns past or present events, it's still conditional on future confirmation.

Having said that, what most of us think of as prediction concerns purported knowledge of some future state; we tend to think that such knowledge is consequential because it can affect behavior by influencing present decisions. Perhaps more forcefully, we could say that purported knowledge of the future drives more of our present judgments and decisions than is often recognized. We want to know how the stock market will fare in the

---

[1] Daniel Kahneman, Oliver Sibony, and Cass R. Sunstein, *Noise: A Flaw in Human Judgement* (New York, 2021), 107.
[2] Ajay Agrawal, Joshua Gans, and Avi Goldfarb, *Prediction Machines: The Simple Economics of Artificial Intelligence* (Boston, 2018), 23-4.

next six months in order to make the best present decisions; we want to understand how geopolitical events will shape government policy over the next two years to determine how best to invest resources; we want to check the weather forecast when packing for vacation in order to pack accordingly. We crave knowledge of the future because it gives us a sense of control in a world that often feels chaotic and *un*predictable. As F. A. Hayek said, most human aims can only be achieved if there is a connected set of actions, and this is based on the assumption that the facts will be what we expect them to be. "It is because, and insofar as, we can predict events, or at least know probabilities, that we can achieve anything."[3] The question for us is: can such "knowledge" be justifiably included in what we can claim to know?

Since it's virtually taken for granted today that knowledge of the future—which we'll refer to as a prediction or a forecast—is best determined by experts, this chapter will focus on the extensive research of Philip Tetlock on expert forecasting accuracy. Among the questions we'll examine, the following will be center stage: How do expert forecasters compare to rough algorithms? Assuming they're less than perfect, what common errors do we find in their assessments of the likelihood of future events? How much better are they, if at all, than novice forecasters? And why are people so drawn to predictions in the first place? Our answers will add some important and often overlooked details to the questions we've posed around the extent and potential limits of human knowledge.

How Forecasts Go Awry

The value of forecasts lies in the fact that they can provide needed answers in a usable form, usually as some sort of probability. However, they too often get lost in transmission and lose the explanatory power they were intended to have, leaving recipients with little more than vague assertions that provide no additional or actionable information. Baruch Fischhoff cites four ways this typically occurs:

1. Ambiguity: not saying clearly what events we're forecasting or how likely we think they are.
2. Irrelevance: not offering forecasts that address one's informational needs.
3. Immodesty: not admitting the limits of our knowledge.

---

[3] F. A. Hayek, *The Constitution of Liberty: The Definitive Edition* (Chicago, 2011), 200.

4. Impoverishment: not addressing the broader context within which forecasts (and contingent decisions) are made.[4]

Scenarios like these can play out in various ways. For instance, forecasters
may use ambiguous terms such as "likely" or "rarely" to indicate some
sort of probability for an event, but such words are too vague to be beneficial.[5] Trouble arises when they fail to express their level of confidence
or uncertainty; recipients are left guessing, which risks their acting in an
unduly aggressive or cautious manner. Part of the problem is that an estimate is only as definite as its knowledge base can warrant. That is, an
estimate might reflect data in a single—and sometimes underpowered—
study (which we noted previously is all too common), data from all similar
studies, or data from all sources the forecaster has available. But people
will be misled if they assume greater or less comprehensiveness than is
warranted.

Even when degree of confidence or lack thereof is stated, recipients
may still be left guessing whether the forecaster has overstated or under-
stated how much he knows. Like other biases we've discussed, these problems can have motivational and cognitive roots. For example, it can lead
to an exaggeration of confidence or an avoidance of public commitment
and accountability, which is only amplified by the fact that people lack the
ability to objectively evaluate themselves. Finally, predicted events may be
so complex that it's difficult to know which parts of them to take seriously,
and under such conditions, it's unclear whether analysts are predicting
anything at all.

Expert Forecasting

The mystique of the expert is so rooted in our culture that failing to
consult one is considered a lapse of judgment and due diligence. We see
this most notably in our 24/7 news cycle, which is full of pundits waxing
on about what to expect on virtually every issue: the economy, world
and local politics, court decisions, election outcomes, and on and on. As

---

[4] Baruch Fischhoff, "What Forecasts (Seem to) Mean" in *Judgement and Decision Making: An Interdisciplinary Reader,* Second Edition, eds. Terry Connolly, Hal R. Arkes, and Kenneth R. Hammond (Cambridge, 2000), 353-5, 360, 362-3, 367.
[5] For examples, see Philip E. Tetlock and Dan Gardner, *Superforecasting: The Art and Science of Prediction* (New York, 2015), 52ff.

prevalent as expertise is, one would be forgiven for thinking that we're more informed about future events than ever before, particularly because so many people watch or read the news. However, research has shown that there's an inverse relationship between notoriety and accuracy, meaning that the more well-known a pundit may be, the more likely it is that his or her predictions will prove false. While that may seem counterintuitive—after all, they're well-known for a reason—what's even more surprising is the actual track record of experts in general, which isn't much better than television personalities.

This was demonstrated by Philip Tetlock in the most comprehensive study on expert forecasting—spanning the years 1984 to 2004—which indicated that, whereas the best human forecasters were hard-pressed to predict more than 20 percent of the total variability in outcomes, crude algorithms could predict 25-30 percent of the variance and the auto-regressive distributed lag models explained 47 percent of the variance. His comments are sobering:

> These results plunk human forecasters into an unflattering spot along the performance continuum, distressingly closer to the chimp than to the formal statistical models ... Surveying these scores across regions, time periods, and outcome variabilities, we find support for one of the strongest debunking predictions: *it is impossible to find any domain* in which humans clearly outperformed crude extrapolation algorithms, less still sophisticated ones.[6]

Tetlock showed that, across all judgments, experts on their home turf made neither better calibrated nor more discriminating forecasts than did "dilettante trespassers." Forecasters, it turns out, display significant noise (a concept discussed in our last chapter).[7] Those who had devoted years of study to a given topic were as hard-pressed as colleagues casually dropping in from other fields to give realistic probabilities to possible futures. Though both groups assign too-low probabilities to the status quo, experts have more big mistakes to explain away than dilettantes do. How do we account for such counterintuitive results? The short answer is that experts

---

[6] Philip E. Tetlock, *Expert Political Judgement: How Good Is It? How Can We Know?* (Princeton, 2005), 38-9, 52-4, 61, 64.

[7] Daniel Kahneman, Oliver Sibony, and Cass R. Sunstein, *Noise: A Flaw in Human Judgement*, 117-22.

are human and therefore not immune from making the same mistakes as the rest of us.

That being true, what mistakes do people generally make? Though space doesn't permit an exhaustive list, we can note a few. To start with, people tend to overestimate the likelihood of low-probability events (death by tornado) while underestimating higher-risk events (heart disease or stroke), thereby ignoring base rate information. Rather than investigating base rates, they ground their probability judgments on how easily compelling causal scenarios come to mind. We're particularly likely to overestimate previously unrecognized risks in the aftermath of an adverse event, which upon cooler reflection may prove to have been a factor with the intense emotional public responses during COVID-19. This may be even more likely, given that risk perceptions can be affected by the visibility of a risk (the availability bias), by the fear associated with it, and by the extent to which individuals and public policy makers believe they can exercise control over it.[8]

Because experience tells us little about low-probability risks, we resort to correlations that too often turn out to have no causal connection. Generally, governmental risk assessments tend to lead people to overestimate the actual risk. For instance, in regulating toxic substances, results from the most sensitive animal species are often used, and government agencies (such as the EPA) routinely focus on the upper end of the 95% confidence interval as the risk level rather than use the mean of the distribution. The trouble is that such assumptions overstate the mean probability of an unfavorable event by several orders of magnitude. Another problem with these types of risk assessments is that they ignore important trade-offs. Restrictions on a "risky" activity, for example, should be based on the relative gains and losses of the activity compared to its alternatives, rather than on an artificial assessment of a single variable.[9]

Part of the problem is that people don't like ambiguity and find it hard not to fill in missing data with ideologically scripted sequences. The desire for certainty by the use of tidy narratives is an enduring human trait. As Kahneman et al. note, anyone who listens to the news knows that few large swings in the stock market go unexplained, even though

---

[8] Richard J. Zeckhauser and W. Kip Viscusi, "Risk within Reason," in *Judgement and Decision Making: An Interdisciplinary Reader,* eds. Terry Connolly, Hal R. Arkes, and Kenneth R. Hammond (Cambridge, 2000), 465, 467, 473-4.

[9] Richard J. Zeckhauser and W. Kip Viscusi, "Risk within Reason," in *Judgement and Decision Making: An Interdisciplinary Reader,* 474-5.

swings involve countless decisions by countless people who operate under countless circumstances.[10] The same is seen by observers of world politics who are often extremely confident in their counterfactual beliefs (i.e., alternate what-if scenarios), declaring with certainty that they know almost exactly what would have happened in counterfactual worlds no one can visit or verify. Because people dislike dissonance, they tend to organize the world into neat systems that couple good causes to good effects, and bad to bad.

Such tendencies were on full display when experts were asked to make predictions in eleven regional forecasting exercises. As their responses indicated, rarely did they think to base their estimates on anything other than their own view of the world. It was as if they were certain they were right and everyone else wrong. Rather than considering—in Bayesian fashion—opposing options and updating their predictions when new information came in, they consulted a gut-level intuition anchored around their own point of view, which they treated as an existential certainty. "In sizing up situations, we have difficulty taking other points of view seriously. Few of us spontaneously factor other views into our assessments—even points of view that, on second thought, we acknowledge have a non-negligible likelihood of being right."[11]

At play here is well-attested research demonstrating the prevalence of certain biases. Among them is the fact that people are reluctant to admit mistakes and update beliefs. They also display what investigators call the "self-serving" attribution bias: the tendency to attribute success to "internal" causes (such as our own abilities) and failure to external ones (such as bad luck or unfair testing conditions). In addition, Tetlock's study showed widespread susceptibility to the hindsight bias, in which people consistently exaggerate what could have been anticipated in foresight—a tendency exacerbated by the norm of reporting history, even by historians, as

---

[10] Daniel Kahneman, Oliver Sibony, and Cass R. Sunstein, *Noise: A Flaw in Human Judgement*, 156.

[11] Philip E. Tetlock, *Expert Political Judgement: How Good Is It? How Can We Know?* 122-3, 128, 138-40, 146, 161-2. This is all on top of the fact that, to improve based on empirical feedback, one needs to have knowledge of task structure, e.g., the rules we used to come up with a prediction in the first place. Otherwise, outcome feedback can be irrelevant, as it potentially leads to the erroneous conclusion that one's methodology was sound. See Hillel J. Einhorn, "Learning From Experience and Suboptimal Rules in Decision Making" in *Judgment Under Uncertainty: Heuristics and Biases,* eds. Daniel Kahneman, Paul Slovic, and Amos Tversky (New York, 1982), 275-6, 278-9.

a good story.[12] Thus, when asked to recall their original likelihood judgments, experts often claimed they attached higher probabilities to what subsequently happened than they did. When they recalled the probabilities that their rivals assigned to the future that materialized, they imputed lower probabilities after the fact than before the fact. In other words, they displayed both the hindsight bias (claiming more credit for predicting the future than they deserved) and the mirror-image hindsight bias (giving less credit to their opponents for anticipating the future than they deserved). This is consistent with research showing that people can convince themselves, within milliseconds, that they knew it all along.

We can summarize Tetlock's research by noting that experts are prone to the same judgmental shortcomings as the rest of us, which he encapsulates as follows: First, they're often too willing to jump to conclusions, too quick to draw strong conclusions from ambiguous evidence, and too slow to change their minds as disconfirming evidence comes in. Beyond a minimum, subject matter expertise translates less into forecasting accuracy than it does into overconfidence,[13] along with the ability to devise elaborate reasons for expecting favored outcomes. Second, experts are reluctant to admit they were wrong and to change their minds based on new evidence. They're adept at strategies for defusing threats to professional self-esteem.[14] Third, experts fall prey to hindsight bias. After the fact, they often claim they knew more about what was going to happen than they actually did. Fourth, they apply higher standards of proof for dissonant than for consonant discoveries. Fifth, valuing closure and simplicity, they're less accurate

[12] See Baruch Fischhoff, "For Those Condemned to Study the Past: Heuristics and Biases in Hindsight" in *Judgment Under Uncertainty: Heuristics and Biases,* eds. Daniel Kahneman, Paul Slovic, and Amos Tversky (New York, 1982), 341-343, 348. Ulrich Hoffrage and Ralph Hertwig have suggested that hindsight bias makes a boundedly rational memory system possible. If we can't remember an original judgment, we reconstruct it by repeating the same process that led to the judgment. But knowledge about the outcome of the event leads to an updating with the relevant knowledge. See "Hindsight Bias: A Price Worth Paying for Fast and Frugal Memory" in *Simple Heuristics That Make Us Smart,* eds. Gerd Gigerenzer, Peter M. Todd, and the ABC Research Group (Oxford, 1999), 195-6.

[13] Paul Slovic, Baruch Fischhoff, and Sarah Lichtenstein, "Facts Versus Fears: Understanding Perceived Risk" in *Judgment Under Uncertainty: Heuristics and Biases,* eds. Daniel Kahneman, Paul Slovic, and Amos Tversky (New York, 1982), 475-7.

[14] Amos Tversky and Daniel Kahneman, "Causal Schemas in Judgments Under Uncertainty" in *Judgment Under Uncertainty: Heuristics and Biases,* eds. Daniel Kahneman, Paul Slovic, and Amos Tversky (New York, 1982), 126.

in forecasting events involving complex social components and more susceptible to overconfidence, hindsight, and belief perseverance effects.

Silver Lining

Despite the dismal results, Tetlock's research reveals some areas of hope.
There are hints that human-versus-mindless-algorithm or expert-ver-
sus-dilettante comparisons mask individual differences in forecasting
skill. In some cases, judgment isn't simply reducible to good luck, meaning
that there's a particular subgroup of people that consistently outperforms
others.[15] The question is: what makes them different? To explain, Tetlock
appeals to Isaiah Berlin's distinction between hedgehogs and foxes and says
that this subgroup thinks and acts more like foxes. In an article entitled "The
Hedgehog and the Fox," Berlin had claimed that there were two types of
people. On the one hand are those who relate everything to a single central
vision and tend to think in grand narrative schemes, while on the other are
those who pursue many ends (even contradictory) and whose thoughts are
scattered and diffused. As forecasters, foxes weave in and out based on evidence and update their projections more frequently than hedgehogs—with
the latter more likely to embrace causal models of reality that give them
too much confidence in their long-range predictions. While foxes derive
modest benefit from expertise in a given area, hedgehogs are harmed, which
goes directly against cultural assumptions that expertise is a *sine qua non*
of good forecasting.

Counterintuitive as the results may seem, they align with a significant
amount of psychological research on cognitive styles and motivated reasoning. Hedgehogs fall within the personality style that needs closure and
structure (and dislikes ambiguity) and is more likely to trivialize evidence
that undercuts their preconceptions and to embrace evidence that rein-
forces them. The reason expertise may handicap this group is because the
more relevant knowledge they have, the more conceptual ammunition they
have to defend preconceived notions. Further, hedgehogs stress parsimony
and believe that deep laws constrain history and that these laws are knowable and lead to correct conclusions when applied to the real world. Along
with this, they tend to admire deductive reasoning that uses abstractions to
organize messy facts and to distinguish the possible from the impossible. In

---

[15] Philip E. Tetlock, *Expert Political Judgement: How Good Is It? How Can We Know?*
65, 81-2, 85, 88, 138-9.

contrast, foxes fit within the personality style that is predisposed to allocate cognitive resources in a more balanced way, in the service of both self-criticism and self-defense. They're more skeptical of deductive predictions, and they qualify analogies by pointing out disconfirming evidence; they're reluctant to make extreme predictions, and they're more motivated to weave together conflicting arguments. Thus, good forecasters tend to be moderate foxes: eclectic thinkers who are tolerant of counterarguments and hedge their bets by not straying too far from base-rate probabilities.

Tetlock would later come to call these superforecasters—who were amateurs that out-predicted even the intelligence community with classified information—and said that what makes them good is less what they are than what they do: e.g., the hard work of research, the careful thought and self-criticism, the gathering and synthesizing of other perspectives, the granular judgments, and relentless updating.[16] They're careful, at least as much as human beings can be, about checking the instant conclusions of System 1 against the critical appraisal of System 2. And they're better than typical experts about consulting what Kahneman has called the "outside view," which translates to gathering base-rate data in order to set an initial forecasting benchmark (the "inside view," in contrast, is the specifics of the particular case). (The inside view is concrete and lends itself to storytelling, which makes it more psychologically compelling, while the outside view is abstract and doesn't lend itself easily to narrative.) It's worth quoting in full Tetlock's composite picture of model superforecasters:[17]

In philosophic outlook, they tend to be:

Cautious: Nothing is certain
Humble: Reality is infinitely complex
Nondeterministic: What happens is not meant to be and does not have to happen

In their abilities and thinking styles, they tend to be:

Actively open-minded: Beliefs are hypotheses to be tested, not treasures to be protected

---

[16] Philip E. Tetlock and Dan Gardner, *Superforecasting: The Art and Science of Prediction*, 117-8, 231.

[17] Philip E. Tetlock and Dan Gardner, *Superforecasting: The Art and Science of Prediction*, 95, 191-2.

Intelligent and knowledgeable, with a "need for cognition": Intellectually curious, enjoy puzzles and mental challenges
Reflective: Introspective and self-critical
Numerate: Comfortable with numbers

In their methods of forecasting, they tend to be:

Pragmatic: Not wedded to any idea or agenda
Analytical: Capable of stepping back from the tip-of-your-nose [e.g., System 1 thinking] perspective and considering other views
Dragonfly-eyed: Value diverse views and synthesize them into their own
Probabilistic: Judge using many grades of maybe
Thoughtful updaters: When facts change, they change their minds
Good intuitive psychologists: Aware of the value of checking thinking for cognitive and emotional biases

In their work ethic, they tend to have:

A growth mindset: Believe it's possible to get better
Grit: Determined to keep at it however long it takes

Tetlock's results echo what we've seen in previous chapters: namely, that there can be no justification for the apparent claims to certain knowledge that so many of today's experts, media, and politicians portray in their accounts of highly complex situations. Standing in sharp relief, superforecasters display cautiousness, humility, and self-reflectiveness. Yet, in that very tentative approach, they also show that some level of forecasting accuracy can in fact be achieved.

Overconfidence and Certainty

Before concluding, it might be helpful to ask: if most forecasters are little better at prediction than a dart-throwing chimp, why do people continue to find them so compelling? Part of the story is that we all want answers. A confident yes or no is much more appealing than a maybe, which helps to explain why the media turns to hedgehogs who are sure they know what's coming, no matter how bad their actual forecasting records are. Another part of the story is that overconfidence is one of the best-documented cognitive biases, and people are biased to correlate confidence with competence.

For example, it's been shown that people trust confident financial advisers over those who are less confident, even when their track records are identical. This exaggerated correlation makes the forecaster who puts a probability on some event less worthy of respect in the eyes of the public. In fact, people see such judgments as indications that the forecaster was incompetent, ignorant of the facts, and unwilling to expend the effort required to gather information that would justify greater confidence.

Another factor is that people mistake their subjective sense of confidence for an indication of predictive validity—yet, too much of the time, this only provides the illusion of validity. For instance, research in managerial decision-making has shown that executives rely extensively on intuition, or gut-feel, which means knowing something but not knowing why. Such instances provide the person with a conviction of being right but without clear justification, which gives him a self-administered reward of achieving closure on a judgment. It's a satisfying emotional experience or a pleasing sense of coherence in which the judgment feels right. Kahneman et al. note that what makes this important and misleading is that it's construed as a belief, not a feeling.[18] Thus, the emotional experience ("the evidence feels right") masquerades as rational confidence in the validity of the person's judgment ("I know, even if I don't know why"). But as we've seen, confidence is a poor predictor of accuracy.

People who believe they're capable of a high level of predictive accuracy aren't just overconfident, however. They don't simply deny the risk of noise and bias in their judgments. The problem is that they believe in the predictability of events that are in fact unpredictable, meaning they implicitly deny the reality of uncertainty, i.e., a denial of ignorance. This is critical because objective ignorance sets a ceiling, not just to our predictions, but also our understanding; the conundrum is that far too many experts seem to underestimate their objective ignorance of the world.

Conclusion

One of the key takeaways from Tetlock's extensive research on prediction is that people, experts included (or perhaps especially), underestimate their objective ignorance of the world. Aggravating this is the fact that we're drawn to those who seem confident in their judgments, since we equate

---

[18] Daniel Kahneman, Oliver Sibony, and Cass R. Sunstein, *Noise: A Flaw in Human Judgement*, 138, 145, 153

confidence with competence. However, we've seen that there's an inverse relationship between notoriety and accuracy, which means that the more well-known a pundit is the more likely his or her predictions will prove false—thus making such claims to knowledge highly illusory.

As the research shows, one of the most basic forecasting errors seems to be the tendency to ignore base-rate information, which causes inflated projections as well as skewed risk assessments. Beyond a minimum, subject matter expertise translates less into forecasting accuracy than it does into overconfidence, and it highlights a person's propensity to devise elaborate reasons for expecting favored outcomes. The research also shows that people are reluctant to admit they were wrong and to change their minds based on new evidence. Experts, in particular, are adept at strategies for defusing threats to professional self-esteem.

While Tetlock's conclusions are sobering—specifically, that it's impossible to find any domain in which humans clearly outperform crude extrapolation algorithms—he also provides evidence that forecasters can achieve a certain level of accuracy. This was evident in the mixed research, which showed ranges from chimp-like results to accuracy levels that outperformed even intelligence experts with classified information. Based on this, we can conclude that knowledge of any future state, while possible, should be considered with a healthy degree of tentativeness. In this, it's not unique and mimics other types of knowledge we've discussed, except perhaps that probability assessments of future events should adjust for time, meaning that the farther out they go, the less predictive value they should be deemed to have. Further, because so many of our claims to know come in the form of prediction—and if prediction is defined as the ability to see otherwise hidden information (past, present, or future)—it should be clear that the attitudes of humility and caution model superforecasters projected are necessary for most (if not all) claims to know. Unfortunately, these are the very attitudes so lacking in today's intellectual environment.

With this brief overview of knowledge out of the way, it's now time to embark on the important question of how and what we can know of God.

Chapter 9
Knowledge of God

In the first quarter of the twentieth century, the logical positivists famously ruled out "God-talk," along with all other metaphysical claims, as meaningless. Recall from our previous chapters that they did so on the basis of a verifiability principle, which proposed that a statement is meaningful only if it can be (at least in principle) empirically confirmed—that is, only if it can be derived from experiment and observation.[1] As they argued, a statement was scientific if it had a determinate meaning, and meaningful statements were those that could be verified. However, as we also noted, despite its simplicity, it wasn't long before critics pointed out that many statements in the sciences aren't open to exhaustive verification (for instance, all universal laws). Further, the majority of non-scientific and pseudo-scientific beliefs have verifiable constituents, and because they're verifiable (in the sense that we can specify some possible observations that would verify them), they're both meaningful and scientific. Consequently, most of the attempts to formulate a verificationist principle came to a rather abrupt end.

With the failure of such attempts to bar claims to a knowledge of God from the outset, debates between theists and critics have tended to take on a more *a posteriori* form, centering around particular arguments and evaluating specific evidence for or against. Thus, as in the other domains of knowledge we've discussed, what and how much we can know of God seems to come only from the strength of the evidence and arguments, not

---

[1] Richard Creath, "Logical Empiricism," The Stanford Encyclopedia of Philosophy (Winter 2021 Edition), ed. Edward N. Zalta, https://plato.stanford.edu/archives/win2021/entries/logical-empiricism/.

by foreclosing the conversation by presupposing what humankind can and can't know.

In light of this, the next four chapters will examine some of these claims and assess not only their evidential strength but their inferential form as well. Chapter ten will explore the resurgence of natural theology based upon developments in Big Bang cosmology, with the following chapter doing the same with recent developments in biochemistry, focusing especially on their relation to standard Darwinian explanations concerning the origin of life on earth. Rounding off our examination, our final chapter will look at a specific argument for God's existence based on the claims of Jesus' followers that he rose (bodily) from the dead after being executed as a Messianic pretender in the first century. To begin this analysis, the present chapter will explore some issues that will set the framework for our subsequent chapters.

Can We Even Begin?

In order to assess any arguments for or against God's existence, we must suppose that arguments and reason are valid. Most of what's presented in this chapter assumes just that, but there exists a rather strong tradition known as fideism that rejects the notion that one can provide arguments for God's existence or for a particular religion. To give this idea a bit more precision, Kai Nielsen has defined the fideist as one who generally believes that fundamental religious beliefs rest solely and completely on faith. Finite and sinful people can't come to know God by the use of their unaided reason, and this implies (logically) for the fideist the parallel assertion that belief and unbelief are intellectually on a par. Religious experience is therefore ambiguous as to the reality of its object, and the existence of God can never be established by empirical investigation or philosophical demonstration. God, according to the fideist, remains a mystery and a scandal to the intellect; i.e., intellectually speaking, many fideists have contended that a belief in God is absurd. The believer can only trust that she's not "whistling in the dark" and not believing in something illusory when she accepts the God revealed in scripture as an ultimate reality. She must simply take the leap of faith without any intellectual assurance that she's leaping in the right direction.[2]

---

[2] Kai Nielsen, "Can Faith Validate God-Talk?" in *New Theology*, no. 1, (eds.) Martin E. Marty and Dean G. Peerman (New York, 1964), 131-132, 135, 138, 143.

From a Protestant perspective, fideism has been represented in both
the Reformed and Lutheran traditions. On the Reformed side, Cornelius
Van Til insisted that when we think about the interpretation of reality,
there are only two possible reference points: God and man. The triune God,
he posited, who created and sustains all things, is the ultimate principle
of interpretation of the universe, which means that a fact is true only if it
receives its interpretation from the God of the Bible. For Van Til, the sinner
is incapable of any knowledge in the proper sense, either in the spiritual
or scientific realms. This is because facts must be correlated with universals, and—apart from God, by whom everything derives its meaning—
understanding anything is impossible, since there is no facticity or truth;
that is, without presupposing the universal of the ontological Trinity. Thus,
for any fact to be truth, it must be a *theistic* fact. In his sinful condition, man
has discarded God as the ultimate universal and has therefore discarded
everything. Hence, there is no epistemological common ground between
the believer and unbeliever. Bruce Demarest explains as follows:

> Because autonomous human reasoning leads nowhere, Van Til asserts that
> the Christian must address the sinner by way of presupposition. ... The
> presentation of isolated facts adduced from nature or history independent of
> God, the ultimate referent, is a futile venture. ... That is, only as one boldly
> begins with the idea of the self-contained God does the data of the space-time
> world become intelligible and reason become a reliable interpretative tool.
> A sound and convincing case for biblical theism cannot be constructed by
> the traditional, empirical, rational, or verificational systems. The commonly
> employed empirical-historical method guarantees the overthrow of biblical
> Christianity.[3]

For Van Til, the only "proof" of Christianity is that, unless its truth is pre-
supposed, there's no possibility of "proving" anything at all. The truth of
the gospel in authoritative scripture is always self-authenticating and self-
validating, meaning that, apart from any inductive or deductive reasoning, the person who allows himself to be confronted by the Word of God
becomes existentially persuaded of it truthfulness. From this it follows that
general revelation (knowledge of God through the workings of nature) gives
the sinner no light.

---

[3]   Bruce A. Demarest, *General Revelation: Historical Views and Contemporary Issues*
(Grand Rapids, 1982), 148-50.

While stating his case differently, the Lutheran dogmatician, Francis Pieper, articulates a similar position. Concerning the question of how we recognize the divine authority of scripture, he begins by distinguishing Christian certainty (*fides divina*) from natural, or scientific, certainty (*fides humana*).[4] Christian certainty, he argues, is created solely by the self-testimony (or "self attestation") of scripture, through which the power of the Holy Spirit creates faith in itself and secures its acceptation. Such certainty isn't accomplished by the employment of human proofs. Scripture is rather an object of perception that creates its own organ of perception, faith. Hence, Pieper admonishes Christians assailed by doubt about the divinity of scripture to have intercourse with it; i.e., they must read, hear, and meditate on scripture and permit it to act on themselves. "Then the self-testimony of the Scriptures, the *testimonium Spiritus Sancti internum*, will dispel all doubts."[5]

Further, because the divine works bear the "divine stamp"—by which human reason can see that they're not the product of human beings—Pieper assigns to the role of apologetics one of proclamation, not defense.

> And as a natural, rational observation of the creation reveals God as its Creator (Rom. 1:18 ff.), so, too, a natural, rational study of Holy Scripture points to God as its author. When we compare the Holy Scriptures according to content and style with other "Bibles" in the world, e.g., with the Koran, the other Sacred Books of the East, etc., when we think of the victorious march of Christianity through the world, though its teaching is an offense to the Jews and foolishness to the Greeks, when we recall the astounding effects of the religion taught in the Scriptures on individuals and whole nations, then a reasonable reason cannot do otherwise than conclude that the Scriptures must be divine and confess that it is more reasonable to grant the divinity of Scripture than to deny it. This is the domain of apologetics.[6]

Thus, the apologist is to preach Christian doctrine to the world, but he doesn't attempt to prove its truth by rational or philosophical arguments.

---

[4] Francis Pieper, *Christian Dogmatics*, vol. 1 (Saint Louis, 1950), 308.

[5] Francis Pieper, *Christian Dogmatics*, vol. 1, 309.

[6] Francis Pieper, *Christian Dogmatics*, vol. 1, 310. Further defining the place of reason, Pieper says: "Arguments of reason, historical arguments, etc., can also be of service in the conversion of a person by inducing those outside the Church to read or hear the Word of God itself and so come to faith in the Word by the operation of the Holy Ghost through the Word" (311).

"And when the Gospel has wrought faith in the Savior of sinners in him, he rejoices in the saving divine truth and does not ask to have this truth demonstrated to him scientifically. That is the meaning of the axiom: 'The best apology of the Christian religion is its proclamation'." The apologist then is only in a position to show that it would appear more reasonable to accept the claims of Christianity as true than to reject them as false. It's not the apologist's business to demonstrate the truth of Christianity to the unbeliever; rather, it's to uncover the insincerity of unbelief, since all who reject Christianity do so because of their evil will and not because of their "pretended" intellectual honesty. Thus, with a long tradition of fideists, Pieper insists that there "are no scientific reasons or rational proofs against the truths of Christianity."[7]

But critics (such as Nielsen) have been quick to point out that, if there can be no scientific reasons or rational proofs of Christianity and if the faith is to be believed because it's absurd (along the lines of Tertullian's famous acclamation "I believe because it is absurd"), how could the believer understand the utterances about God at all? How could he accept or reject them, for he literally wouldn't understand what he's accepting or rejecting? If such utterances are to be meaningful at all, they must be intelligible to at least some men. But if we don't understand what "God" means or what it would be like for "There is a God" to be true or false, then to say that we accept God on faith is logically equivalent to saying we accept "There is an Irglig" on faith. That is, before we can make the leap, or before we can accept a claim on faith or refuse to accept it on faith, we must at least have some minimal understanding of what it is we're accepting or rejecting. Thus, despite the fideists claims, faith can't at this level be a way to understanding. As Nielsen points out, "Faith cannot ensure the meaningfulness of religious utterances; quite the contrary, faith presupposes that the discourse in question is itself meaningful (intelligible)."[8] If the fideist still maintains that it is a

---

[7] Francis Pieper, *Christian Dogmatics*, vol. 1, 109-110. In a similar fashion, Pieper claims the following: "We do not wait for science to establish a foundation for us. We have it already; and prior to all scientific investigation and scrutiny it stands as firm as our God, who has laid it. The findings of science can neither give us the faith nor rob us of it. We stand on a rock; we know that not even the gates of hell, much less human science, can prevail against it. Therefore we laugh at all enemies and their scientific battering rams and siege artillery with which in insane rage they attack this rock towering over the turbulent waters of this world, towering as high as heaven" (163).

[8] Kai Nielsen, "Can Faith Validate God-Talk?" 135: "It is this last question [i.e., granting religious utterances are intelligible, why should we accept them when we cannot

fact that there's a God, that he created the world, that he loves us, etc.—and it seems that if he has a truly Christian theology, he must—then how can we meaningfully assert that they're statements of fact if we have no idea of what it would be like for such statements to be either true or false? It's generally accepted that, in order for a sentence to serve as the vehicle for a factual assertion, one must be able to say what would count for the truth or falsity of this putative assertion. It must, in other words, have *that* much meaning.[9]

We should note that the question isn't whether reason has any place in religious belief, for fideists of most stripes would answer that question in the affirmative;[10] it seems that all fideist religious thinkers make use of reason in the process of teaching the religion's belief-system. In a more general sense, the real controversial question is this: What role—if any—should reason play in the *validation* of religious belief-systems? Or, should having faith depend on having good reasons to believe that one's faith is *true*?[11] From the fideist viewpoint, an objective, rational inquiry is a process by which one comes closer and closer to the truth. But because there's always more evidence one can and should consider, the person seeking truth can never quite reach it. So the decision for or against a belief-system is put off indefinitely. Yet, the fideist argues, for the person who is concerned with his soul, every moment that passes by without God is wasted. "In fact [for the fideist] if we could *prove* God's existence and his love for us it would then be impossible to have *faith* in God—so even if our inquiry were successful, it would frustrate rather than facilitate the goal of coming to know God!"[12]

---

establish their truth or even establish that they are probable?] that Pascal, Kierkegaard, and Barth wrestle with, while (in effect) assuming that there is no puzzle about the *meaning* of religious utterances. But it is just this logically prior question that disturbs contemporary philosophers when they think about religion, and to this question it would seem that fideism is no answer at all nor is it a way around the problem. We are, whether we like it or not, left with the crucial question: Are religious utterances intelligible, can we meaningfully assert or deny there is a God? This logically prior question remains a question of first importance in an examination and defense of religion" (136).

[9] Kai Nielsen, "Can Faith Validate God-Talk?" 138, 143.

[10] For example, see Francis Pieper's discussion of the ministerial use of reason, *Christian Dogmatics*, vol. 1, 197-200.

[11] Michael Peterson, William Hasker, Bruce Reichenbach, David Basinger, *Reason and Religious Belief: An Introduction to the Philosophy of Religion* (New York, Oxford; 1991) 33.

[12] Michael Peterson, et al., *Reason and Religious Belief: An Introduction to the Philosophy of Religion* 38.

On top of these considerations, critics will point out that many religions claim that their founding documents are self-authenticating, so how would the unbeliever—no matter how sincere—decide which to believe? If no external criteria can be brought to bear on the issue, then it seems he's left with nothing but emotion/intuition—but, as we'll see, these are no answers at all. At very best, the claim to self-authenticity is circular, taking something like the following form: We know the Bible is true because it guarantees (via the Holy Spirit) an internal testimony of its own truth; the internal testimony is true because the Bible guarantees it. Such arguments only beg the more central question of how we know that the "internal testimony" is truly that of the Holy Spirit and, by extension, that the Bible is truly the word of God. We've seen that both Van Til and Pieper marshal a similar claim to the self-authenticity of the Bible, but it's important to note that Joseph Smith (the nineteenth-century founder of Mormonism) used the same argument for the *Book of Mormon*: "And when ye shall receive these things, I would exhort you that ye would ask God, the Eternal Father, in the name of Christ, if these things are not true; and if ye shall ask with a sincere heart, with real intent, having faith in Christ, he will manifest the truth of it unto you, by the power of the Holy Ghost" (Moroni 10:4). The Christian fideist may object to the comparison, but the method employed by Smith is exactly the same: namely, knowing that their respective "Scriptures" are truly God's word by their own inner subjective illumination of the Holy Spirit.

But how does one know whether he's received this internal testimony? Fideists' answer: by the consequent presence of faith. Pieper, for example, argued that Scripture is an object of perception that creates its own "organ" of perception: faith. It's this inward faith that justifies belief in the divinity of scripture. But what does it mean to say that faith is an organ of perception, or that it's self-validating? The critic might object that faith is a relational term, always involving an object of belief. So the issue isn't the person's faith itself, for one could no more doubt that than he could doubt a person's claim to be in pain. It's rather the *object* of belief that stands at the center of dispute. We're compelled to distinguish sound from unsound objects of faith. Belief in and of itself is neither good nor bad, but beliefs can be true or untrue, noble or demonic. "To believe fervently," John Montgomery has commented, "that a medicine bottle contains aspirin when in fact it contains arsenic is a very dangerous practice; to consume tablets from the bottle on the ground that faith is self-validating could be fatal. … The answer to the question, 'Can Faith Validate God-Talk?' (Kai Nielsen) is thus a resounding negative; whether Deity exists and is the proper object of faith must be determined apart from the fact of faith. ...Without any test for truth but the 'leap of faith', how can one avoid the live possibility of autointoxication by metaphysical poison?"[13]

As a final point, Nielsen notes that the fideist would—indeed, *must*, if he has a genuinely Christian theology—maintain it as a fact that there is a God. That is, the fideist assumes in the way he uses language that he asserts something meaningful (factual). He wouldn't want to say that he's uttering empty tautologies. Rather, he implicitly claims something about the external world by insisting it was created by God and that this Creator entered human history in the person of Jesus. Yet he can't have it both ways. Either Christianity makes an existential claim or it doesn't. Of course, even a cursory reading of the New Testament reveals that it makes existence claims: i.e., they state something of a factual nature. Its numerous reports of miracles—especially the centrality of the resurrection—*presuppose* their factual, historical nature. Thus, it would seem inescapable that, at its core, contrary to the wishes of the fideist, Christianity *is* a falsifiable belief system. Given this, fideism is an inadequate expression, not only of the nature of the Christian claim to truth, but also of the epistemological and linguistic considerations inherent in such assertions about the existence of God and his attributes.

Religious Experience

Fideism has been one way of dealing with uncertainty, which it has often done by appealing to the reality of a religious experience it takes as self-authenticating. Yet there have been, both recently and throughout history, arguments for God's existence based upon the fact that people have religious experiences, which typically involve a claim to know something about God through a direct encounter with him. While the notion of experience varies, it can take the form of a vision, a dream, or a strong sense of emotion, whether that arises in private or in a communal setting. Often thought of as self-authenticating, such experiences are claimed to be direct, intuited, and unmediated by concepts, ideas, beliefs, and practices. Because of this, adherents frequently say they can't describe them and claim them to be beyond the rational, known only by feeling. Though one

---

[13] John Warwick Montgomery, *Tractatus Logico-Theologicus* (Bonn, 2002), 26, 28.

could point to more obvious proponents of experience such as Friedrich Schleiermacher or Rudolf Otto, or to Mormons who claim to know God via a "burning-in-the-bosom," it might be safe to say that a large contingent of the religiously inclined claim knowledge of God along such lines. In addition to its purported self-authenticating nature, part of the appeal of religious experience as a justification for a belief in God is the claim that such experiences can't be explained by natural causes and must therefore have been caused by God.

But can religious experience justify religious belief? Michael Peterson et al. have pointed out several difficulties with these proposals. First, they note that if religious experience is indescribable, then it can't be used to ground beliefs, since there's no rational content to hold up the grounding. On the other hand, if the experience has conceptual content, then it can't be independent of conceptual expression or exempt from criticism. Those who claim to have even the vaguest knowledge of God through experience can't have it both ways. Second, the very designation of an experience as religious requires at the outset certain beliefs about what the person takes to be as its cause; i.e., the identification of the cause is part of the experience's description. That being so, the religious experience can't be used to justify belief in the cause's existence. To do so would be to argue in a circle: "The experience is religious because someone perceived it as being caused by God; and that person has good reason to believe God exists because of his religious experience."[14]

In response, experience proponents could argue that, if the fact that our experiences reflect our beliefs means that those experiences can't be used to justify our beliefs, then none of our experiences can justify our beliefs, since all experiences invoke our belief structures. Thus, my experience of seeing a bird in the tree outside my window wouldn't justify my belief that there's a bird in the tree. If that's so, what would justify such a belief? Such a view, proponents argue, leaves all experiential beliefs unjustifiable. This of course doesn't mean that the religious experiencer might not be mistaken any more than an experiencer might not be mistaken in his perception of a bird in the tree. But, absent special considerations, religious experience should be taken by experiencers as grounds for belief in God.

However, as Peterson et al. point out, the critic might note that there seems to be a uniformity in the way we report ordinary perceptual

---

[14] Michael Peterson et al., *Reason & Religious Belief: An Introduction to the Philosophy of Religion*, 14-7, 26-9.

experiences and the beliefs about their objects, but religious experiences are reported in very diverse ways in that people give incompatible descriptions of the reality they experience. Mormons and Christians, for example (both of whom have religious experiences), describe them and the God who stands behind them in radically different terms. Thus, if people claim radically incompatible views of God and the world, what justification can religious experience give for any particular belief? It would seem that, for religious experience to have any epistemic value, it would have to be supported by something other than the experience itself: something else that would justify the believer's claim about God. This isn't to say that experience couldn't be meaningful in some sense, but it could never by itself provide the justification for assertions about God.

Beyond these analytical concerns, the critic might also point to specific instances that highlight the practical problems with using religious experience as a basis for belief and action. To take a particularly poignant example, on July 24, 1984, Allen Lafferty came home from work to his American Fork, Utah, home to find his young wife Brenda and their toddler daughter with their throats slashed. Brenda's body was found sprawled on the kitchen floor drenched in a lake of blood, while their daughter was lying dead in a blood-soaked crib. In separate trials, Allen's brothers Ron and Dan Lafferty were convicted of the double murders. Ron claimed he had an experience with God and that he'd received a "revelation" to remove his sister-in-law and niece, who he believed were an obstacle in his path.[15] If, the critic will ask, religious experience can justify belief in God, how do we know Ron's experience wasn't genuine while others are? Though the religious experience proponent might object to such an extreme example, the case highlights the fundamental epistemic problem with using experience as a basis for belief. How are we to tell which experiences to trust given their inherently subjective nature? For the critic, it would seem impossible to conceive of any objective criteria that could separate the true (assuming there are any) from the false experiences.

Natural and Revealed Knowledge of God

Moving beyond the previous approaches, various traditions argue that we can gain at least some knowledge of God from nature (natural revelation),

---

[15] For a full account see Jon Krakauer, *Under the Banner of Heaven: A Story of Violent Faith* (New York, 2004).

on the one hand, and God's more deliberate revelation of himself through Jesus Christ and the Bible (special revelation, or revealed knowledge), on the other. Most who concede that we have knowledge from these two sources see them not as mutually exclusive, but complementary. For the most part, natural revelation is thought to show not only God's existence but also some of his divine attributes, while special revelation via scripture makes known how God intends to save fallen sinners. With special revelation as the key to salvation, natural revelation is often seen, because of human sin, as something that has limited value in terms of what knowledge it provides (if any, as with Van Til).

From a Reformed perspective, Michael Horton argues that how we know (generally) depends on what we think there is to be known. In this sense, epistemology follows ontology.[16] We always, he suggests, presuppose a particular view of reality before we ask how to examine it, which means that there's no such thing as a neutral epistemology. Thus, with questions that ask if there's a God and how we might know him, the answers will follow the narrative we embrace, which is the case whether we recognize our basic assumptions or not. We know the world only as participants but never as detached observers. At the heart of Horton's position is the contention that we shouldn't attempt to ascend to heaven and know God by our own reason, will and works, but rather meet God where he has promised to descend to us: the covenant of grace, which is mediated by Christ who serves as the only door to God's presence. The reason for this is because God isn't an object for study as are the planets in our solar system. He can't be manipulated or subjected to repeatable experiments and so must condescend to reveal himself in a way we can understand; this means that, for Horton, his approach is opposed to rationalism and mysticism. Thus, against our distorted intuitions, the gospel (through which we come to know God's grace) doesn't encourage us to climb to heaven through intellectual, mystical, or moral striving. As he states:

A covenantal ontology requires a covenantal epistemology. We were created as God's analogy (image bearers) rather than as self-existent sparks of divinity; therefore, our knowledge is also dependent rather than autonomous. So there is indeed such a thing as absolute, perfect, exhaustive, and eternal truth,

---

[16] Michael Horton, *The Christian Faith: A Systematic Theology for Pilgrims On the Way* (Grand Rapids, 2011), 47, 49, 49-51, 53, 78.

but this knowledge is possessed by God, not by us. Rather we have *revealed* truth, which God has accommodated to our capacity.[17]

God has revealed himself through creation (general revelation), meaning that no one is without excuse concerning his existence, even though humans may suppress that knowledge. But there is no way we could come to know of God's saving purposes in Christ from this general revelation alone. Because total depravity means that there wasn't any part of humanity left unsullied by the fall into sin, even what we glean from general revelation is corrupted by our fallen heart. So even though we're swimming in general revelation, there can be no true natural theology (i.e., true knowledge of God through creation). A true theology (even of nature) requires a revelation other than what Calvin called the *sensus divinitatis* (sense of divinity, or natural revelation) to announce God's grace through the mediation of Christ. Hence, natural theology always takes some form of our native theology of glory (our attempt to ascend to God by way of reason or mysticism), while the gospel reveals the theology of the cross (the proclamation of God's descent to sinners in the flesh by grace alone by Christ alone). Reformed systematicians Charles Hodge and Louis Berkhof roughly agree with Horton and affirm that the works of God in creation reveal his being and attributes, but also affirm that natural theology fails in answering how human beings can be just with God. This is something only known through scripture.[18]

Lutheran dogmatician, Francis Pieper, argues in the same way that human beings know by nature that there is a creator and preserver of the universe and that this God is holy and just, demanding and rewarding the good while condemning and punishing the evil. They know this by (1) pondering the divine works of creation, (2) from God's continuous operation in nature and human history, and (3) from the divine law written into the hearts of all people. He explains that, in nature and history, God approaches people from without, while, in the law which is in all people, God confronts them directly from within their nature. Thus, a natural knowledge of God is both acquired and innate. However, like his Reformed counterparts, Pieper affirms that, in our present sinful condition, the natural knowledge of God

---

[17] Michael Horton, *The Christian Faith: A Systematic Theology for Pilgrims On the Way*, 54, 139-46.

[18] Charles Hodge, *Systematic Theology* (Grand Rapids, 1986), vol. 1, 24-9; Louis Berkhoff, *Systematic Theology* (East Peoria, IL, 2005), 36ff. See also Benjamin B. Warfield, *The Inspiration and Authority of the Bible* (Grand Rapids, 1948), 79ff.

is insufficient for salvation, which is revealed to us through the words of holy scripture. "This Christian knowledge of God is brought to us and is wrought in us not by God's self-revelation in nature, history, and man's conscience, but solely by God's self-revelation in his Word. For in Holy Scripture, which is God's Word, God speaks to us and with us and there reveals His innermost being and His loving heart."[19]

Ludwig Ott, from the Roman Catholic perspective, stresses that God can be known by human beings in their condition of fallen nature from (1) creation, through which the knowledge of God is a natural, certain, immediate, and easily achieved knowledge; (2) conscience, through which even unbelievers know naturally—without supernatural revelation—the essential content of the Old Testament law, i.e., the law has been written in the human heart; and (3) history, through which God reveals himself in beneficent works, even to the unbeliever. On this basis, Ott argues that the existence of God can be proved through the natural light of reason by means of the principle of causality, i.e., "as a cause is known by its effects, from those things that are made, that is by the visible works of creation."[20] However, only supernatural faith in revelation is effective for salvation. The supernatural revelation of God's existence confirms the natural knowledge of God and enables his existence to be known without any admixture of error. That is, the "naturally achievable knowledge of God is deepened and extended by supernatural revelation."[21]

Stating things a little differently, the *Catechism of the Catholic Church* adds that the proofs of God's existence can predispose a person to faith and help her see that faith isn't opposed to reason. Echoing the idea that people can know God with certainty from the created world by the natural light of human reason, it goes on to say that they have this capacity because they're created in the image of God. However, with Ott, the catechism affirms that we stand in need of being enlightened by God's revelation, which is a knowledge we can't arrive at by our own powers.[22] In addition to these, the Second Vatican Council reiterated that God provides human

---

[19] Francis Pieper, *Christian Dogmatics*, vol. 1, 371-7.

[20] Ludwig Ott, *Fundamentals of Catholic Dogma: A One-Volume Encyclopedia of the Doctrines of the Catholic Church, showing their Sources in Scripture and Tradition and their Definitions by Popes and Councils* (Rockford, 1960), 13-20.

[21] Ludwig Ott, *Fundamentals of Catholic Dogma: A One-Volume Encyclopedia of the Doctrines of the Catholic Church, showing their Sources in Scripture and Tradition and their Definitions by Popes and Councils*, 18.

[22] *Catechism of the Catholic Church*, Second Edition (New York, 1997), 20, 23.

beings with constant evidence of himself in creation, but that Jesus Christ reveals the words of God and accomplishes the saving work the Father gave him to do. As the section *Dei Verbum* states: "As a result, he himself—to see whom is to see the Father (cf. Jn. 14:9)—completed and perfected Revelation and confirmed it with divine guarantes. He did this by the total fact of his presence and self-manifestation—by words and works, signs and miracles, but above all by his death and glorious resurrection from the dead, and finally by sending the Spirit of truth. He revealed that God was with us, to deliver us from the darkness of sin and death, and to raise us up to eternal life."[23]

In terms of how we understand that knowledge, Ott maintains that our natural knowledge of God isn't an immediate, intuitive cognition, but a mediate knowledge because it's attained through a knowledge of creatures. Thus, in contrast to ontologism, which asserts that even in this life we have an immediate, intuitive knowledge of God, Ott argues that our knowledge is analogical (with immediate intuitive knowledge of God being possible only for the blessed in heaven). Analogical cognition, instead of knowing an object by immediate vision, comprehends an object through an "alien form." So, in our knowledge of God (in this world), we use concepts derived from created things to conceptualize God on the basis of a particular similarity of the created things to him as their efficient cause. This relation of analogy between the creature and the creator holds because the creature is necessarily made in the likeness of the creator—and it's this analogy that is the basis of all natural knowledge of God.

Additionally, Ott suggests that our knowledge of God comes by the three-fold way of affirmation, negation, and eminence. Affirmation (or causality) proceeds from the fact that God is the efficient cause of all things, and that efficient cause has in itself every perfection within the effect. It follows that God, who is origin of all creatures, has every perfection of the creatures. While the pure perfections are ascribed to God, the mixed perfections—which contain something finite in their concept—are ascribed

---

[23] Austin Flannery, ed., *Vatican Council II: The Conciliar and Postconciliar Documents, New Revised Edition*, (Collegeville, 2014), Kindle Edition, Location 16443-16458 of 22287. Recently, Mauro Gagliardi has contended that faith has no fear of reason: just as grace builds on and brings nature to fulfillment, so faith builds upon and perfects reason. He adds, however, that while it's clear that certain but limited knowledge of God can be obtained via natural theology, we can only know the truths that pertain to the gospel through God's self-revelation in Jesus Christ. See *Truth Is a Synthesis: Catholic Dogmatic Theology* (Steubenville, 2020), 127ff.

to God only in a "transferred" sense (e.g., metaphorically or anthropo-morphically). Negation denies to God every imperfection found in created things, and eminence enables us to deduce, from the finite perfections of creatures, God's possession of infinite analogous perfections. Because our knowledge of God in this world is composed of various inadequate con-cepts, it's necessarily limited and imperfect. However, Ott also insists that our knowledge of God is nevertheless true, because he really possesses the perfection attributed to him, and because we're aware of the analogous character of our knowledge of him.

Warrant and Knowledge

Many will concede that the above approaches to natural and special reve-lation are all well and good, but how can any purported knowledge of God have warrant (i.e., how is it justified)? Philosopher Alvin Plantinga has been at the forefront of dealing with the question of human knowledge of God and its epistemic status, and he has proposed a "Reformed Epistemology" through what he calls the Aquinas/Calvin (A/C) model. In this, he argues that theistic belief (belief in God) has sufficient warrant for it to be consid-ered as knowledge. At the heart of the model is the idea that God has cre-ated human beings with a belief-producing process or source of belief, the *sensus divinitatis* (an immediate, natural knowledge of God), which works under various conditions to produce beliefs about God, including beliefs that immediately entail his existence. Plantinga's contention is that beliefs produced in this way can meet the conditions for warrant, which he defines as the property enough of which is what distinguishes knowledge from mere true belief (given, as we've already seen, that you can have a true belief that isn't a case of knowledge).[24] (Note: Jeremy Koons has suggested that, for Plantinga, warrant functions like justification and the Gettier condition in traditional theories of knowledge.[25]) More technically, for Plantinga, a belief has warrant for person S only if that belief is produced in S by cogni-tive faculties that are functioning properly (i.e., with no dysfunction) in a cognitive environment that is appropriate for S's kind of cognitive faculties, and according to a design plan that is successfully aimed at truth.

---

[24] Alvin Plantinga, *Knowledge and Christian Belief* (Grand Rapids, 2015), 25, 28, 45ff.
[25] Jeremy Randel Koons, "Plantinga on Properly Basic Belief in God: Lessons from the Epistemology of Perception," 4. Published in *The Philosophical Quarterly* 61:245 (October 2011), 839-850, https://faculty.georgetown.edu/koonsj/papers/Plantinga.pdf.

Pursuant to the A/C model, we have a natural knowledge of God that's not arrived at by inference or argument, but in a more immediate way via the *sensus divinitatis*, which resembles the faculties of perception, memory, and *a priori* knowledge. That is, knowledge of this sort can be considered as properly basic, since it isn't based on other beliefs. Plantinga asks us to consider the following perceptual and memory beliefs:

(a) I see a tree,
(b) I had breakfast this morning.

Though these beliefs are typically and properly taken as basic, it would be a mistake to regard them as groundless. My having that sort of experience plays a central role in the formation and justification of that belief. Thus, the experience is what justifies me in holding it, meaning that this is the ground of my justification and, by extension, the ground of the belief itself. The same holds for beliefs that ascribe mental states to other persons and memory beliefs. In each of these cases, a belief is taken as properly basic in that there's some circumstance that confers justification; i.e., there is a circumstance that serves as the *ground* of justification. This of course doesn't imply that if I'm wearing rose-colored glasses, I'm still justified in saying that I see a rose-colored wall in front of me. The same goes for memory, if I know I have a bad memory. Plantinga's point is that we typically take such beliefs to be basic, and properly basic at that.

He then argues that similar things may be said about beliefs in God. Appealing to Calvin, he contends that God has so created us that we have a disposition to see his hand in the world around us. "More precisely, there is in us a disposition to believe propositions of the sort *this flower was created by God* or *this vast and intricate universe was created by God* when we contemplate the flower or behold the starry heavens or things about the vast reaches of the universe."[26] Yet there are many circumstances that call forth belief in God: guilt, danger, gratitude, a sense of God's presence, and a sense that he speaks. Though none of these beliefs involves the simple belief that God exists, they serve the purposes of entailing that he exists. The types of properly basic beliefs Plantinga has in mind are as follows:

(a) God is speaking to me,
(b) God has created all this,

---

[26] Alvin Plantinga, "Is Belief in God Properly Basic?" *Nous*, 15 (1): 1981, 45-7.

(c) God disapproves of what I have done,
(d) God forgives me,

And

(5) God is to be thanked and praised.

The *sensus divinitatis* to which he refers doesn't involve inferences from circumstances that trigger it, meaning it's not that we behold the night sky and draw the conclusion that God exists. It's rather that, upon perception of the night sky, these beliefs just arise within us; i.e., they arise in such circumstances but aren't conclusions from them. These beliefs, according to Plantinga, are to be considered properly basic in that they're not accepted on the evidential basis of other propositions, which he articulates as follows:

> We could put it by saying that *theistic belief can be properly basic with respect to justification*. According to the A/C model I am presenting, theistic belief produced by the *sensus divinitatis* can also be properly basic with respect to *warrant*. It isn't just that the believer in God is within her epistemic rights in accepting theistic belief in the basic way. That is indeed so; more than this, however, this belief can have warrant for the person in question, warrant which is often sufficient for knowledge.[27]

As to how this all works, Plantinga suggests that the *sensus divinitatis* is a belief-producing faculty that produces (under the right conditions) belief that isn't evidentially based on other beliefs. This is because, according to the model, our cognitive faculties have been designed and created by God and provide a blueprint for our cognitive functioning. The purpose of the *sensus divinitatis* is to give us the ability to have true beliefs about God, and, when it functions properly, it ordinarily does so. Because of this, Plantinga argues, these beliefs meet the conditions for warrant, and if they're strong enough, they constitute knowledge. By stipulating the idea of proper functioning, he concedes that our natural knowledge of God has been compromised by sin and—prior to faith and regeneration—is narrowed in scope and partially suppressed.

---

[27] Alvin Plantinga, *Knowledge and Christian Belief*, 35-7.

Broad and Narrow Image of God

The A/C model stipulates that God created human beings in his own image, as beings with intellect and will, which Plantinga calls the broad image of God. Yet, in addition to having an intellect and a will that has aims and intentions, humans also—as originally created—had a narrow image, meaning they had extensive and intimate knowledge of God, along with the right affections and gratitude for God's goodness. Part of the broad image was the *sensus divinitatis*. However, human beings have fallen into sin and require a salvation they're unable to accomplish by their own efforts. This sin has alienated us from God and has had disastrous consequences that envelop both our intellect and will, with our hearts now harboring deep and radical evil. Instead of loving God above all, we love ourselves. In this way, the narrow image was nearly destroyed. Further, the *sensus divinitatis* has been damaged and deformed, and we no longer know God in the same natural way and even resist the *sensus divinitatis*.

Because we're unable to extricate ourselves from sin, God provided a remedy through the life, suffering, death, and resurrection of Jesus Christ. Being that it's the principal work of the Holy Spirit to produce in us the gift of faith, it's by virtue of the internal testimony of the Holy Spirit that we come to see the truth of the central Christian affirmations. While the condition of sin brings damage to the *sensus divinitatis*, it doesn't obliterate it, and it remains functional in most of us. We thus have some grasp of God's presence and properties and demands, but this knowledge is impeded or suppressed.[28]

Given all this, how does the A/C model explain the way in which Christian belief could have justification or warrant? Plantinga responds by saying that these beliefs don't come just by way of memory, perception, reason, testimony, or the *sensus divinitatis*; they come rather by way of the work of the Holy Spirit, who gets us to accept and see the truth of the great truths of the gospel. Thus, these beliefs don't simply come by way of the normal operation of our natural faculties; they're rather a supernatural gift. Even so, the Christian who has received the gift of faith will be *justified* (in the basic sense of the term) in believing as he does.

---

[28] Alvin Plantinga, *Knowledge and Christian Belief*, 47-51.

Faith and Proper Basicality

A central part of Plantinga's model involves a concept of faith he inherits from Calvin, that faith is a special case of knowledge ("a sure and certain knowledge"), which means that it shouldn't be contrasted with knowledge. Faith is knowledge, though of a certain and special kind. However, it's unusual in the sense that its object/content is known by way of an extraordinary cognitive belief-producing mechanism, which involves the divinely inspired scripture and the internal instigation of the Holy Spirit. If this is so, how can it be considered "knowledge"? Plantinga responds by saying that when the believer encounters the great truths of the gospel, he comes to see—by the activity of the Holy Spirit—that these things are true. This means, he contends, that faith is a product of a belief-producing process like perception or memory. The activity of the Holy Spirit involves a means by which belief is produced in regular ways, which resembles memory, perception, reason, sympathy, and induction. Yet it differs from these in that it's not a part of our natural epistemic equipment.

Based on his criteria for what constitutes knowledge—i.e., that a belief be produced by cognitive faculties that are working properly, in an appropriate epistemic environment, according to a design plan successfully aimed at truth—Plantinga argues that what one believes by faith meets these conditions. Thus, (1) when these beliefs are accepted by faith and come from the instigation of the Holy Spirit, and when they're produced by cognitive processes working properly (i.e., they're not malfunctioning), the whole process can be said to be working as designed, since it was God himself that created them to produce this very effect (just as vision is designed by God to produce certain types of perceptual beliefs). And when it produces this effect, it's working properly and therefore produces beliefs that satisfy the condition of warrant, (2) our environment that includes the cognitive contamination by sin is precisely the environment for which this process is designed, (3) the process is designed to produce true beliefs, and (4) the beliefs it produces are in fact true in that this is a reliable belief-producing process, so that the process is successfully aimed at the production of true beliefs.

All of this means that Christian belief is *immediate* and formed in a basic way in that it doesn't proceed by way of evidential argument. It's rather a kind of intuitive and immediate evidence, making Christian belief properly basic. "On the model the believer is justified in accepting these beliefs in the basic way and is rational in so doing; still further, the beliefs can have warrant, enough warrant for knowledge, even when they are accepted in that basic way."[29] This means that a person can have warrant sufficient for knowledge even if he can't make a good historical case for the reliability of the biblical writers or their teachings. Hence, there's no need for a good argument for the resurrection of Christ, and so on. Warrant floats free of such questions in that it doesn't require validation by some source of belief other than faith. This also means that Scripture is self-authenticating.

But Is It True?

In making his case, Plantinga discusses several potential defeaters of Christianity—e.g., biblical criticism, postmodernism, and the problem of evil—and concludes that none of them are successful if Christianity is held as firmly as is warranted by the processes that produce it as a basic belief. And if the belief is true, it is warranted. Noting that Plantinga concedes that it's beyond the competence of philosophy to show that Christianity is true, in the same way that it couldn't demonstrate that there's an external world or a world that has existed more than five minutes—which is why his concern is to show that there's no good reason for believers not to continue to hold their Christian beliefs—Richard Swinburne highlights a potential problem with the A/C model:

> There is, however, a monumental issue which Plantinga does not discuss, and which a lot of people will consider needs discussing. This is whether Christian beliefs do have warrant (in Plantinga's sense). He has shown that they do, if they are true; so we might hope for discussion of whether they are true.[30]

The question, in other words, that concerns the sceptic isn't Plantinga's question about whether Christian belief is warranted (in his sense), but whether it's rational, i.e., whether it's probably true, given our evidence.

Going even further, Koons challenges the idea that any belief can be properly basic in Plantinga's sense. In making his case, Koons casts doubt

---

[29] Alvin Plantinga, *Knowledge and Christian Belief*, 63-5.
[30] Richard Swinburne, "Plantinga on Warrant," *Religious Studies* 37, 206-7. Swinburne notes Plantinga's puzzling distinction between a *de iure* question about religious beliefs (whether people are "warranted" in having religious beliefs) and the *de facto* question (whether those beliefs are true), 209.

KNOWLEDGE OF GOD   177

over the idea that perception (which Plantinga uses as an analogy to the *sensus divinitatis*) produces properly basic belief. His reason concerns the theory-ladenness, or background theories, of the observational predicates we employ, which stand or fall with the theories that stand behind them— meaning that their use in observation is only warranted if the corresponding theories are warranted. The theory of the world we hold plays a significant role in determining what beliefs we form in response to particular stimuli. Consider an example. If I'm in Utah and believe I see a deer, I may be right. But if I believe I see a unicorn, I'm certainly wrong, because the theories that embed these observation terms lack evidential support (and they face much counter-evidence). If I think I experience the presence of God or see his handiwork, then whether such a belief is warranted depends on the prior question of whether I'm warranted in using such a theoretical entity in my non-inferential judgments in the first place.

The crucial point is that our observation reports have an epistemic dependence on our background theories—which are inherently contestable and the proper subject for challenge and defense—in that their warrant depends on the warrant of the theories standing behind the observational terms embedded in our observational reports. (Koons concedes that perceptual beliefs can and do serve as evidence for and against background theories, which would be absurd to deny. But the credibility of any particular perceptual belief is always to be assessed in the light of the background theory.) So these observation reports aren't basic at all, but are *epistemically dependent* upon an entire body of theory. Koons concludes from this the following:

> So the real issue here is general: theistic belief can't be properly basic, but only because no kind of belief can be properly basic. And no belief can be properly basic because of the relation of epistemic dependence on theory. ... Whether a (psychologically) non-inferential belief is warranted cannot depend solely on whether the cognitive mechanism in question has operated properly in the appropriate cognitive environment; it must also depend on the warrant of the relevant background theory, which may well (and probably will) depend on all kinds of evidential relations.[31]

---

[31] Jeremy Randel Koons, "Plantinga on Properly Basic Belief in God: Lessons from the Epistemology of Perception," 839-850. Koons notes that Plantinga isn't arguing for fideism, just against the idea that evidence is the only possible source of warrant for theistic belief (17).

To sharpen the point, Koons highlights a well-known objection to Plantinga's model, which asserts that, if one is entitled to belief in God without evidence or argument, then the floodgates seem to be open for the most absurd claims. Plantinga had dealt with this himself by asking, "What about the belief that the Great Pumpkin returns every Halloween? ... If we say that belief in God is properly basic, won't we be committed to holding that just anything, or nearly anything, can properly be taken as basic, thus throwing wide the gates to irrationalism and superstition?"[32] In response, Plantinga says that to recognize that *some* of our beliefs are properly basic (with respect to warrant) doesn't commit one to thinking all *other* kinds are. While the Great Pumpkin objection is weak as stated, it does seem that there should be some epistemic criteria to sort out the types of psychologically non-inferential judgments we make. That's because if we're allowed to make judgments without evidential constraint, wouldn't anything be allowed? But what we've seen, says Koons, is that the epistemic controls operating on our psychologically non-inferential beliefs (the candidates for properly basic beliefs) come from above, from the level of theory.

Thus, even if we grant Plantinga's contention that belief in God is warranted, it still inherits part of its warrant from the warrant of Plantinga's theory of the Christian God, that is, from his inferentially articulated background theory.[33] What critics wonder is why others who approach belief from Plantinga's perspective couldn't also just as easily claim their religion is properly basic. Perhaps more disturbingly, why couldn't the Lafferty brothers use the same argument to justify their claims of revelation? Certainly Plantinga would object, but it seems that, if beliefs of this sort come via their being properly basic and without evidential support, and further through the internal testimony of the Holy Spirit, exactly how—epistemically—is that different from their claims to know God's will by their own internal testimonies?

A primary concern for Koons is that Plantinga's model has epistemic warrant flowing only in one direction: from psychologically non-inferential judgments to the superstructure of theory. While warrant may flow in this direction, it just as surely flows in the other direction too, meaning that warrant is in part a top-down phenomenon. But because Plantinga recognizes only the former, he doesn't allow theory to provide a sufficient check

---

[32] Alvin Plantinga, "Is Belief in God Properly Basic?" 48.
[33] Jeremy Randel Koons, "Plantinga on Properly Basic Belief in God: Lessons from the Epistemology of Perception," 839-850.

on cognitively spontaneous judgment. And without this downward check (from theory to these spontaneous judgments), says Koons, anything goes.

Conclusion

We started this chapter by asking if reason, or evidence, can legitimately be brought to bear in discussing human knowledge of God. Against this, fideists argue that neither reason nor evidence has any place in the validation of religious beliefs, which must simply be accepted on faith. We saw that critics ask: if we don't understand what "God" means or what it would be like for "There is a God" to be true or false, then how can we say it's different than any other absurd statement? We must at least have some minimal understanding of what it is we're accepting or rejecting, meaning that, despite the fideists' claims, faith can't at this level be a way to understanding. Unfortunately, arguments from religious experience, while perhaps meaningful in some sense, fare no better because of their inherently subjective nature.

Moving to more traditional ideas, we've seen that there are a variety of positions regarding if and how much we can know of God from creation—whether, in other words, a natural theology is possible—with much convergence within the Christian world around the fact that saving knowledge can come only through God's special revelation in Jesus Christ and scripture. Finally, we explored Alvin Plantinga's vigorous attempt to show that Christians have a warranted knowledge of God based upon how man was created and via the internal testimony of the Holy Spirit. Yet we also saw how Plantinga's argument could open the door to virtually any claim, meaning that if we're allowed to make judgments without evidential constraint, wouldn't anything be allowed? To many atheists and theists alike, Plantinga has failed to address the more central question: whether Christian beliefs can be shown to be in fact true. But these questions turn us back to the evidential status of the Christian claims about God and the world.

It's precisely this question that will take up the remaining chapters of this book, beginning first with Big Bang cosmology and the re-emergence of natural theology.

Chapter 10

Resurgence of Natural Theology

Since it has become increasingly implausible to foreclose any discussion about God before it even begins, recent debates between theists and atheists have turned on the relative strength or weakness of arguments for or against his existence. As we saw in the last chapter, logical positivists came up short when trying to disallow God-talk at the outset, leaving once again—at least philosophically—the question about his existence open to *a posteriori* arguments.

However, it wasn't only the logical positivists with their verificationist principle that cast shadows over the possibility of a natural theology. That had already been in the works some time before Darwin's publication of *On the Origin of Species* in 1859, but general acceptance of Darwin's evolutionary hypothesis sent natural theology into serious decline—to the extent that many thought it would never recover, since the origins of life had now been explained in completely naturalistic terms, requiring no ultimate cause other than those uncaused elements of physics and biology. God had effectively been pronounced dead by science. That is, until relatively recently, when, beginning with certain discoveries in 1926, scientists uncovered hitherto unknown facts that had profound implications on how we understand the origin of the universe. For the first time in decades, it wasn't theologians—who seem to have shamelessly gone into retreat—that were attempting to articulate something beyond the physical universe as an ultimate cause, but rather the very scientific community that had so confidently announced such a search to be archaic and unnecessary.

It's this resurgence of God as an ultimate cause that will preoccupy us in the present chapter, beginning with the notable revival of the traditional proofs for God's existence.

Traditional Theistic Arguments Revisited

Oxford University professor Richard Swinburne has been on the forefront of the question of knowledge as it relates to God. Arguing on the basis of the traditional proofs for God's existence, he makes the case that we can have justified knowledge that God exists.

Briefly stated, Swinburne suggests that various occurrent phenomena are such that they're more probable, and more to be expected, if there is a God than if there isn't. The universe's existence, its order, the existence of animals and people (along with our ability to acquire knowledge), the pattern of history and the evidence of some miracles are "all such as we have reason to expect if there is a God, and less reason to expect otherwise."[1] Posed as the simplest explanation—which he regards as an important criterion of explanation—theism postulates the existence of the simplest kind of person there could be (a being with capabilities, beliefs, and intentions). What the theist is saying is that God has capacities as great as they logically can be: he is infinitely powerful (i.e., omnipotent). That there is an omnipotent God is a simpler hypothesis than the hypothesis of a God who has limited power, the latter of which would then require further explanation. This is because a finite limitation cries out for an explanation of why there is just that particular limit in a way that limitlessness doesn't.

To make his case, he explores various arguments for God's existence (cosmological, teleological, consciousness, and morality), while offsetting those against potential defeaters such as the problem of evil, and concludes that, on the basis of our total evidence, theism is more probable than not. His argument notwithstanding, he concedes that the phenomena considered are strange and puzzling and that theism doesn't make their occurrence very probable; but nothing else makes their occurrence in the least probable, and they cry out for explanation (in that they don't adequately explain themselves). A priori, he says, theism may be unlikely, but it's far more likely than any rival hypothesis. "Hence our phenomena are substantial evidence for the truth of theism."[2] To clarify his point, Swinburne notes that a theory may not make the occurrence of its data (or evidence e) very probable and the theory may not have very high prior probability (according to Bayes' theorem). But if it provides the only possible/plausible explanation of e,

[1] Richard Swinburne, *The Existence of God* (Oxford, 1979), 277, 282-3
[2] Richard Swinburne, *The Existence of God*, 277, 288-91.

and if the uncaused occurrence of *e* would be a great puzzle, then *e* is very strong evidence for the theory. Matter is complex but regular in its behavior, and its existence and behavior need explaining in the same way that regular chemical combinations need explaining. It may seem strange that there exists anything at all, but if there is to exist anything, it's far more likely to be something with the simplicity of God than something like the universe with all its characteristics crying out for explanation without there being God to explain it.

To better understand Swinburne's argument, it will help to touch on his analysis of the cosmological argument, which starts from the existence of a finite object—i.e., any other object than God—to the existence of God. He begins with the existence of a complex physical universe and contends that, whether the universe had a beginning or is of infinite age, with no explanation outside itself, then it would simply be an inexplicable brute fact. That's because, if the only causes of its past states are prior past states, the set of past states as a whole will have no cause and thus no explanation. In the case of infinite age, though each state of the universe will have a complete scientific explanation (unlike if the universe is finite where its first state won't have an explanation), the whole infinite series will have no explanation because there won't be any causes of members of the series lying outside the series. There will be an explanation of why, once it's in existence, it continues to exist, but the non-existence of a time before its existence will be inexplicable. Thus, as to a question like why the world contains just this amount of energy (no more, no less), science would explain the reason whatever energy there is remains the same. However, it doesn't explain why there is just this amount of energy.

He concludes from this that, if each state of the universe at each instant of time has a complete scientific explanation, then the existence of the universe at each instant of time and its having certain permanent features have no explanation at all. Why should there be any world rather than none? The existence of the universe is something too large for science to explain. If we're to explain it, however, personal explanation must be appealed to and an explanation given in terms of a person who isn't part of the universe and acting from without. This can be done, he says, if we suppose that such a person (through an intention of his) brings it about at each instant of time. And if we're to postulate a person G who does so, we should postulate the simplest kind of G, and that means a G of infinite power, knowledge, and freedom. He sums the argument up as follows:

There is quite a chance that if there is a God he will make something of the finite and complexity of a universe. It is very unlikely that a universe would exist uncaused, but rather more likely that God would exist uncaused. The existence of the universe is strange and puzzling. It can be made comprehensible if we suppose that it is brought about by God. This supposition postulates a simpler beginning of explanation than does the supposition of the existence of an uncaused universe, and that is grounds for believing the former supposition to be true.[3]

It's important to note that, in arguing from the existence and order of the world to the existence of an agent, God, who brought it about, the theist may or may not claim to know what the intention was, i.e., why he did so. But even though the explanation is only partial, Swinburne contends that it's a legitimate explanation nonetheless.

Science and the Re-emergence of Natural Theology

Since Swinburne made his case for a knowledge of God through traditional theistic proofs, some scholars have turned in a more scientific direction and suggest that we can glean God's existence through the intricate laws and cosmic constants of the universe. While these are obviously related to traditional proofs, they take on a much more empirical nature in recent debates and have accelerated a comeback of natural theology, which had been largely discredited by Darwinism. Occurring not so much through the work of theologians, who seem to have been in retreat on such matters since Darwin, this resurgence of natural theology has taken its cue largely from scientists, asking what we can know of the creator by looking at his creation.

Theoretical physicist John Polkinghorne made this clear when he said that theology can't be simply left to the theologians, as every form of human understanding must make its contribution to it, and that's because a theological view of the world is a total view of the world. "It is as idle," he says, "to suppose that one can satisfactorily speak about the doctrine of creation without taking into account the actual nature of the world, as it would be to think that the significance of the world could be exhaustively conveyed in the scientific description of its physical processes."[4] For him,

---

[3]   Richard Swinburne, *The Existence of God*, 50, 116, 124-32.

[4]   John Polkinghorne, *Science and Creation: The Search for Understanding* (London, 1988), 2-3, 15.

this implies an urgent need for dialogue between science and theology. The arena for their interaction is natural theology, which can be defined as the search for the knowledge of God by the exercise of reason and the inspection of the world. Though there are those on both the religious and anti-religious sides who deny the possibility of such knowledge, Polkinghorne suggests that, if theism is true, creation is potentially a vehicle for God's self-disclosure. It may not be able to bring us to a knowledge of God the Father and our Lord Jesus Christ, but its insights shouldn't for that reason be disregarded. For the atheist who fails to see theism as credible and coherent, natural theology may be for him a necessary starting point. Unlike their pre-Darwinian predecessors, which focused on particular occurrences such as the coming-to-be of life or of the eye, contemporary cases for a revised natural theology point to the fundamental laws and constants of the universe.

Before getting to these, however, it's important to note that this has all happened against the background of a growing popularity of scientific materialism, which affirms that matter, energy, and the laws of physics are the entities from which everything else came and which serve as the uncreated foundation of all that exists.[5] According to this view, matter and energy organized themselves by strictly naturalistic processes to produce the complex forms of life we know today, and it also means that there exists no immaterial entities such as God, free will, the soul, and a human mind that are distinct from mere physiological processes in the brain. While materialism is nothing new and has a long history going back to ancient Greece, it has received renewed vigor through the writings of the New Atheists. Led by such writers as Richard Dawkins, Daniel Dennett, Lawrence Krauss, Christopher Hitchens, and Stephen Hawking,[6] the New Atheists popularized materialism for an entirely new generation and have had profound influence on the popular discourse on science and religion.

---

[5] Stephen C. Meyer, *Return of the God Hypothesis: Three Scientific Discoveries That Reveal The Mind Behind The Universe* (New York, 2021), 3-5, 13-4.

[6] See, for example, Richard Dawkins, *The Blind Watchmaker: Why the Evidence of Evolution Reveals a Universe Without Design* (New York, 1996) and *The God Delusion* (Boston, 2006); Daniel Dennett, *Breaking the Spell: Religion as a Natural Phenomena* (New York, 2006) and *Darwin's Dangerous Idea: Evolution and the Meaning of Life* (New York, 1995); Lawrence Krauss, *A Universe from Nothing: Why There is Something Rather Than Nothing* (New York, 2012); Christopher Hitchens, *God Is Not Great: How Religion Poisons Everything* (New York, 2007); Stephen Hawking and Leonard Mlodinow, *The Grand Design* (London, 2010).

As one of the New Atheists' more outspoken proponents (one might even say an atheist evangelist), Dawkins insists that science has demonstrated that there's no evidence of an actual design to the universe (i.e., no Grand Designer, God) but only the illusion or appearance of design. The evolutionary mechanism of mutation and natural selection has the power to mimic a designing intelligence without itself being designed or guided (what Dawkins calls the "blind watchmaker").[7] Even further, he contends that the universe we see has exactly the properties we would expect if there is no purpose, no design, no evil, no good, "nothing but blind, pitiless indifference."[8] Hawking, on the other hand, argues that because there is a law such as gravity, the universe will spontaneously create itself from nothing.

Central to the New Atheists is a commitment to reductionism, which reduces all things to simple physics and chemistry. Such a reductionism is in some ways understandable in that—as Roy Bhaskar pointed out—the historical order of the development of knowledge of the different levels of reality is opposite to the causal order of their dependence in being. In other words, as Polkinghorne notes, scientists have a difficult time starting with complexity. Because of our limited intellectual powers, we're forced to think from bottom to top, from underlying simplicity to overall complexity, at least at first, and this retains a hold upon our minds as controlling the metaphysical picture, because it's hard to dispel reductionist tendencies from our thinking altogether.[9] Nevertheless, we've given reasons throughout this book to question reductionism and suggested that the idea of emergence fits better with what we see in the real world.[10] Recall that, for Bhaskar, emergence theories are "those that, while recognizing that the more complex aspects of reality (e.g., life, mind) presuppose the less complex (e.g., matter), also insist that they have features which are irreducible, i.e., cannot be thought in concepts appropriate to the less complex levels—and that not because of any subjective constraints on our thought, but because of

---

[7] Richard Dawkins, *The Blind Watchmaker: Why the Evidence of Evolution Reveals a Universe Without Design*, 1.

[8] Richard Dawkins, *River Out of Eden: A Darwinian View of Life* (New York, 1995), 133.

[9] John Polkinghorne, *Reason and Reality: The Relationship Between Science and Theology* (London, 1992), 34-5, 39. We should note that Polkinghorne also takes a critical realist position, meaning that what we know and what is the case should be closely allied, i.e., epistemology and ontology are intimately connected (41-2).

[10] See also the discussion on reductionism by John C. Lennox in *God's Undertaker: Has Science Buried God?* (Oxford, 2009), 52ff.

the inherent nature of the emergent strata."[11] Biology has its own concepts that aren't reducible to physics or chemistry, and this means that subatomic particles have no more privileged share in determining the nature of reality than a bacterial cell.

At any rate, it will help to keep in mind that reductionism plays a significant role in the works of the new atheists and helps to explain the contours of their arguments, particularly as we see them in the written works of Dawkins below.

The Emerging Role of Complexity

By the mid-twentieth century, it was starting to be recognized that the science of the seventeenth, eighteenth, and nineteenth centuries was largely concerned with two-variable problems of simplicity. As such, it was concerned with the application of the scientific method, which chiefly involved the collection, description, classification, and observation of concurrent and correlated effects. However, as Warren Weaver noted in 1948, the progress in fields such as biology was of a different character in that the problems of living organisms are rarely those where one can rigidly maintain constant all but two variables. Living systems are more likely, he said, to present situations in which several dozen quantities are all varying simultaneously, and in interconnected ways. Weaver refers to these types of problems as those of organized complexity, which he defines as "problems which involve dealing simultaneously with a *sizable number of factors which are interrelated into an organic whole.*"[12]

He includes in this class of problems questions such as: Is a virus a living organism? What is a gene, and how does the original genetic constitution of a living organism express itself in the developed characteristics of the adult? On what does the price of wheat depend? What unifies these is that they involve a substantial number of relevant variables which are all interrelated in a complex, but not helter-skelter, fashion. These problems, along with a whole range of similar problems in the medical, biological, economic, psychological, and political sciences are much too complicated to

---

[11] Andrew Collier, *Critical Realism: An Introduction to Roy Bhaskar's Philosophy,* 107-13.

[12] Warren Weaver, "Science and Complexity," *American Scientist,* 36:536 (1948), 2-3, 5, https://people.physics.anu.edu.au/~tas110/Teaching/Lectures/L1/Material/WEAVER1947.pdf.

yield to nineteenth-century techniques that were successful on two-to-four-variable problems of simplicity. In a 1967 article, F. A. Hayek concurred and added that earlier theories (in physics) succeeded because they dealt with phenomena that we consider simple—but a simple theory of phenomena that are complex in their nature is probably false.

Both Weaver and Hayek recognized that we have the means of dealing with the problem of large numbers via statistics (what Weaver calls disorganized complexity), where the system as a whole possesses certain orderly and analyzable average properties. Statistics handles such cases by eliminating complexity and deliberately treating individual elements as if they weren't systematically interconnected; i.e., it disregards the fact that the relative position of the different elements may matter. But it is for this reason that it's irrelevant to problems of organized complexity in which the relations between individual elements with different attributes are what matters. Statistics, Hayek contends, treats the structure of the elements as "black boxes" that are presumed to be of the same kind but about whose identifying characteristics it doesn't have anything to say. He goes on to note that "Nobody would probably seriously contend that statistics can elucidate even comparatively not very complex structures of organic molecules, and few would argue that it can help us to explain the functioning of organisms. Yet when it comes to accounting for the functioning of social structures, that belief is widely held."[13] It's on this basis that Hayek had argued the futility of a centrally planned state (such as we saw in the murderous failure of twentieth-century Soviet Russia or in today's China). This is because, as we don't have a full knowledge of the particular circumstances that determined the emergence of existing forms or institutions, we have no way of predicting what will determine the selection of future developments. The way our imperfect knowledge of the past limits our ability to predict the future holds as well in biology. Hayek puts it thus:

> The theoretical understanding of the growth and functioning of organisms can only in the rarest of instances be turned into specific predictions of what will happen in a particular case, because we can hardly ever ascertain all the facts which will contribute to determine the outcome. Hence, "prediction

---

[13] F. A. Hayek, "The Theory of Complex Phenomena: A Precarious Play on the Epistemology of Complexity," Studies in Philosophy, Politics and Economics (London, 1967), 22-42. https://bazaarmodel.net/ftp/Project-C/Bazaarmodel/Materiaal/Xtradetail/pdf/Theory%20of%20Complex%20Phenomena.pdf, 5-7.

and control, usually regarded as essential criteria of science, are less reliable in biology." It deals with pattern-building forces, the knowledge of which is useful for creating conditions favourable to the production of certain kinds of results, while it will only in comparatively few cases be possible to control all the relevant circumstances.[14]

What's important here is that the idea of complexity came to play a significant role in many theistic arguments for a knowledge of God. While perhaps more implicit in arguments from Big Bang cosmology, complexity serves as an explicit reason not just for doubting pure Darwinian and neo-Darwinian approaches, but also serves as a springboard for a positive case that life (and the universe itself) is best explained by intelligent design.

Big Bang Cosmology

At about the same time that theoretical work was positing an expanding universe, observational cosmology led by Edwin Hubble was coming to the same conclusion. In 1926, Vesto Slipher had discovered that the optical spectra of the light from distant galaxies were shifted toward the red end of the spectrum, which was thought to be a result of the Doppler effect.[15] When a source is moving toward an observer, there's a blue shift in the spectral lines, and when it's receding, a red shift occurs. Then, in 1929, Hubble showed not only that all measured galaxies are receding but that their velocity of recession is proportional to their distance from us, i.e., the greater the distance, the greater the source's red shift. But it wasn't only that Hubble and his colleagues established that the universe is expanding, just as

---

[14] F. A. Hayek, "The Theory of Complex Phenomena: A Precarious Play on the Epistemology of Complexity," Studies in Philosophy, Politics and Economics, 22-42. https://bazaarmodel.net/ftp/Project-C/Bazaarmodel/Materiaal/Xtradetail/pdf/Theory%20of%20Complex%20Phenomena.pdf, 8. Hayek continues by saying that "the insight into the impossibility of such full knowledge induces an attitude of humility and reverence towards that experience of mankind as a whole that has been precipitated in the values and institutions of existing society" (11). The real problem with central planning is a naive assumption that society's "experts" have full knowledge of the limitless parts of the system relevant to the planning process, which Hayek rightly sees as impossible.
[15] William Lane Craig, "The Finitude of the Past and the Existence of God" in William Lane Craig and Quentin Smith, Theism, Atheism and Big Bang Cosmology (Oxford, 1995), 37-43.

the theoretical models predicted, but also that it's expanding the same in all directions. What made this all the more profound was the discovery that, if the acceleration of the expansion is always decreasing, then the further we go into the past, the greater the increase of the acceleration and the smaller the radius of the universe, until a time when the entire universe is squeezed into a point of infinite density, i.e., a spacetime singularity.[16]

Thus, if the velocity of the galaxies has remained unchanged, then the universe began with a great explosion from a state of infinite density in what has been termed the "Big Bang" (about 15 billion years ago). Beyond these early observations, one of the most important pieces of evidence confirming the Big Bang theory was the discovery of a microwave background radiation that permeates the entire universe by Penzias and Wilson in 1965. Though we don't have space for details here, it was shown that this cosmic radiation is the relic of an early era of the universe in which the universe was very hot and dense.

What concerns us here is that two lines of argument have ensued since these discoveries, each of which have opposite metaphysical consequences—with one implying the existence of a creator who caused the universe to come into existence and the other that the universe spontaneously came into existence uncaused. Quentin Smith argues the latter, suggesting that the singularity at t_0 isn't part of the universe and therefore is not the earliest part of the universe.[17] Rather it's a source of the universe, with the universe itself beginning some time after t_0. On this basis, Smith argues that the beginning of the universe is the explosion of four-dimensional spacetime out of the earliest singularity, which, for him, means that the Big Bang is the beginning of the universe. This also means that he takes the singularity to be real. Though a unique sort of reality, it's real, nonetheless, with Smith contending that the singularity is a *physical singularity*. He further suggests that there are uncaused events that follow from Heisenberg's uncertainty principle, which states that for magnitudes such as the position and momentum of a particle, it's impossible in principle to precisely measure both simultaneously. Even if it's objected that this type of quantum acausality only applies at the microscopic level and not the macroscopic states, Smith argues that, because the physical processes of the Big Bang are

---

[16] Quentin Smith, "The Uncaused Beginning of the Universe" in William Lane Craig and Quentin Smith, *Theism, Atheism and Big Bang Cosmology* (Oxford, 1995), 111.

[17] Quentin Smith, "The Uncaused Beginning of the Universe," 116, 119, 121, 123-4, 129.

all microscopic, they occur at dimensions in which quantum-mechanical principles apply. In other words, classical notions of space and time and all known laws of physics break down at the singularity, which means that it's impossible to predict—and not simply unpredictable *by us* but unpredictable *in principle*—what will emerge from the singularity. This implies, for Smith, a strong probabilistic argument for an uncaused beginning of the universe consistent with atheism.

A possible objection to Smith's contention might be that God could have intervened in the initial lawlessness of the Big Bang singularity to constrain it, so that it would emit a life-producing configuration. But Smith responds by saying that the objection is incompatible with the rationality of God.[18] If God intended to create a universe that contains human beings, then there's no reason to begin with an inherently unpredictable singularity. In fact, it seems irrational and a sign of incompetence to create as the first state something requiring immediate supernatural intervention to ensure it leads to the desired result, not to mention that the requirement for God's intervention doesn't agree with an efficient creation. The rational thing would have been to create a state that leads to a life-producing universe by its own lawful nature. Yet everything we know suggests that it's highly *improbable* that an animate universe would result from a Big Bang singularity, which is often seized upon by theists as evidence for a designer. To counter the theist here, Smith argues that this is inconsistent with the conclusion that God created the singularity, because it's illogical that he would have created something whose natural evolution would lead with high probability only to inanimate states. Thus, he states, the following two propositions seem to be logically incompatible:

(a) God is a rational and competent creator, and he intends to create an animate universe.
(b) God creates as the first state of the universe a singularity whose natural tendency is towards lifelessness.

The problem, as Smith sees it, is a problem of divine interference in or a correction of his creation. Since there are countless, logically possible initial states that lead by a natural and lawlike evolution to animate states, God,

---

[18] Quentin Smith, "Atheism, Theism, and Big Bang Cosmology" in William Lane Craig and Quentin Smith, *Theism, Atheism and Big Bang Cosmology* (Oxford, 1995), 202-6, 208, 212.

if he created the universe, would have selected one of those. But given that the initial state posited by Big Bang cosmology isn't one of these, it follows that Big Bang cosmology isn't consistent with a divine creation.

Theist William Lane Craig has challenged Smith's conclusions. In sharp contrast to Smith's contention that the singularity is real, Craig argues that "infinite density" is equivalent to "nothing." There can be, he suggests, no object in the real world that possesses infinite density; if it had any size at all, it wouldn't be *infinitely* dense. An object having no spatial dimensions and no temporal duration can hardly qualify as a physical object, as Smith contends. It's rather a mathematical conceptualization/point.[19] The creation of matter, Craig argues, came from nothing, in that, if we follow the expansion back in time, we reach a time at which the universe was shrunk down to nothing at all. "This is the state of 'infinite density'. What a literal application of the Big Bang model really requires, therefore, is creation *ex nihilo*."[20]

In his case for theism, Craig defends the causal proposition that whatever begins to exist has a cause, and this proposition is constantly verified and never falsified, meaning that it's an empirical generalization enjoying the strongest support experience can provide. The motions of elementary particles that quantum-mechanical laws describe (even if uncaused) aren't an exception to this principle. Smith's use of vacuum fluctuations is misleading because virtual particles don't literally come into existence spontaneously out of nothing. "Rather," Craig notes, "the energy locked up in a vacuum fluctuates spontaneously in such a way as to convert into evanescent particles that return almost immediately to the vacuum."[21] He suggests that, even if Smith's argument is successful, in no way does it prove that the universe began to exist without a cause, but only that its beginning was unpredictable. But this is something with which the theist is already in complete agreement; theism affirms that creation is the freely willed act of God, so it necessarily follows that the beginning and structure of the universe were, in principle, unpredictable, even though they were caused by God. However, to be uncaused in the sense of an absolute beginning,

---

[19] William Lane Craig, "Theism and Big Bang Cosmology" in William Lane Craig and Quentin Smith, *Theism, Atheism and Big Bang Cosmology* (Oxford, 1995), 227.

[20] William Lane Craig, "The Finitude of the Past and the Existence of God," 44, 61.

[21] William Lane Craig, "The Caused Beginning of the Universe" in William Lane Craig and Quentin Smith, *Theism, Atheism and Big Bang Cosmology* (Oxford, 1995), 143, 145.

an existent has to lack any non-logical necessary or sufficient conditions whatsoever. Craig presses his point as follows:

> Now at this juncture, someone might protest that such a requirement is too stringent: "For how could *anything* come into existence without *any* non-logical necessary or sufficient conditions?" But this is my point exactly; if nothing existed—no matter, no energy, no space, no time, no deity—if there were absolutely nothing, then it seems unintelligible to say that something should spring into existence.[22]

The fact that the universe originated in a naked singularity only shows that we can't predict what sort of universe will emerge, but it doesn't show that anything and everything can come into existence uncaused. In the end, Craig notes, while this is all dressed up in the guise of a scientific theory, the real issue here is a philosophical one: can something come out of nothing?

As to Smith's argument about God's creating the universe according to his (Smith's) notion of efficiency, Craig asks why we would think God is incompetent because he doesn't conform to our standards of efficiency. The only way to draw such a conclusion would be to know all the relevant divine goals and values that would be operative in the creation and governance of a world like ours. It could be that, given God's intentions, he's been perfectly efficient in his creation of our universe. As an illustration, Craig notes that, on Smith's principles, a chef ought to prefer simply having (if he could) his gourmet meal to eat instantaneously over going through all the effort of preparing the meal, as if there might be no inherent value in the process itself. Smith discounts the fact that the end of some activity may not exhaust the agent's reasons for doing something. The chef isn't deemed irrational or incompetent since it was part of his intention to enjoy the activity itself. Perhaps God wanted to leave a general revelation of himself in nature by creating a world that wouldn't have (in terms of probability) resulted from its natural tendencies alone. Simply put, how does Smith know that God doesn't also have his own reasons for his being causally engaged in creation?

Craig also notes something Smith has entirely overlooked, namely, that efficiency is a good property to have if one has limited power or limited time. However, apart from these limitations, it's not at all clear that

---

[22] William Lane Craig, "The Caused Beginning of the Universe," 146, 156. Craig notes that Smith's statements concerning the models he cites are much bolder than the proponents of the models themselves (140).

efficiency is the type of property it's better to have than to lack. It seems that the only reason Smith thinks that God's intervention in the natural order is incompetent is because it's inefficient, but this imposes an inappropriate, anthropomorphic standard upon God. What Smith misses entirely here is that the Christian theist welcomes the case for the necessity of divine intervention in both the creation and conservation of the world, maintaining, as he does, that God is living and active within it (in sharp contrast to the deist). Craig concludes thus:

> The universe (including, in Smith's view, the initial singularity) simply sprang into being out of nothing without a cause, endowed with a set of complex initial conditions so fantastically improbable as to defy comprehension, and as it evolved through each symmetry-breaking phase cosmological constants and quantities continued to fall out wholly by accident so as to accord with this delicate balance of life-permitting conditions. Such an interpretation seems implausible, if not ridiculous. The metaphysician can hardly be regarded as irrational if he reposes more confidence in the principle *ex nihilo nihil fit* than in Smith's mootable premises.[23]

Fine Tuning

More recently, Stephen Meyer has argued for a theistic conception of the world's origins on precisely the grounds Craig lays out, namely, from the fine tuning of the laws of physics and chemistry. Fine tuning refers to the discovery that many properties of the universe fall within extremely improbable and narrow ranges that have been shown to be absolutely necessary for complex forms of life to exist. Since the 1950s, physicists have discovered not only that life depends on a highly improbable set of forces, but also an extremely improbable balance among many of them. The precise strengths of the fundamental forces of physics, the arrangement of energy and matter at the beginning of the universe (among others) seem to be delicately balanced to allow for the possibility of life. So, if any of these properties were altered to even a slight degree, complex chemistry and life wouldn't exist. What has puzzled physicists is that they could have been different without violating either the fundamental laws of physics or any necessity of logic or mathematics. The universe appears to have been created with human beings in mind.

---

[23] William Lane Craig, "Theism and Big Bang Cosmology," 228-31.

Meyer observes that all the equations describing the fundamental forces of physics include force constants, which measure or quantify the net effect of all the other factors affecting the magnitude of the forces in question. And this is the fact that ends up so surprising because these force constants have one of the rare sets of values that make life in the universe possible; meaning that the constants in the equations describing the fundamental forces are exquisitely fine-tuned within extremely fine tolerances. Thus, as physicist Paul Davies once said, the amazing thing isn't that life on earth is balanced on a knife-edge, it's that the entire universe is balanced on a knife-edge.

In addition to the fact that (as astrophysicist Fred Hoyle discovered) a multitude of factors had to occur in exactly the way they did to produce carbon (the basis of life) in stars—which had to last long enough to form solar systems capable of sustaining life—there are many other constants that exhibit fine-tuning. For instance, the ratio of the electromagnetic force to gravity must be accurate to 1 part in 10^{40}. If this ratio had been a little higher, the gravitational attraction would be too strong compared to the contravening force of electromagnetism pushing nuclei apart. In such a case, stars would burn too quickly and unevenly to allow for the formation of long-lived stars and stable solar systems. If it had been a bit lower, gravitational attraction would be too weak in comparison to electromagnetism, which would have prevented stars from burning hot enough to produce the heavier elements needed for life. In short, even slight differences in the strength of any of these constants (and there are more) or their ratios would preclude the possibility of life.

Beyond these considerations, a life-permitting universe depends on its precise expansion rate. Meyer notes that, since the discovery of the red shift of the light coming from distant galaxies, astronomers have discovered that if the universe had initially expanded even slightly faster or slower, either stable galaxies wouldn't have formed, because matter would have dissipated too quickly for galaxies to congeal, or else the universe would have quickly collapsed in on itself. Moreover, the expansion rate in the earliest stages of the universe would have depended on the density of mass and energy at those early times, and the density of the universe one nanosecond (a billionth of a second) after the beginning had to have the precise value of 10^{24} kilogram per cubic meter. If the density were smaller or larger by only 1 kilogram per cubic meter, galaxies would never have developed, which corresponds to a fine-tuning of 1 part in 10^{24}.

Yet, as impressive as these figures are, the cosmological constant requires an even greater degree of fine-tuning, which physicists now agree is no less than 1 part in 10^{90}. To illustrate what this number means, Meyer asks us to imagine searching the vastness of the visible universe for one specially marked subatomic particle. Consider also that the visible universe contains around 200 billion galaxies, each with about 100 billion stars, along with a plethora of asteroids, planets, moons, comets, and interstellar dust. Assume now that you have the power to move instantly anywhere in the universe to select—blindfolded and at random—any subatomic particle you want. The probability of finding a specially marked subatomic particle (1 chance in 10^{80}) is still 10 billion times better than the probability (1 part in 10^{90}) that the universe would have happened upon a life-permitting strength for the cosmological constant.[24] Puzzling over the almost incomprehensible complexity involved in the universe's development and the eventual existence of human beings, Meyer comments:

> We apparently live in a kind of "Goldilocks universe," where the fundamental forces of physics have just the right strengths, the contingent properties of the universe have just the right characteristics, and the initial distribution of matter and energy at the beginning exhibited the right configuration to make life possible. These facts taken together are so puzzling that physicists have given them a name—*the fine-tuning problem*.[25]

Concurring with this stunning complexity and improbability, Alister McGrath has provided a summary of six critical constants, which are worth citing here because of their conciseness:

1. The ratio of electromagnetic force to the force of gravity, which measures the strength of the electrical forces holding atoms together, divided by the force of gravity between them. If this were even slightly smaller than its observed value, only a short-lived miniature universe could exist: no creatures could grow larger than insects and there would be no time for biological development.
2. The strong nuclear force, which defines how firmly atomic nuclei bind together. This force, having a value of 0.007, controls the power from the

---

[24] Stephen C. Meyer, *Return of the God Hypothesis: Three Scientific Discoveries That Reveal The Mind Behind The Universe*, 131, 141-2, 151-2.

[25] Stephen C. Meyer, *Return of the God Hypothesis: Three Scientific Discoveries That Reveal The Mind Behind The Universe*, 131, 141-2, 151-2.

sun and how stars transmute hydrogen into all the atoms of the periodic table. Again, the value of this constant is critical: if it were 0.006 or 0.008, we couldn't exist.

3. The amount of matter in the universe. The cosmic number Ω (omega) is a measure of the amount of material in our universe (e.g., galaxies, diffuse gas, dark matter, and dark energy) and tells us the relative importance of gravity and expansion energy in the universe. If this ratio were too high, the universe would have collapsed long ago, and if it were too low, no galaxies or stars would have formed. Thus, the initial expansion speed seems to have been finely tuned.

4. Cosmic repulsion. Cosmologists now know the importance of cosmic antigravity in controlling the expansion of the universe and its increasing importance as our universe becomes darker and emptier. As it just so happens (which was surprising to theorists), λ is very small.[26] Otherwise, its effects would have stopped galaxies and stars from forming, meaning that cosmic evolution would have been stifled before it even began.

5. The ratio of gravitational binding force to rest-mass energy is fundamentally important in determining the "texture" of the universe. If it were smaller, the universe would be inert and structureless and if it were much larger, it would be a violent place, in which no stars or solar systems could survive (dominated by vast black holes).

6. The number of spatial dimensions, which is three. String theory argues that of the 10 or 11 original dimensions at the universe's origins, all but three were compactified. Life couldn't exist if this were two or four.[27]

McGrath also notes that, according to the anthropic principle, very small variations in any of these fundamental specifications would have rendered the world anthropically sterile.[28] Hence, he suggests, a contemporary understanding of the origins of the universe reveals an entity that came into existence and was instantaneously endowed with potentialities for anthropic development. And since life is fundamentally a physicochemical phenomenon, it depends upon the fundamental laws of physics and chemistry as well as the availability of fundamental materials required to

---

[26] This represents the cosmological constant associated with dark energy in empty space that explains the accelerating expansion of space against the attractive effects of gravity.

[27] Alister E. McGrath, *A Fine-Tuned Universe: The Quest for God in Science and Theology* (Louisville, 2009), 119-20, 125, 180.

[28] John Polkinghorne, *Reason and Reality: The Relationship Between Science and Theology* (London, 1992), 77.

achieve certain biologically necessary outcomes, a point that's consistently overlooked in many accounts of evolution. But this biological process so frequently taken for granted requires the availability of a stable planet, irradiated by an energy source capable of chemical conversion and storage, and the existence of a diverse array of core chemical elements (with certain fundamental properties) before life can begin. While biology has come to see these as core assumptions, McGrath points out that they're in as much need of explanation as anything else.

Adding to this, Polkinghorne emphasizes the fact that these delicate balances are required at all stages of the cosmos process and don't simply refer to its beginning stages.[29] Significant "coincidences" seem to have been necessary at every stage of the world's development if its history was going to be capable of anthropic development. This means that there appear to be ample reasons for a revised form of the argument from design, not along the lines of Paley's cosmic craftsman who serves as a necessary explanation of every process, but as a cosmic planner who endowed the world with a potentiality embedded within the delicate balance of the laws of nature themselves (which science can't explain since it *assumes* them as the basis for its explanation of the process). It's on the basis of this extraordinary complexity and improbability that many scholars have insisted on an updated natural theology that makes the case for intelligent design, or theism.

Our Minds and the Universe

In addition to the facts we've just explored, Polkinghorne adds another point often overlooked by those arguing for naturalistic explanations. He notes that, while we take it for granted that we can understand the world, it could have been otherwise. The universe might have been a disorderly chaos rather than an orderly cosmos, or might have had a rationality that wasn't accessible to human beings.[30] Yet our minds have shown themselves able to understand the problems which the physical world presents. That is, there's a congruence between our minds and the universe, between the

---

[29] John Polkinghorne, *Reason and Reality: The Relationship Between Science and Theology* (London, 1992), 77-8. We should note that Polkinghorne rejects deistic notions and insists that at every moment of existence, the universe is held in being by the will of God (80).

[30] John Polkinghorne, *Science and Creation: The Search for Understanding* (London, 1988), 20-1.

rationality experienced within and the rationality we observe outside of us. A particular example concerns the fact that scientists commonly recognize that mathematics is the abstract key which turns the lock of the physical universe—what Eugene Wigner has called "the unreasonable effectiveness of mathematics"[31]—but this congruence between the human mind and the world can't be explained by science since it assumes that very congruence.[32] Evolution has often been invoked as an explanation, but it seems incredible that (for instance) Einstein's ability to conceive the General Theory of Relativity was simply a consequence of the human struggle for existence. What possible survival value does the ability for abstract knowledge provide? And how is it that abstract concepts of pure mathematics happen to fit perfectly with the patterns of the subatomic world of quantum theory or the cosmic world of relativity, neither of which has provided any practical benefits for the human evolutionary struggle to survive?[33]

For Polkinghorne and many others, the meta-question of the unreasonable effectiveness of mathematics needs to be answered.[34] Recognizing that this can't be done by science, which has to assume it in order to get started, he argues that a coherent and elegant explanation lies in the rationality of the creator. The physical universe, he says, seems embedded with signs of mind. Thus, for the theist, it's God's mind that stands behind the universe's rational beauty.

Conclusion

After being relegated to the dustbin of history, we've now seen how natural theology has made a startling comeback from an unlikely source: discoveries by the very scientific community that had so confidently asserted God to be an unnecessary postulate. While we shouldn't take this to mean that a large contingent of scientists have become theists—in fact, it's probably safer to say most are functioning materialists—it has meant a fundamental

---

[31] Wigner, Eugene. "The Unreasonable Effectiveness of Mathematics in the Natural Sciences," *Communications in Pure and Applied Mathematics*, vol. 13, no. 1 (February, 1960). New York: John Wiley & Sons, Inc, 1-14.

[32] John Polkinghorne, *One World: The Interaction of Science and Theology* (London, 1986), 46.

[33] See also John Polkinghorne, *Science and The Trinity: The Christian Encounter with Reality* (New Haven, 2004), 62ff.

[34] John Polkinghorne, *Reason and Reality: The Relationship Between Science and Theology*, 76-7.

shift not only in the problems being discussed but also in the visible shift of at least some scientists.

And it seems there is good reason for this. For many, the nature of such a finely tuned, mind-bogglingly complex universe, which seems to have been created with human beings in mind, can have but only one reasonable cause: an all-powerful being, God, who stands outside the universe. While materialists such as Smith balk at such a notion, theists insist that it seems inconceivable that something so complex and delicate—a universe that, as Paul Davies said, balances on a knife-edge—should arise uncaused out of nothing and by pure chance. This appears all the more improbable given all the things that had to have occurred, not just simultaneously, but also throughout the universe's long development—things and events that could have very easily been different, thereby making human existence an impossibility. For the theist, that all of this occurred in the face of incalculable improbability makes the case for God as the cause the best explanation of the evidence at hand.

So far so good for the theist, it seems. But up to this point we haven't touched on the theory that has been the greatest source of trouble for theistic explanations: namely, the Darwinian account of the origin of life on earth. Perhaps no other scientific theory has caused theistic accounts such heartache, with scientific materialist explanations gaining in popularity and causing a rather sharp decline in the number of those who formerly claimed some sort of religious affiliation. Because of its profound influence on both scientific and popular culture, it's to this we turn next.

Chapter 11
Origin of Living Things on Earth

According to Pew Research data, 59% of Americans say that science and religion conflict, up 4% from the previous survey.[1] Among the three in ten adults who report that their own religious beliefs conflict with science, evolution and the creation of the universe are the most common areas of contention. Further, a full 76% of those not already affiliated with a religious tradition are especially likely to think that science and religion conflict. This correlates with the fact that 65% of Americans now believe that humans evolved over time, with 35% of those saying that humans evolved through natural processes and 24% that humans evolved with the guidance of "a supreme being."[2] An interesting question that arises from these figures, then, is: to what extent has materialism affected people's attitudes toward religion and church attendance?

While it's not our goal here to explore this particular issue, or to analyze evolutionary theory *per se*, it does seem likely that materialistic evolutionary explanations have played a role in the decline in church attendance over the past decades. No doubt the popularity achieved by the New Atheists helped to accelerate that trend. However, based upon current origin of life research, there's a new breed of scholars questioning whether materialism is a sufficient answer to the causal questions

---

[1] Pew Research Center, https://www.pewresearch.org/science/2015/10/22/perception-of-conflict-between-science-and-religion/. Ironically, when it comes to their *personal* religious beliefs and science, 68% of American adults say there is no conflict between the two.

[2] Pew Research Center, https://www.pewresearch.org/fact-tank/2015/10/22/5-facts-about-the-interplay-between-religion-and-science/.

surrounding the beginnings of life on earth. In fact, many of these scholars have flipped the materialist script and vigorously argue that God's existence as life's ultimate designer is the best explanation of the data we now posses. Because of the profound importance of evolutionary theory on scientific and popular culture, this chapter will investigate theistic arguments based on design.

As mentioned previously, the idea of complexity surfaces in these debates as the backbone of the arguments against materialism. But it will also take center stage in the case being made that God, as the designer of life, is the only explanation with enough explanatory power to function as a sufficient cause of that complexity. As such, these arguments will challenge the standard Darwinian account.

Biology and Irreducible Complexity

Standard Darwinism has argued that all biological forms came into existence by a gradual, cumulative, step-by-step transformation from simpler things, which consist of primordial objects sufficiently simple to have come about by chance.[3] As we've noted, this gradualist view has been evangelized with admirable effectiveness by the best-selling books of the New Atheists, which have doubtless made materialism somewhat popular (even hip) for recent generations. However, in part beginning with Michael Behe's book *Darwin's Black Box*, various theistic challenges to the standard Darwinian view, based upon recent biochemical discoveries, have arisen.

In this book, Behe disputes the Darwinian explanation on the grounds that it has given no account of the mechanisms capable of gradually producing complex biochemical systems. Noting that Darwin himself had recognized that "If it could be demonstrated that any complex organ existed which could not possibly have been formed by numerous, successive, slight modifications, my theory would absolutely break down," Behe argues that Darwin's criterion of failure is met in any system that can be shown to be

---

[3] As a side note to these debates, William Lane Craig has argued recently that the biblical creation narratives—specifically, chapters 1-11, which he considers "mythohistory"—can be seen as consistent with an evolutionary viewpoint. Assessing current literature on human history, Craig concludes that it's plausible to identify Adam and Eve as members of Homo heidelbergensis and as the founding pair of human species. In doing so, he situates Adam and Eve prior to the divergence of Homo sapiens, Neanderthals, and other species. See William Lane Craig, *In Quest of the Historical Adam: A Biblical and Scientific Exploration* (Grand Rapids, 2021), 509.

irreducibly complex, i.e., a single system that's composed of several well-matched, interacting parts that contribute to the basic function, wherein to remove any one of the parts causes the system to effectively cease functioning.[4] The problem with an irreducibly complex system is that it can't be produced directly (by continuously improving initial function, which continues to work by the same mechanism) via small, successive modifications of a precursor system, because any precursor missing a part is by definition nonfunctional. That is, such a system needs to have it all in order to have anything that works properly. Because natural selection only has the ability to choose systems that are already working, then, if a system can't be produced gradually, it would have to spring up as an integrated unit, all at once, for natural selection to have anything to act on. Further, mutations can't be appealed to for explanation of how these irreducibly complex systems arise, since mutations can't change every set of instructions in one step.

Behe notes that, as biochemists have started to understand what at first appeared to be simple structures, they've discovered "staggering complexity," with sometimes hundreds of precisely tailored and interrelated parts. But as the required parts increase, the idea that the system was gradually put together via natural selection working on mutations encounters insurmountable problems. Even apparently simple systems seem to have no Darwinian explanation. Michael Denton has agreed, adding that, in terms of their basic biochemical design, no living system can be thought of as being primitive or ancestral with respect to any other system. Nor is there any hint of an evolutionary sequence among all the very diverse cells on earth, with the basic design of the cell system essentially the same in all living systems from bacteria to mammals.[5] Envisaging how a living cell could have gradually evolved through a sequence of simple proto-cells appears to have insuperable problems. To get a cell by chance, Denton says, requires at least one hundred functional proteins to appear simultaneously in one place. That's one hundred simultaneous events each of an independent probability that could hardly be more than 10^{-20}, and giving a maximum combined probability of 10^{-2000}. Based upon these and other considerations, Behe—with many others—argues for intelligent design, which he suggests rests on the same principles we use when we detect design in anything else:

---

[4] Michael J. Behe, *Darwin's Black Box: The Biochemical Challenge to Evolution* (New York, 1996), 39, 41, 73.
[5] Michael Denton, *Evolution: A Theory in Crisis* (Chevy Chase, MD, 1985), 250, 323.

the ordering of separate components to achieve an identifiable function that depends on the components.[6]

Behe highlights several poignant examples within known biological systems that require an astonishing amount of exactness and complexity to be useful to a living cell. One of those involves the function of the cilium, the purpose of which is to be a motorized paddle. Yet, for it to work, micro-tubules, nexin linkers, and motor proteins all have to be precisely ordered, meaning they have to recognize each other and interact exactly such that the function can't occur if any of the components is missing. Beyond this, for the system to be useful for a living cell, the cilium has to be in the right place, oriented correctly, and turned on or off depending on the cell's needs. Another example concerns the blood-clotting system, which functions as a strong but transient barrier. Ordered to that end, the many components of the system do something together that none of them could do alone, cutting and aligning with each other in precise places and ways. Still another example involves the intracellular transport systems that carry cargo from one place to another. To do so, packages have to be labeled, destinations recognized, and vehicles equipped. Further, there are mechanisms that have to be in place to leave one enclosed area of the cell and enter a different enclosed area. Any failure of a system would mean a lack of critical supplies for the cell's proper functioning. "Because the functions depend critically on the intricate interactions of the parts we must conclude that they, like a mousetrap, were designed."[7]

Design Arguments Refuted?

Before going any further with recent debates, we need to step back briefly and talk about the philosophical baggage critics associate with the idea of design. Much of the criticism surrounding these arguments is centered around William Paley's argument for God's existence, which he constructed by appealing to purported instances of design in nature. Though the argument wasn't original to him, the teleological (from the Greek word *tēlos*, meaning end or goal) argument for God's existence came under increasing attack shortly after it was proposed in Paley's *Natural Theology*.[8] In it, Paley

---

[6] See also Michael J. Behe, *Darwin Devolves: The New Science About DNA That Challenges Evolution* (New York, 2019).

[7] Michael J. Behe, *Darwin's Black Box: The Biochemical Challenge to Evolution*, 204-5.

[8] William H. Halverson, *A Concise Introduction to Philosophy* (New York, 1981), 161ff.

contended that whenever we observe something composed of several parts that are framed and put together for a purpose (for instance, a watch), we naturally conclude that it has been created for this purpose by some intelligent designer. "There cannot be design," he contended, " without a designer, contrivance, without a contriver, order, without anything capable of arranging ... Arrangement, disposition of parts, subserviency of means to an end, relation of instruments to a use, imply the presence of intelligence and mind."[9] This being so, he pointed out that the universe is chock-full of phenomena that exhibit teleological order, with his favorite example being the eye, which exhibits incredible intricacy and delicacy and is ordered for the purpose of sight. The conclusion, he suggests, is that design in nature points to the existence of an intelligent designer of nature in the same way that design in a watch (or any other machine) points to the existence of a designer.

Unpacking Paley's argument, William Halverson notes that it contains two premises, with the first consisting of the purported fact (at least as theists see it) that nature exhibits instances of means ordered to ends. The second is that the ordering of means to ends presupposes the existence of a designer whose intelligence and ability is sufficient to do the ordering. The second premise is an inductive generalization that, the theist contends, is backed by substantial experience and never shown to be false. But critics have pointed out several objections, the first of which is that the alleged analogy to nature—which "exhibits a number of instances of means ordered to ends"—appears to be a case of syllogistic smuggling. What nature seems to exhibit is a high degree of lawlike regularity, but the idea of "means ordered to ends" suggests purposiveness and therefore subtly smuggles in an allegedly factual premise: the suggestion that we should look for a purposer, or orderer.[10] Perhaps more to the point, however, is that the alleged analogy between the lawlike regularity of nature and what we find in human contrivance is weak. David Hume argued that, if this suggests any analogy, it's that of an organism rather than a machine, the former of which has an internal principle of life and organization. Thus, the fact that machines require a designer is irrelevant. Hume puts it this way:

I have still asserted, that we have no *data* to establish any system of cosmogony. Our experience, so imperfect in itself, and so limited both in extent

---

[9] William Paley, *Natural Theology*, ed. Frederick Ferrè (Indianapolis, 1963), 10.
[10] William H. Halverson, *A Concise Introduction to Philosophy*, 170-1.

and duration, can afford us no probable conjecture concerning the whole of things. But if we must needs fix on some hypothesis; by what rule, pray, ought we to determine our choice? Is there any other rule than the greater similarity of the objects compared? And does not a plant or an animal, which springs from vegetation or generation, bear a stronger resemblance to the world, than does any artificial machine, which arises from reason and design?[11]

As W. T. Jones notes, for Hume, an impartial observer wouldn't be able to infer either *one* cause or an *intelligent* one. Further, it may be true that we posit human intelligence whenever we see something that serves some purpose and isn't a product of nature, but none of this applies to the regularities we find in nature. Isn't it possible, the critic asks, that these laws themselves are the ultimate facts we should appeal to? Couldn't the universe itself be the model of regularity to which every other instance of regularity is only a pale analogy? Additionally, even if the argument were valid, this wouldn't at all establish an all-powerful, all-wise, all-good being. It would only imply a being with sufficient knowledge and architectural ability, and because an architect doesn't create the materials he works with, it would only establish that he's a sufficient craftsman. In fact, because we know there's evil in the world, the argument would imply that this craftsman is less than perfectly good, or maybe worse. Lastly, since a watchmaker is only required to exist at the time the watch was made, the teleological argument would only establish such a craftsman's past existence, not present.

However, Meyer challenges Hume's objections on several grounds. First, we know now that organisms come from organisms because they possess information-rich macromolecules and a complex information-rich system for processing and replicating the information stored in these cells. But we also know that systems capable of copying and processing other information arise from intelligent design. As to Hume's contention (elsewhere) that uniform experience suggests that organisms arise from an infinite regress of primeval organisms, we now know from Big Bang cosmology that the universe is finite, beginning in the relatively short past, which means that biological life also had a beginning. Any Humean appeal, Meyer argues, to uniform experience actually suggests intelligent design, not an undirected material process, because experience only affirms the

---

[11] W. T. Jones, *A History of Western Philosophy: Hobbes to Hume* (Fort Worth, 1969), 331-3.

former as it relates to information-rich systems capable of processing and copying information.

Beyond that, Meyer points out that his own argument for intelligent design isn't analogical.[12] It rather constitutes an inference to the best explanation and compares the explanatory power of competing causes with respect to a single kind of effect—and doesn't compare degrees of similarity between different effects. Hence, his argument doesn't depend on the similarity of DNA to a computer program, but upon the presence of an *identical* feature in both DNA and intelligently designed artifacts. Taking a different approach, Behe maintains that the argument from analogy is still valid, despite Hume's objections. The reason is that analogies are set up so that they explicitly or implicitly propose that A is like B in some restricted subset of properties. Any complex machine is like the blood-clotting system in that each is irreducibly complex, even though they may have many differences. Still, the analogy is based on the shared property that any irreducibly complex machine requires an intelligent designer to produce it, which means that the irreducibly complex blood-clotting system also requires a designer. Behe notes that Hume's objection was based on the notion that the design argument rests on a close similarity in *accidental details* of biological organisms. But such thinking would destroy all analogies, since any two nonidentical objects will inevitably differ more than in the ways they're similar.

In an interesting turn, Behe suggests that even by Hume's own criteria, the analogy between a watch and a living system could be strong, in that modern biochemistry could conceivably make a time-keeping device out of biological materials. There are many biological systems that keep time, and we know of many biochemical components that act as gears and flexible chains, along with various feedback mechanisms. "Hume's criticism," he says, "of the design argument that asserts a fundamental difference between mechanical systems and living systems is out of date, destroyed by the evidence of science which has discovered the machinery of life."[13] That said, Hume also objects to the design argument on the basis that it's an inductive argument, which would require that we have experience of living things being designed. Because we haven't observed the designing

---

[12] Stephen C. Meyer, *Signature in the Cell: DNA and the Evidence for Intelligent Design* (New York, 2009), 384-6.

[13] Michael J. Behe, *Darwin's Black Box: The Biochemical Challenge to Evolution*, 218-9.

of living systems, we have no basis for making such an inductive inference about the necessity of a grand designer. While, here again, Meyer skirts the issue by saying the argument for design isn't an inductive inference but an inference to the best explanation, Behe goes on the offensive and points out that—here too—science has proved Hume wrong. Biochemistry routinely designs biochemical systems, which means that we've observed the intelligent design of components of life, e.g., experiments in which new biochemical systems were put together.

However, taking Hume's objections to the next level, atheist biologist Richard Dawkins has maintained—with an almost religious-like fervor—that the analogy between the eye or watch and living organisms is false. Despite any appearance of design (which Dawkins concedes), the only watchmaker in nature is the blind forces of physics, albeit deployed through mutation and natural selection. A watchmaker has a purpose in mind; he has foresight as he designs cogs and springs and thinks through their interactions. This isn't so with biological mechanisms:

> Natural Selection, the blind, unconscious, automatic process which Darwin discovered, and which we now know is the explanation for the existence and apparently purposeful form of all life, has no purpose in mind. It has no mind and no mind's eye. It does not plan for the future. It has no vision, no foresight, no sight at all. If it can be said to play the role of watchmaker in nature, it is the *blind* watchmaker.[14]

Thus, for Dawkins, all biological forms came into existence by a gradual, cumulative, step-by-step transformation from simpler things, which consist of primordial objects sufficiently simple to have come about by chance. Recognizing that complex things (such as we see in biological forms) have a quality that is highly unlikely to have arisen by random chance alone, Dawkins insists that Darwinian cumulative selection is nonrandom. That is, each change in the gradual evolutionary process was simple enough (relative to its predecessor) to have come about by chance. However, the whole sequence of cumulative steps is anything but a chance process, being directed as it is by nonrandom survival. To make his case, he draws

---

[14] Richard Dawkins, *The Blind Watchmaker: Why the Evidence of Evolution Reveals a Universe Without Design* (New York, 1996), 9, 22, 29, 61, 68-9. It's interesting, in light of our previous discussion, that Dawkins simply takes the facts of physics for granted (23).

a distinction between cumulative selection (where each improvement is used as a basis for future building) and single-step selection (where each new attempt is a fresh one). If evolutionary progress had to rely on the latter, it could never have gotten anywhere. Fortunately, he suggests, that's not how cumulative selection occurs, because its necessary conditions were set up by the blind forces of nature. "Chance," says Dawkins, "is a minor ingredient in the Darwinian recipe, but the most important ingredient is cumulative selection which is quintessentially *non*random."[15]

To show how this would work, he highlights a computer simulation that purports to demonstrate how natural selection, enacting random mutations, could explain the origin of biological forms. In the simulation, Dawkins and his collaborators provided a program with target sequences (to represent a functional polymer) involving English phrases, one of which was "Methinks it is like a weasel" (from Shakespeare's *Hamlet*). Confirming that little, if anything, could evolve via single-step selection of random variation, they then tested cumulative selection. The program began with a random sequence of 28 letters. As Dawkins describes it, the program "breeds from" this random phrase and duplicates it repeatedly, but with a chance of random error ("mutation") in the copying. The computer then looks at the mutant nonsense phrases that most resemble the target phrase METHINKS IT IS LIKE A WEASEL. The short of it is that, after 43 generations, the target was finally reached, thus showing how cumulative selection could work in nature.

Challenges to Gradualism

Despite Dawkins' simulation, which purports to show how gradualism works in nature, some have remained skeptical, with Meyer, for one, noting that this and other such simulations conceal an obvious flaw: molecules don't have a target sequence "in mind." Nothing in nature corresponds to the role the computer plays in selecting functionally nonadvantageous sequences that just happen to be slightly closer to a target sequence.[16] This is because, in biology, survival depends upon maintaining function, and selection can't occur until functional sequences arise. In the case of a molecule in

---

[15] Richard Dawkins, *The Blind Watchmaker: Why the Evidence of Evolution Reveals a Universe Without Design*, 70-1.

[16] Stephen C. Meyer, *Signature in the Cell: DNA and the Evidence for Intelligent Design*, 281-4.

which a sequence happened to be slightly closer to some unrealized target protein, it would in actuality not be preserved but eliminated, stopping the evolutionary process in its tracks. Yet these simulations show early generations of variant phrases deluged with nonfunctional gibberish. A large part of the problem is that genetic algorithms need a forward-looking memory to succeed, but Darwinian natural selection lacks any form of foresight. Thus, Meyer concludes that if computer simulations demonstrate anything, it's precisely the need for an intelligent agent to retain some options and dispense with others. This simulating of a goal-directed foresight is precisely what natural selection doesn't possess, and it has bedeviled other more sophisticated attempts—such as Ev[17]—to show the same thing.

In addition to Meyer's critique, Behe has pointed out that variation, selection, and inheritance will work only if there's a smooth evolutionary pathway from biological point A to point B. To illustrate, he asks us to imagine that we had to walk blindfolded from point A to point B.[18] It's safe to say that the greater the distance between the two points, and the more rugged the intervening landscape, the bleaker the odds for success are for a blindfolded walk—especially if following a simple rule of always climbing higher and never backing down (which mimics natural selection). The same problem attends evolution. We now know that life is highly complex and intricate, meaning that Darwinian pathways to life are long and rugged. Worse, random mutation and natural selection may simply keep a species staggering down genetic dead-end alleys, on top of the fact that all of it needs to occur in a relatively reasonable time. And even with thousands or millions of organisms for natural selection to act on (the more there are, the more opportunities random mutation has to pass beneficial change to natural selection), a mutation occurs relatively rarely, and few of those are helpful.

As an example, Behe notes that *E. coli* has been studied for over a century, with its genetics and biochemistry being better understood than any other organism. In fact, it has recently received the most extensive laboratory evolution study ever conducted. Duplicating around seven times per day, the bug has been grown continuously in flasks for over thirty thousand

---

[17] Ev is an evolutionary algorithm that attempts to simulate how mutation and selection—chance and necessity—can generate new information. See Stephen C. Meyer, *Signature in the Cell: DNA and the Evidence for Intelligent Design*, 283.

[18] Michael J. Behe, *The Edge of Evolution: The Search for the Limits of Darwinism* (New York, 2007), 5-7, 11.

generations, equivalent to about a million human years. Behe comments on the results as follow:

> And what has evolution wrought? Mostly devolution. Although some marginal details of some systems have changed, during that thirty thousand generations, the bacterium has repeatedly thrown away chunks of its genetic patrimony, including the ability to make some of the building blocks of RNA. Apparently, throwing away sophisticated but costly molecular machinery saves the bacterium energy. Nothing of remotely similar elegance has been built. The lesson of *E coli* is that it's easier for evolution to break things than make things.[19]

In addition, concerning microbes as diverse as HIV and malaria, and despite their huge population numbers and intense selective pressure, he notes that they yield only minor evolutionary responses. While Darwinists have touted studies in finch beaks showing modest changes over time, genetic studies covering thousands upon thousands of generations, of trillions upon trillions of organisms, demonstrate little biochemical significance.

Denton, for his part, has argued against the gradualist understanding of evolution on the basis that the natural system is a natural discontinuum rather than a Darwinian adaptive gradualism (functional continuum). The taxa (a classified group) are more analogous to distinct geometric figures, such as triangles or quadrilaterals, which can't be approached via small successive steps from some other class of geometric figure.[20] Accordingly, he defends the typological view that taxa (or Types) are ontologically real and distinct components of nature. With that said, he points out that significant recent advances in evo-devo (evolutionary developmental biology) have been touted as providing a causal explanation of how homologs—a unique biological characteristic or trait shared by all the members of a particular group (such as the pentadactyl ground plan of the tetrapod limb shared by all tetrapods)—developed along Darwinist (via cumulative selection) lines, thus purportedly solving the problem of evolution noted above.

But he challenges the claims as erroneous in that, while evo-devo has made great strides in giving an inventory of the genetic changes involved

---

[19] Michael J. Behe, *The Edge of Evolution: The Search for the Limits of Darwinism*, 15-6, 140. See also Behe's discussion of the sickle and HbC mutations, among others (33-43, 49-51, 59-62).

[20] Michael Denton, *Evolution: Still a Theory in Crisis* (Seattle, 2016), 11-3, 88-91.

in the actualization of a novelty (which is always incomplete), it hasn't provided a causal account. Behe agrees and objects to the idea that evo-devo discoveries make undirected development of life any easier to explain. "The need for a foreman," he contends, "and subsequent subcontractors to coordinate construction does not make it easier to explain how unintelligent processes could make a building out of bricks and wood and pipes and wiring. It shows it to be impossible."[21] Part of the challenge, says Denton, of giving an adequate causal account of the actualization of the homologs isn't just that many genetic changes still have to be documented, but also that the ontogeny of every organ or complex morphological structure (including homologs) involves all the complex epigenetic changes. The assembly of gene products into the final phenotypic form of any organ or structure also involves the complex set of integrated self-organizing emergent processes, which are invisible from the perspective of genes. As an example of this, there's a necessity for tight control of organ size during development, e.g., to ensure that a human hand is seven centimeters across and a fly wing a few millimeters. Organs somehow know what size they should be, and they stop growing when they reach their target size, based upon higher-order emergent properties of cells and tissues. But not only do organs know their target adult size, they also keep the size at all states of development at then appropriate dimensions.

If evo-devo has demonstrated anything, Denton argues, it's that there are internal constraints that play a far more important role in the actualization of evolutionary innovations than cumulative selection. Underlying the development of all organisms "is a set of highly conserved gene circuits and integrated development modules that guide and constrain phylogeny without regard for the immediate adaptive needs of species."[22] Not only has this revelation challenged prevailing views of evolutionary processes, but it has undermined the neo-Darwinian mechanistic view that organisms are analogous to LEGO blocks which can be used in an infinite number of circumstances. Against this, evo-devo has shown that there are profound constraints that work contrary to such a notion. Major evolutionary novelties could only have occurred if they were compatible with the pre-existing inner developmental logic of the organism. Denton adds that the really radical part of this is that the constraints restrict the paths of evolution without

---

[21] Michael J. Behe, *Darwin Devolves: The New Science About DNA That Challenges Evolution*, 118.

[22] Michael Denton, *Evolution: Still a Theory in Crisis* (Seattle, 2016), 96-8.

any regard for immediate adaptive function. "If true," he comments, "this would mean that the constraints and internal factors are parts of the natural order, and the evolutionary paths they have facilitated were built into nature from the beginning, precisely as structuralism implies."[23]

The Fossil Record: The Burgess Shale

No review of the status of the standard Darwinian account would be sufficient without mention of the fossil record, particularly as it manifests itself in the Cambrian explosion—an event during a remote geological period in which numerous animal forms appear to have arisen suddenly and without any evolutionary precursors in the fossil record. Meyer observes that, while Darwin was aware of the problem and was convinced that future fossil discoveries would eliminate it, the problem for a Darwinian account was only intensified when Charles Doolittle Walcott discovered in 1909 a rich trove of middle Cambrian-era fossils—which included many previously unknown animal forms. Preserved in exquisite detail, the Burgess Shale was one of the most dramatic discoveries in the history of paleontology and suggested an event of even greater suddenness than had been known in Darwin's time. It also manifested a greater diversity of biological forms and architecture than researchers had imagined up to that point.

Meyer reports that since its initial discovery, and as paleontologists have analyzed the pattern of the Precambrian-Cambrian fossil record, they've uncovered several characteristics of the Cambrian explosion that, from a Darwinian perspective, are unexpected. First is the sudden appearance of new animal forms. Second is an absence of transitional intermediate fossils that connect the Cambrian animals to simpler Precambrian forms. Third is a startling array of completely novel body plans. And fourth is a pattern displaying radical differences in form in the fossil record which arise before more minor, small-scale diversification and variations. "This pattern," he notes, "turns on its head the Darwinian expectations of small incremental change only *gradually* resulting in larger and larger differences in form."[24] And it's not just the increase in complexity that's the problem; it's the sudden quantum leap in complexity. To make matters worse, each new Cambrian creature required its own series of transitional ancestors.

---

[23] Michael Denton, *Evolution: Still a Theory in Crisis* (Seattle, 2016), 100.
[24] Stephen C. Meyer, *Darwin's Doubt: The Explosive Origin of Animal Life and The Case for Intelligent Design* (New York, 2014), xii, 28, 34, 36, 38, 69-71.

To explain this complete lack of transitional forms, many researchers have suggested that we're not getting a valid representation of the fossil record and thus the intermediate forms are probably still there to be found. However, as Michael Foote's (University of Chicago) statistical analysis demonstrates, it's improbable that there ever existed a myriad of as yet undiscovered intermediate forms that could fill in the gaps. In other words, according to his analysis, we have a representative sample of morphological diversity and can rely on patterns already documented in the fossil record. One way of overcoming this yawning chasm has been to propose saltationalism, which posits that new types of organisms arise suddenly. Along these lines, the punctuational equilibrium model of Niles Eldredge and Stephen Jay Gould suggested that evolution consists of an episodic process of fits and starts interspersed with long periods of stasis. Denton notes that, while the model is a reasonable explanation of the gaps between species, it's doubtful it can explain the larger systematic gaps. Gaps that separate species of dog/fox are trivial compared with major phyla such as molluscs and arthropods. As he explains:

> Such major discontinuities simply could not, unless we are to believe in miracles, have been crossed in geologically short periods of time through one or two transitional species occupying restricted geological areas. Surely, such transitions must have involved long lineages including many collateral lines of hundreds or probably thousands of transitional species. To suggest that the hundreds, thousands or possibly even millions of transitional species which must have existed in the interval between vastly dissimilar types were all unsuccessful species occupying isolated areas and having very small population numbers is verging on the incredible![25]

He notes that, ironically, while punctuated equilibrium has been widely publicized, its major effect has been more to draw attention to the gaps in the fossil record than to provide a reasonable explanation of them.

Specified Information and DNA

On the heels of the discovery of the structure of DNA during the 1950s and early 1960s, molecular biologists became increasingly aware of the fact

---

[25] Michael Denton, *Evolution: A Theory in Crisis* (Chevy Chase, MD, 1985), 162, 192-4.

that DNA and proteins carry information comprising two features: complexity and functional specificity (or specified information, which means it has instructions to do something specific). Meyer notes that complex sequences are different from ordered sequences, with the former—such as those exhibiting an irregular, nonrepeating arrangement—defying expression by a general law or algorithm, and the latter sequences—those that exhibit a clearly repeatable pattern (such as ABCABCABCABC)—capable of being characterized in an algorithm or general law. Information scientists usually equate complexity with improbability, while regarding repetitive sequences as highly probable, meaning that information and probability are inversely related. Thus, high-probability repeating sequences like ABCABCABCABC have little information, meaning that once we've seen the first triad of ABCs, the rest are redundant. However, the information of DNA and proteins is both complex and has functional complexity (as opposed to mere complexity).

As an example, Meyer points out that the sequences of nucleotide bases in DNA and the sequences of amino acids in proteins are highly improbable and have large information-carrying capacities. While some have mistakenly seen this as evidence of mere complexity, like meaningful sentences or lines of computer code, the bases in DNA and amino acids in proteins are also specified with respect to function. "Thus, molecular biologists beginning with Francis Crick have equated biological information not only with improbability (or complexity), but also with 'specificity', where 'specificity' or 'specified' has meant 'necessary to function'."[26]

In addition to the fact that DNA carries specified information, biologists have also come to understand that living organisms must contain systems for processing genetic information. Just as information stored on a floppy drive is useless without a device for reading it (such as a properly configured computer installed with an operating system capable of reading it), DNA is useless without the cell's information-processing system. That is, the cell contains not only molecular repositories of genetic information but also a code for translating the information in the DNA molecule (and its RNA transcript) into the construction of a protein. This, however, requires a physical medium of information transfer—which occurs through a complex information-processing system composed of many types of nucleic acids (such as mRNAs and tRNAs) and many specific enzymes. Thus, the

---

[26] Stephen C. Meyer, *Signature in the Cell: DNA and the Evidence for Intelligent Design*, 106-10.

information-processing system of the cell depends on a highly integrated system of components, with transcription and translation systems dependent on numerous proteins, many of which are jointly necessary for protein synthesis to occur at all. Yet, and this is part of the mystery, all of these proteins are made by this very process. As Meyer puts it:

> Proteins involved in transcription such as RNA polymerases, for example, are built from instructions carried on an RNA transcript. Translation of the RNA transcript depends upon other specialized enzymes such as synthetases, yet the information to build these enzymes is translated during the translation process that synthetases themselves facilitate.[27]

The cell's translation machinery has at least fifty macromolecular components that are themselves coded in DNA, yet the code can't be translated other than by products of translation. As we might imagine, this has raised a significant "chicken and egg dilemma" because the cell needs proteins to process and express the information in DNA in order to build proteins. But the construction of DNA molecules (during DNA replication) also requires proteins. "So which came first, the chicken (nucleic acids) or the egg (proteins)? If proteins must have arisen first, then how did they do so, since all extant cells construct proteins from the assembly instructions in DNA. How did either arise without the other?"[28] What's striking in all of this is that, like software, the coding regions of DNA direct operations within a complex material system, through highly variable and improbable—yet precisely specified—sequences of chemical characters.

Meyer's contention is that repeated experience about the origin of information-rich systems suggests two possibilities. Either they arise from pre-existing systems of information through a mechanism of replication, or they arise from minds.[29] Though we have repeated experience of both, we also know that systems capable of copying and processing other information ultimately come from intelligent design. Computer hardware that can copy and process information in software originated in a programmer's

---

[27] Stephen C. Meyer, *Signature in the Cell: DNA and the Evidence for Intelligent Design*, 132-3.

[28] Stephen C. Meyer, *Signature in the Cell: DNA and the Evidence for Intelligent Design*, 110,134, 384-6.

[29] Stephen C. Meyer, *Signature in the Cell: DNA and the Evidence for Intelligent Design*, 385-6.

mind. Making this even more likely is the fact that our understanding of planetary and cosmic evolution rules out the possibility that biological life has always existed. The Big Bang theory implies that the universe itself is finite. The real question becomes whether life originated from a purely undirected material process or whenever a mind also had a role. Between the two options, Meyer argues that our uniform experience (as Hume put it) affirms only the latter as an adequate cause for information-rich systems capable of processing and copying information (meaning that a Humean appeal to uniform experience actually suggests intelligent design). We know intelligent agents can and do produce complex and functionally specified sequences of symbols and arrangements of matter, which implies that intelligent agency qualifies as an adequate causal explanation for the origin of this effect. The case for intelligent design is bolstered by the fact that materialistic theories have proven inadequate for explaining the origin of such information. Thus, whether or not these systems resemble human artifacts in other ways, the presence of specified information in living systems points to intelligent design as the best explanation of it.

God-of-the-Gaps?

Critics have contended that arguments for design fall prey to the "God-of-the-gaps" objection, which states that arguments like the ones just discussed use gaps in scientific knowledge as support for God's action and hence his existence. Here, the charge is that if science can't explain how something occurred, then theists insist on that basis alone that God must be the explanation. However, critics insist, with the continuing advance of science, God-of-the-gaps explanations often get replaced by natural mechanisms. In this case, the argument for intelligent design functions as a placeholder for ignorance, and one that its proponents fill by proposing the activity of a creative intelligence.[30] In other words, critics charge those arguing for intelligent design with arguing from ignorance. Though, admittedly, this has been the case with some design proponents in the past, is that what recent proponents are doing? Meyer, for one, says no.

To dispel the charge, he notes that arguments from ignorance occur when evidence *against* one proposition is offered as the *sole grounds* for accepting an alternative, which proceeds along the following lines:

---

[30] Stephen C. Meyer, *Return of the God Hypothesis: Three Scientific Discoveries That Reveal The Mind Behind The Universe* (New York, 2021), 412-6.

Premise: Cause A can't produce or explain evidence E.
Conclusion: Therefore, cause B produced or explains evidence E.

Arguments such as this commit a logical error because they fail to include a premise that provides affirmative support for the preferred conclusion. But recent arguments for intelligent design don't commit this error, as they not only show that materialistic explanations can't account for the origin of the universe or specified information in DNA, but also because we know that intelligent agents can and do produce information of that kind. We have positive experience-based knowledge of an alternative cause sufficient to produce the effect in question. Thus, the argument takes a different logical form:

> *Premise One*: Despite a thorough search, no materialistic causes have been discovered with the power to produce large amounts of specified information necessary to produce the first cell.
> *Premise Two*: Intelligent causes have demonstrated the power to produce large amounts of specified information.
> *Conclusion*: Intelligent design constitutes the best, most causally adequate explanation for the origin of the specified information in the cell.

Here, in addition to the premise stating that materialistic causes lack causal adequacy, the argument affirms the demonstrated causal adequacy of intelligent agency. It therefore doesn't appeal to ignorance or commit a gaps fallacy.

We should note that Meyer's argument (along with McGrath's) self-consciously rests on inference to the best explanation, in which—as Peter Lipton notes—we begin with the evidence available to us and infer what would, if true, best explain the evidence. As we discussed previously, Lipton suggests that good explanations are typically causal.[31] Thus, in the case of particular events, they cite a prior cause that's part of the causal history of the event in question—and to identify the cause of an event, scientists must identify something within the causal history of the event that accounts for the difference between what did occur and what could have occurred otherwise. Philosophers of science and historical scientists

---

[31] Peter Lipton, *Inference to the Best Explanation* (London, 2004), 32ff., 75ff.

emphasize the causal adequacy criteria as a condition of a successful explanation, in which—when evaluating competing hypotheses—they identify causes that are known to have the power to produce the kind of effect or event in question. Causes that are known to produce the effect are judged to be better candidates than those that don't.[32]

But, as Meyer points out, philosophers have also noted that this leads to sound inference only when scientists can infer a uniquely plausible cause. When such a cause can be identified, they can avoid the fallacy of affirming the consequent (the error of ignoring other possible causes with the power to produce the same effect).[33] An archeologist, for instance, who knows that scribes are the only known cause of linguistic inscriptions, will infer scribal activity when discovering a tablet with ancient writing. When a particular past cause is known to be necessary to produce a subsequent effect, the occurrence of the effect is taken as sufficient to establish the occurrence of the cause. While experimental scientists use a different method (by testing theories through predictions about what will happen under controlled laboratory conditions), historical scientists use a distinctive method, as follows: identify the causes of past events, formulate distinctive types of explanations (in which they cite past events as causes), and make inferences with a distinctive (abductive) logical form.

In his contention for a theistic cause of the universe, Meyer (along with other recent works) argues that all materialistic theories of the origin of the material universe face a fundamental problem given the evidence we have of a cosmic beginning. Namely, before matter and energy exist (before the initial Big Bang), they can't cause or be invoked to explain the origin of the material universe. "Instead, positing a materialistic process to explain the origin of matter and energy assumes the existence of the very entities—matter and energy—the origin of which materialists need to explain. No truly materialistic explanation can close this particular causal discontinuity or gap—the gap between either nothing or a preexisting *im*material or mathematical reality, on the one hand, and a material universe, on the

---

[32] Stephen C. Meyer, *Signature in the Cell: DNA and the Evidence for Intelligent Design*, 159, 161, 163, 169.

[33] It might be noted here that McGrath argues that inference to the best explanation doesn't require the explanation to be *causal*. To demonstrate that A causes B one could simply show that A explains B. Explanatory power is thus seen to reside not primarily in causality, but in *ontology*—an understanding of the way things are, or of the fundamental order of things. See Alister E. McGrath, *Darwinism and the Divine: Evolutionary Thought and Natural Theology* (West Sussex, 2011), 200.

other."[34] A similar criticism applies to appeals (such as that by Stephen Hawking) to the laws of nature, which simply describe how nature operates and how its different parts interact; they don't cause the natural world to come into existence in the first place. But this means that no law of nature can close the causal discontinuity between nothing and the origin of nature itself. McGrath concurs, pointing out that the laws of nature didn't come into being by a gradual process of cumulative selection.[35] The universe that emerged out of the Big Bang was already governed by laws that were fine-tuned to prompt the rise of carbon-based life forms.

Having established the inadequacy of materialistic accounts for the universe's origins, Meyer then provides positive evidence for the causal adequacy of intelligent agency as a cause of the kind of specified information needed to produce life. He further argues that any cause capable of explaining the origin of the universe and its fine-tuning must stand causally separate from the universe; i.e., it must transcend matter, space, time, and energy. God, as conceived by theists, possesses the attribute of transcendence and qualifies as a causally adequate explanation for the origin of the material universe (more so than competing materialistic or pantheistic worldviews).

Conclusion

Despite the materialist claims of the New Atheists, recent arguments for theism in relation to origin of life research have pointed to the stunning complexity we now know exists in even the simplest biochemical structures. Using this complexity and the probabilities of life on earth evolving by pure chance and without an "end" in mind, these scholars have contended that the only cause with sufficient explanatory power to bring life about is a supreme being capable of doing such ordering.

As with the arguments based on Big Bang cosmology that we examined in the previous chapter, these researchers rely not on strict deduction or simple enumerative induction (in which a conclusion is based on the number of instances supporting it), but rather on an abductive inference which examines opposing hypotheses and concludes that God as the cause

---

[34] Stephen C. Meyer, *Return of the God Hypothesis: Three Scientific Discoveries That Reveal The Mind Behind The Universe*, 418-20.

[35] Alister E. McGrath, *A Fine-Tuned Universe: The Quest for God in Science and Theology* (Louisville, 2009), 118.

of life is the best explanation. In so doing, they call attention to the fact that abductive reasoning is widely used in the historical sciences and elsewhere. Meyer specifically has argued that the causal adequacy criterion (or a uniquely plausible cause) concerning the origin of life on earth is best accounted for by postulating theism, with materialism failing to meet the challenge in light of recent advances in our understanding of biochemistry.

The epistemic status of such theistic arguments will then depend not only upon the relative strength of the evidence brought to bear, but also on the validity of abductive reasoning overall. But the researchers we've discussed believe that inference to the best explanation is fully justified and supplies a relatively strong argument for theism, not to mention that abduction was used by Darwin himself in formulating his theory, so disallowing it entirely would cut both ways. The one thing these theistic arguments don't do, no matter how strong, is provide knowledge about who such a God might be and what, if anything, he desires of human beings. Because of that inherent deficiency and because, to many, these are questions of paramount importance, some scholars have proposed a supplemental case for theism. For that, we'll want to turn to their argument involving claims for the historic bodily resurrection of Jesus of Nazareth.

Chapter 12

Historical Argument

Thus far, we've concerned ourselves with arguments for a knowledge of God through natural theology. Through the use of inference to the best explanation, various scholars have weighed materialistic and theistic explanations and have concluded, based upon recent evidence, that God is the best explanation for the existence of both the universe and life on earth. Viewed optimistically, these arguments could potentially provide some knowledge, for instance, that a God exists and created (and perhaps still conserves) the universe and life on earth. While some, like the scholars we've discussed, argue for the importance of such knowledge, others have expressed more skepticism about how much these arguments can really tell us.

Wolfhart Pannenberg, for instance, has contended that, given the debatability of the existence of God arising from such arguments, one could hardly maintain that this type of purported knowledge is present in the fact of the world. To be fair, he doesn't survey the arguments presented here, but his caution is shared by many. "The results," he says, "of the history of the proofs and discussions of their force show that they cannot decisively change the situation regarding the debatability of God's existence."[1] Generally agreeing with Pannenberg, others have added that even if these arguments are able to give us some reason to believe there was a designer involved in the origin of the universe and human beings, they lack any particular information about who such an artificer might be.

In light of this perceived shortcoming, various scholars have developed a case for God's existence based upon a specific historical event they

---

[1] Pannenberg, Wolfhart. *Systematic Theology,* vol. 1, trans. by Geoffrey W. Bromiley (Grand Rapids, 1988), 95.

claim to have occurred in the first century: the bodily resurrection of Jesus of Nazareth.[2] Though these approaches vary, recent works assess the evidential merit of primitive traditions within the New Testament Gospels and epistles. Arriving at certain bedrock/minimal facts[3] supported by a wide range of scholars—atheist, agnostic, and Christian—they then argue that God's having raised Jesus from the dead best accounts for the claims of his followers to have seen him alive shortly after his crucifixion and death. It's this argument for God's existence that will occupy the present and final chapter of this book.

Historical Core

Though the particular facts may vary slightly from one researcher to another, the following are generally agreed to be part of the historical core supporting the resurrection argument: (1) Jesus died by crucifixion and his body was buried. After his execution, the disciples were devastated because they had expected him to redeem Israel, and they fled in fear. (2) Shortly

---

[2] We should note that various scholars have offered an alternative account of the nature of Jesus' resurrected body. James Tabor, for instance, has argued that—for Paul—the resurrected Christ dwells in a spiritual body as a life-giving Spirit, which means that "we can say with assurance that the Christ that Paul claimed to have 'seen' was not Jesus' physical corpse revived." As such, Tabor suggests that Jesus' physical body returned to the dust and had nothing to do with the new spiritual body he received. See James D. Tabor, *Paul and Jesus: How the Apostle Transformed Christianity* (New York, 2012), 64. For a detailed critique of these views, as well as (from the present author's perspective) for a more comprehensive treatment of the evidence, see N. T. Wright's *The Resurrection of the Son of God* (Minneapolis, 2003), 209ff. Because we're focused primarily on the epistemological questions concerning God's existence, and because a discussion of the nature of Jesus' resurrected body falls outside our scope, we'll leave the question to other more thorough works on the topic.

[3] See for example Michael R. Licona, *The Resurrection of Jesus: A New Historiographical Approach* (Grove, Illinois, 2010); Gary R. Habermas, "Jesus' Resurrection and Contemporary Criticism: An Apologetic" in *Criswell Theological Review*, part 1, vol. 4, no. 1 (Fall 1989), and "The Minimal Facts Approach to the Resurrection of Jesus: The Role of Methodology as a Crucial Component in Establishing Historicity" in *Southeastern Theological Review*, 3/1 (Summer 2012) 15-26; William Lane Craig, *Assessing the New Testament Evidence for the Historicity of the Resurrection of Jesus* (New York, 1989); Richard Bauckham, *Jesus and the Eyewitnesses: The Gospels as Eyewitness Testimony* (Grand Rapids, 2006); N. T. Wright, *The Resurrection of the Son of God*; Richard A. Burridge, *What Are the Gospels? A Comparison with Graeco-Roman Biography* (Grand Rapids, 2004).

afterwards, the disciples had experiences they believed were appearances of the risen Jesus which occurred in private and communal settings over an extended period of time. Convinced that Jesus was alive, they were transformed from being hopeless to fearless proclaimers of Jesus' resurrection, even to the point of martyrdom. Not only this, but they preached the message in Jerusalem, the very city where Jesus had been crucified and buried only a short time before. (3) One to three years later, Saul of Tarsus (Paul) claimed to have had an encounter with the risen Jesus on the road to Damascus. Having been commissioned by the Jews to arrest Christians, Paul was a persecutor of early believers and had been complicit in the stoning of Stephen (and probably others). Breathing threats against Christians, he rode into Damascus and was stopped in his tracks by what he described as a sudden encounter with the risen Jesus. (4) Belief in Jesus' resurrection is attested in our earliest Christian formula found in 1 Corinthians 15:3-8. Scholars agree that it's to be dated no later than just a few years after the crucifixion, meaning that belief in Jesus' resurrection erupted suddenly with a sort of religious Big Bang. Further, Jesus' resurrection was *the* central Christian message from the beginning. (5) There was a sudden and very early eruption of the belief that Jesus is fully divine—that he's actually YHWH, Israel's God. Making this fact even more enigmatic is that no evidence exists of any evolutionary development in the idea, and it appears to have originated alongside belief in Jesus' resurrection.

As we noted, one of the central things scholars have focused on in their analysis concerns the primitive traditions found in the New Testament documents. While there are many such traditions in our earliest documents, 1 Corinthians 15:3-8 has been widely recognized as especially significant. Containing a pre-existing formula—i.e., to be dated prior to Paul's reporting of it—scholars have concluded that it's to be dated within the first five years after Jesus' crucifixion, making it one of the earliest formulae attesting the historicity of Jesus' resurrection.[4] In addition to its early date, scholars have pointed to the importance of its origin. In the letter, Paul (1 Corinthians 15:11) states that the apostles preached the same tradition, which points to Jerusalem as the place of origin for the resurrection formula. Since the church began in Jerusalem, the Twelve, which included Peter, would have acted as guarantors of the tradition. We know that Paul probably received the formula in Damascus immediately after his conversion.

---

[4] William Lane Craig, *Assessing the New Testament Evidence for the Historicity of the Resurrection of Jesus,* 15-20.

We also know from Galatians 2 that Paul personally met with Peter and James in Jerusalem three years after his conversion, spending two weeks with Peter in particular. Since Paul had been educated as a Pharisee, his natural inclination would have been to seek out doctrinal authorities able to transmit authentic tradition, which is exactly what Jewish teachers and students did. Hence, there seems to be little doubt why Paul went to Jerusalem: to gather and validate the tradition he'd already received from first-hand eyewitnesses.

What's important about the timing of his visit is that it was only six years after Jesus' crucifixion and, given the incredibly short period, it would be infeasible to regard the formula—with its list of named eyewitnesses, who were still alive and could be questioned—as legendary. Further, because the formula is a unity, scholars believe that the original apostolic preaching included the naming of eyewitnesses. Hence, based on its early date and Jerusalem origin, it seems likely that it goes back to the apostles themselves.[5] From this, proponents of the historical argument conclude that, with the formula, Paul was passing on first-hand eyewitness testimony of Jesus' resurrection from the dead. Emphasizing that this was a common practice for handing down tradition in the ancient world, these scholars note that Greek historians like Herodotus regularly employed the method of naming witnesses to demonstrate historical trustworthiness. As Dodd comments, "There can hardly be any purpose in mentioning the fact that most of the 500 are still alive, unless Paul is saying, in effect, 'the witnesses are there to be questioned'." Proponents also point out that the majority of the appearances and the sequence of events—death, burial, resurrection, appearances—are multiply attested in other Gospel sources.

Beyond the Corinthians tradition, Samuel Byrskog has argued that it's highly likely there were written accounts with eyewitness reports integrated into small narratives well before any New Testament writings appeared.[6]

---

[5] Birger Gerhardsson, *Memory and Manuscript: Oral Tradition and Written Transmission in Rabbinic Judaism and Early Christianity with Tradition and Transmission in Early Christianity* (Grand Rapids, 1998), 297-8.

[6] Samuel Byrskog, *Story As History—History As Story: The Gospel Tradition in the Context of Ancient Oral History* (Boston, 2002), 269-72. Byrskog also notes that the early Christian teachers and authors were well educated, and that their oral practices intersected with scribal practices. See "A New Perspective on the Jesus Tradition: Reflections on James D. G. Dunn's *Jesus Remembered*" in *Memories of Jesus: A Critical Appraisal of James D. G. Dunn's Jesus Remembered*, eds. Robert B. Stewart and Gary R. Habermas (Nashville, 2010), 75.

One of the clearest examples is the passion narrative found in the Gospel of Mark, which reflects a "pre-Markan" account of Jesus' crucifixion that Mark used to compile his Gospel. It's extremely early and may date back to the time of the crucifixion itself. The reason for such a claim lies in the details of places and names that situate the narrative in Jerusalem, probably originating with the Galilean members of the early church in Jerusalem soon after Jesus' death, no later than 37 A.D. (it's important to remember that Jesus' disciples were identified as Galileans in Jerusalem). Because of its early date, scholars have argued that it's unlikely it would have been corrupted so early on. Another thing to note is that the narrative doesn't name the high priest, which the parallel accounts in the other Gospels do. Such a strange omission seems explicable only if the account was circulating between 18-37 A.D., the time in which everyone would know Caiaphas currently held the office. In terms of the eyewitness authority behind the tradition, it has been argued that Peter probably stands behind the narrative (and Mark's Gospel generally), which is where its Galilean imprint comes to the foreground. Scholars have noted that the combination of its early date, its Jerusalem location, and the eyewitness testimony behind it makes it an extremely important witness, in that within it we have an unadorned account of Jesus' crucifixion with high historical value that few question.[7]

Further building their case, resurrection proponents point out that Jews and some of the early Christians of the period venerated the tombs of prophets and martyrs.[8] After the person's burial, friends and family would meet at the tomb regularly to pray and have commemorative meals in honor of the deceased. However, there's no evidence that Jesus' tomb was ever venerated, which is inconceivable given his status as a great prophet among his followers. Adding to this, we also have evidence that Christians continued the first-century Jewish practice of secondary burial in caves and catacombs. It was customary to collect the bones of the deceased after the flesh decomposed and place them in careful order in an ossuary, which was then stored in a special compartment in a cave or tomb. Reflecting belief that the bones of the deceased continued to matter, the practice affirmed continued hope of the resurrection. There were pragmatic reasons as well

---

[7]   Craig L. Blomberg has suggested that there were probably other private written notes of the disciples and other witnesses which may have been worked up into written sources. See "Orality and the Parables: With Special Reference to James D. G. Dunn's *Jesus Remembered*" in *Memories of Jesus: A Critical Appraisal of James D. G. Dunn's Jesus Remembered*, eds. Robert B. Stewart and Gary R. Habermas (Nashville, 2010), 126.

[8]   N. T. Wright, *The Resurrection of the Son of God*, 579, 707-8.

for the custom, in that tomb space was limited and had to be consolidated for future family members. Nobody who owned a burial cave would leave it with only one body, which would have included Joseph of Arimathea, who laid Jesus' body in his own tomb.

As N. T. Wright observes, Jesus' burial, which is so carefully described in the Gospels, was intended to be the first stage of a two-stage burial. The body was wrapped in graveclothes with significant amounts of spices to offset the smell of decomposition, all on the usual assumption that other shelves in the cave would be required by the same family or group. After six months to two years, the body would be completely decomposed with only the bare skeleton remaining. It would then be collected and reverently folded, according to a traditional pattern, and placed in an ossuary, which would be either stored in the same cave or another nearby location. Joseph of Arimathea would have expected to carry out this practice with the bones of Jesus.

Yet what's striking is that not even a trace of evidence suggests either that Jesus' tomb was venerated or that his bones were collected and placed in an ossuary, further corroborating the multiply attested New Testament claims that the tomb was empty. Historical proponents are also quick to point out that all this would have occurred at the same time Jesus' follow- ers were busily proclaiming him as the Messiah on the grounds that he had been raised from the dead. Evidence of this is found in our earliest accounts of Christian preaching in the book of Acts, where, for example, Peter in 2:22ff. specifically asserts that Jesus' body didn't undergo decay because God raised him from the dead. This claim was easily refutable. All one had to do is point to the tomb where Jesus' body laid; but no one did. Moreover, during the same period, a persecutor of the early Christians, Saul of Tarsus, made an about-face on the grounds that he'd been confronted by the risen Jesus. All this evidence, resurrection proponents say, points in one direction: the tomb was empty because Jesus had been raised from the dead, as he had foretold.

Alternative Explanations

As one would expect, there have been many alternative explanations of the disciples' claims, but before examining them, we should note that some have barred discussion of Jesus' resurrection at the outset due to a commitment to naturalism (which, again, denies the existence of any entities or events lying outside the scope of science). As an axiom, it excludes any notion of the supernatural, making miracles an impossibility. However, as we've already noted, naturalism's strong metaphysical claims go beyond what can be reasonably claimed as a scientific outlook. As McGrath observes, "Naturalism smuggles an essentially materialist philosophy into its allegedly 'scientific' account of reality. It places an embargo on the transcendent, without offering any scientific justification for doing so."[9] In other words, in advance of any evidence, naturalism precludes all miracles and predetermines what can and cannot occur in the known universe, which is something that can only be assessed on the basis of empirical evidence. In light of this, critics of materialism charge it with circularity, since it assumes that miracles are impossible and then concludes, on that basis, that we can't justify any miracle. But how could we know no miracle has ever occurred unless we examine the evidence for or against a particular claim? Science's success, they say, and its remarkable progress can't be explained by sweeping assumptions. On the contrary, the success of science rests on its refusal to make *a priori* judgments about what can and can't be known, and the manner by which that knowledge is established.

Historically, the natural sciences accumulated an understanding of reality primarily in an *a posteriori* manner—i.e., as a result of our actual experience of the world—and as a consequence of empirical testing and assessment of evidence. "The fundamental point to be made here is that the natural sciences have not allowed themselves to be inhibited by a preconceived epistemology, which lays down what can and what cannot be known in advance of an engagement with the natural world."[10] Accordingly, the only way one could know if a miracle has occurred in history is to evaluate the evidence for and against it. Merely stating that Jesus' resurrection is impossible as a matter of course is an unjustified opinion, not an argument.[11] It simply highlights one's presuppositions about what can and can't happen in the world.

Materialism aside, there have still been various alternatives proposed to explain the resurrection claims. A popular hypothesis is that Jesus' disciples stole the body (which Matthew records in his Gospel). But proponents of the historical argument object that such a theory seems implausible. Not

---

[9] Alister E. McGrath, *A Scientific Theology* (Grand Rapids, 2001), vol. 1, 128-30.
[10] Alister E. McGrath, *A Scientific Theology* (Grand Rapids, 2002), vol. 2, 270-2.
[11] Michael R. Licona, *The Resurrection of Jesus: A New Historiographical Approach*, 506-7.

only was the tomb guarded by one of the most highly trained soldiers of the day, but our earliest documents report that—much to their embarrassment (which makes it likely historical)—the disciples fled after Jesus' arrest. Only Peter remained, and only until he denied Jesus during the trial. It's the women who tarry and follow Joseph of Arimathea to the tomb, and it's to them that Jesus first appears. The vast majority of scholars grant that the disciples fled in terror, so from a locational standpoint, they couldn't have stolen the body. Further, the record shows that they were in no psychological state to confront a Roman guard, concoct a story they knew to be a lie, and then preach the resurrection fearlessly to the point of their own martyrdom. In short, the theory is untenable and contradicts well-attested facts. Similar problems attend the claim that a third party stole the body.[12] At any rate, the fact that the graveclothes remained in the tomb seems to preclude theft of the body (Luke 24:12).

Another popular alternative (though not among specialists) is the swoon theory, which claims that Jesus lost consciousness on the cross, causing onlookers to conclude he was dead. When taken down, some say, he revived in the cool of the tomb and was treated. But resurrection proponents have been quick to note the absurdity that Jesus survived the long process of Roman torture and crucifixion, and it seems nonsensical that, after brutal torture and crucifixion, Jesus' disciples believed after seeing him that he was resurrected. Equally implausible is the idea that the women went to the wrong tomb. Are we to believe that some of Jesus' most devout followers were so careless that, after having gone to the lengths of being present at the crucifixion, failed to follow Joseph to the tomb as reported? There's little doubt they would have wanted to anoint Jesus' body and wouldn't have made a mistake about the tomb's location. In addition, as with the other alternatives, the Jews would have been only too happy to point out the correct tomb with Jesus' body still in it. Yet there's no hint of such a suggestion, a fact corroborated by the concocted story we hear related about the disciples stealing the body.

Perhaps the most popular alternative explanation for the past one hundred years is a variation of the hallucination theory. Hallucinations can be defined as false sensory perceptions that have the sense of reality despite the absence of external stimuli. Or more simply, they're subjective experiences of something that doesn't exist outside the person experiencing

---

[12] For a more detailed assessment of the evidence, see William Lane Craig, *Assessing the New Testament Evidence for the Historicity of the Resurrection of Jesus*, 371-8.

the vision. This theory postulates that the disciples were inflicted with various psychological conditions that brought about experiences of the risen Jesus. The second-century critic, Celsus, was the first to propose that the resurrection of Jesus was the "cock and bull story" of a "hysterical female" who "through wishful thinking had a hallucination due to some mistaken notion."[13] As Michael Licona points out, hallucination theories today usually begin with Peter and suggest that he experienced a hallucination of Jesus because of his sorrow and guilt. Unable to cope, his unconscious mind created a hallucinatory experience of the risen Jesus in order to ease his intense anguish.[14] Peter shared his experience with the other disciples who then had similar experiences in groups of various sizes. These constituted shared hallucinatory fantasies that assured them of forgiveness for their desertion of Jesus at his time of need. However, in reality, they were victims of self-deception.

Plausibility of the hypothesis aside for the moment, how are we then to account for Paul's claim to have seen the risen Jesus, since he wouldn't have had the same guilt over abandoning Jesus that the disciples had? Adherents to the hallucination theory have entertained the idea that Paul was secretly harboring doubts about Christianity and had a growing distaste for Judaism. Given his later references to the law as a "yoke" that places one in "spiritual bondage," it's argued that he felt bondage to the strict form of Pharisaism with which he was aligned. His vehement response to Christians reflects the fact that it had a powerful effect which unconsciously attracted him to the movement. Railing against his subconscious, he projected his inner struggle against the early believers all the more savagely. These factors led him to flee from his painful situation and he experienced a hallucination of the risen Jesus on the road to Damascus. Like Peter and the others, Paul was a victim of self-deception. Fortuitously, he was also able to capitalize on the situation by assuming the exalted position of apostle to the Gentiles, something that fulfilled his tendency to be a competitive overachiever.

As the theory goes, thirty to seventy years later, there were tensions within Christian groups about what else may have happened. As speculations flourished, people started to fill in the gaps, which led eventually

---

[13] Joseph W. Bergeron and Gary Habermas, "The Resurrection of Jesus: A Clinical Review of Psychiatric Hypotheses for the Biblical Story of Easter" in *Irish Theological Quarterly*, vol. 80, no. 2, 2015, 4, http://www.garyhabermas.com/articles/irish-theological -quarterly/Habermas_Resurrection%20of%20Jesus.pdf.

[14] Michael R. Licona, *The Resurrection of Jesus: A New Historiographical Approach* (Downers Grove, 2010), 479-82, 496-505.

to myths such as a prominent person burying Jesus, an empty tomb, and then physical resurrection appearances to his disciples (resulting from their Jewish belief in a physical resurrection). According to this perspective, Jesus' tomb contained a decomposing body. Paul's reference to Jesus' appearance to more than five hundred is assumed to be an instance of mass ecstasy stimulated by one or a few of the others. Adherents of the theory argue that modern communal delusions, such as sightings of Mary, Big Foot, and UFOs give plausibility to the group experiences of the disciples being hallucinatory. The bottom line is that all of the appearances were visionary in nature and induced some sort of individual and group hallucinations. On this view, we could only conclude that they were no more than a fantasy of the disciples' minds, making early Christianity a history of self-deception.

However, resurrection proponents contend that there are several problems attending hallucination proposals. First and foremost is that, by their very nature, hallucinations are individual, private experiences. Given this fact, Joseph Bergeron and Gary Habermas ask, "What are the odds that separate individuals in a group could experience simultaneous and identical psychological phenomena mixed with hallucinations?"[15] It would require a mind-boggling number of coincidences, they point out. Despite the fact that hallucinations are experienced by roughly fifteen percent of the general population, an incredible one hundred percent of the Twelve would have had to simultaneously experience the exact same phenomena around the risen Jesus. As Licona states, "It would be an understatement to claim that such a proposal has only a meager possibility of reflecting what actually occurred. Embracing it would require an extraordinary amount of faith."[16]

Bergeron and Habermas also point out that hallucination proposals for the appearances are far outside mainstream clinical thought. The concept of collective hallucination isn't found in peer-reviewed medical or psychological literature—and there's no mention of such phenomena in the *Diagnostic and Statistical Manual of Mental Disorders*. It's simply not part of current psychiatric understanding or accepted pathognomy. "This is noteworthy since these hypotheses propose hallucinatory symptoms which

[15] Joseph W. Bergeron and Gary Habermas, "The Resurrection of Jesus: A Clinical Review of Psychiatric Hypotheses for the Biblical Story of Easter" in *Irish Theological Quarterly*, vol. 80, no. 2, 2015, 3, 8-10, http://www.garyhabermas.com/articles/irish-theological-quarterly/Habermas_Resurrection%20of%20Jesus.pdf.
[16] Michael R. Licona, *The Resurrection of Jesus: A New Historiographical Approach*, 479-82, 485-6.

imply an underlying medical condition."[17] So where do the theories come from if not from the medical literature? The answer is primarily from New Testament scholars who lack the appropriate medical background. That's not to say that collective hallucinations don't occur on rare occasions, but the features characterizing such events don't explain the disciples' encounters with the risen Jesus. The reason, resurrection proponents suggest, is that in these rare cases we find a group sense of "expectation" and "emotional excitement." However, not everyone in the group experiences a hallucination, and those that do see something have different hallucinations from one another. In this sense, they're a lot like dreams; a person can't share in the dream of another. Also important is the fact that apparitions in hallucinations don't tend to carry on conversations, but none of these facts are consistent with the early accounts of Jesus' appearances.

Another problem with the hallucination theory is that the disciples were far from expecting Jesus' resurrection (as the Gospels make embarrassingly clear). Interpreting Jesus within the context of their first-century Jewish beliefs, they were unable to make the necessary connections for them to expect his imminent resurrection. Further, because they already understood the category of being translated directly to heaven on the model of Enoch and Elijah (Gen. 5:24; 2 Kings 2:11-18), historical proponents argue that, even if they had hallucinations, it's unlikely they would have concluded Jesus rose from the dead; it would have contradicted their Jewish belief in the resurrection at the end of time.[18] Rather, they would have likely concluded that God had translated him to heaven. Yet the fact that the disciples proclaimed—not the translation of Jesus—but contrary to their Jewish belief, the physical resurrection from the dead, strongly suggests that the origin of the disciples' belief can't be accounted for by visions or hallucinations. No experiences consistent with hallucinations were present, nor were they psychologically able to experience such an event.

What about the contention that their sorrow and guilt led to a wish-fulfillment regarding Jesus' appearance? Historical proponents point out that this claim implicitly smuggles in the unstated assumption that the disciples *expected* Jesus to rise from the dead before the end time. Implicit

---

[17] Joseph W. Bergeron and Gary Habermas, "The Resurrection of Jesus: A Clinical Review of Psychiatric Hypotheses for the Biblical Story of Easter" in *Irish Theological Quarterly*, vol. 80, no. 2, 2015, 3, 10, http://www.garyhabermas.com/articles/irish -theological-quarterly/Habermas_Resurrection%20of%20Jesus.pdf.

[18] William Lane Craig, *Assessing the New Testament Evidence for the Historicity of the Resurrection of Jesus* (New York, 1989), 414, 417.

also is the assumption that they could have connected the ideas of crucifixion and Messiah, and Messiah and YHWH. However, nothing supports
this, either from our general knowledge of the period or from what we
know about the disciples themselves. In order to avoid the most plausible
explanation that Jesus rose from the dead, resurrection proponents suggest,
hallucination theories have to propose ideas flatly contradicted by the bedrock facts accepted by the vast majority of scholars. In addition, resurrection proponents balk at the suggestion that Paul subconsciously desired a
leadership position in the early church. Not only is there no hint of such as
desire, but considering his lofty stature as a Pharisaic Jew at the time of his
conversion, this fails to make sense. He already had a leading position and
was on his way to being notable among his contemporaries. The only thing
to be won by converting to this despised little movement was persecution
and threat of death—and this was certainly no way to advance his career.
It would have been a huge step in the wrong direction.

Finally, resurrection proponents object to the claim that the physical
resurrection of Jesus was a late invention by subsequent believers on the
ground that it's attested in our earliest resurrection formulae. We've seen
that the pre-Pauline formula in 1 Corinthians 15:3-8 is universally recognized as being extremely early, to be dated no later than one to three years
after Jesus' crucifixion—much too early to bear the stamp of pure myth.
There are also other early formulae that corroborate the early Christian
claims of the physical appearances of Jesus.

Beyond these alternatives, there is one more philosophically oriented
objection worth noting. Resurrection critics might complain that, even if
it could be established that Jesus rose from the dead, this wouldn't by itself
entail either that it was accomplished by the Father of whom Jesus spoke
or that Jesus is God. In other words, even if Jesus was raised from the dead,
there's no way of knowing for certain that the explanation of the earliest
believers is the correct one. There could conceivably be numerous explanations of what really caused Jesus' being raised after his crucifixion and
death. Here, it's possible that the resurrection proponent may concede the
critic's point insofar as he (critic) means that a resurrection doesn't *necessarily* entail (in the deductive sense) that the Christian God raised Jesus
from the dead. Being in the form of inference to the best explanation, the
Christian isn't suggesting some deductive type of proof, only that, given
all the relevant evidence, Jesus' contention that the Father raised him from
the dead—and, further, that Jesus is himself the Son of God, Second Person
of the Trinity—appears to be the most likely causal explanation vis-a-vis

opposing hypotheses. Not only is it Jesus' own explanation, who had sufficient authority to command nature itself, but those who were eyewitnesses to his appearances and who spent many days with Jesus after that first Easter would have been in a better position to evaluate the evidence. At any rate, the resurrection proponent might complain that such a criticism seems little more than a last-straw attempt to avoid the full implications of such a historically significant event.

Having evaluated these and other objections, historical proponents conclude that the theory more accurately accounting for the all the data (data agreed upon by the majority of scholars) is the physical resurrection of Jesus of Nazareth.

Form of the Argument

In both the arguments from Big Bang cosmology and from origin of life research, we noted that proponents used inference to the best explanation to establish their case for theism. But how do we evaluate the logical structure of the resurrection argument? From the preceding discussion, it now seems clear that resurrection proponents proceed in much the same fashion, arguing on the basis of abductive reasoning and not by strict deduction or simple enumerative induction. As recently developed, the argument advances by pointing out that, despite a thorough review of alternative explanations, no purely natural causes have been shown to adequately explain the bedrock facts the majority of scholars accept. However, a supernatural being (God) capable of raising the dead would provide an adequate causal explanation. From this, proponents conclude that God's raising Jesus from the dead constitutes the best, most causally adequate explanation for the claims of Jesus' disciples and Paul, i.e., core historical facts.

With that said, we should point out that a difference exists in the way abduction is used here compared with the way it was used in our previous chapter. Recall that Peter Lipton had suggested that good explanations are typically causal.[19] Thus, in the case of particular events, they cite a prior cause that's part of the causal history of the event in question, and to identify the cause of an event, scientists must identify something within the causal history of the event that accounts for the difference between what did occur and what could have occurred otherwise. Philosophers of science and

---

[19] Peter Lipton, *Inference to the Best Explanation* (London, 2004), 32ff., 75ff.

historical scientists emphasize the causal adequacy criterion as a condition of a successful explanation—in which, when evaluating competing hypotheses, they identify causes that are known to have the power to produce the kind of effect or event in question. Causes that are known to produce the effect are judged to be better candidates than those that don't.[20] Stephen Meyer had added that this leads to sound inference only when scientists can infer a uniquely plausible cause. When such a cause can be identified, the fallacy of affirming the consequent can be avoided—that is, a scientist can avoid the error of ignoring other possible causes with the power to produce the same effect.

The difference between the argument of this and the previous chapter is easily seen in premise two of Meyer's argument, which stated that "Intelligent causes have demonstrated the power to produce large amounts of specified information." This is a premise based on our vast experience of seeing intelligent agents, and only intelligent agents, produce specified information (or things ordered to a specific end, as suggested in the fact that the universe seems to have been created with human beings in mind). However, the critic might argue that the resurrection argument doesn't satisfy the criterion of appealing to an already known cause that accounts for the difference between what did occur and what could have occurred otherwise. How can we be justified in appealing to a supreme being as having already demonstrated the causal power to raise a person from the dead? Is there anything in our experience to which we could make such an appeal, independent of the claim that Jesus rose from the dead? The resurrection proponent could respond by saying that divine power was indeed demonstrated already within the causal history of Jesus of Nazareth, as, for example, in his many miracles. But the skeptic will probably object on the ground that these examples are tied to the very case in question. However, the resurrection proponent might retort that the case for Jesus' resurrection postulates a truly unique event, and since it can't be precluded simply on the materialist premise that miracles can't occur, arguments about it have to proceed by some sort of inference to the best explanation whether or not they meet the causal history criterion.

But resurrection proponents could also argue—as Alister McGrath does—that inference to the best explanation doesn't require the

---

[20] Stephen C. Meyer, *Signature in the Cell: DNA and the Evidence for Intelligent Design*, 159, 161, 163, 169.

explanation to be *causal*.[21] As we noted, McGrath had suggested that, to demonstrate that A causes B, one could simply show that A explains B. Explanatory power should thus be seen to reside not primarily in causality, but in *ontology*: an understanding of the way things are, or of the fundamental order of things. Thus, the resurrection argument could be formulated along these lines. Again, though, however it's formulated, the resurrection proponent will doubtless argue that given the core facts—and given that a thorough review of possible natural causes has brought us to a dead end—God's raising Jesus from the dead is, in matter of fact, the best explanation, despite that it may have uncomfortable metaphysical implications for the critic.

Conclusion

Given that natural theology, at its best, could only arrive at a knowledge of God's existence and perhaps of some of his attributes, the resurrection argument can be seen as a way of supplying—on evidential grounds—knowledge of God that's highly specific. Basing the argument on the fact that the primitive resurrection formulae we find in the New Testament—with their naming of eyewitnesses—are much too old to have been mythologized, resurrection proponents contend that we have trustworthy historical accounts of the appearances originating from the disciples themselves.

Proponents add that in light of the fact that none of the disciples—despite the embarrassment it presented to the early church—expected Jesus to rise from the dead, and that none of them were psychologically or locationally capable of pulling off an elaborate hoax, the historic physical resurrection of Jesus seems to best account for their consequent claims. It also seems to account best for the claim of Paul, who was a fierce persecutor of the early Christian faith, to have had an encounter with the risen Jesus on the road to Damascus. Not only this, but proponents point out that there's no evidence that Jesus' tomb was ever venerated, as would have been expected during this period. The reason, they say, is that Jesus' tomb was empty, as the disciples claimed. On this basis, and after a thorough review of alternative explanations, resurrection proponents conclude—by abductive inference—that the resurrection hypothesis best accounts for the core facts the vast majority of scholars accept.

---

[21] Alister E. McGrath, *Darwinism and the Divine: Evolutionary Thought and Natural Theology* (West Sussex, 2011), 200.

In terms of the knowledge question, resurrection proponents would argue that we possess historically credible, multiply attested, accounts of Jesus' death, burial, resurrection, and appearances in the New Testament documents. This being the case, they further argue that we have justified knowledge that God forgives the world of its sins through the life, death, and resurrection of Jesus Christ, Second Person of the Holy Trinity. Thus, vis-a-vis the other arguments for God's existence we've surveyed, the resurrection hypothesis promises the most detailed validation not only of the existence of God, but also his specific intent for humankind.

Conclusion

If there's one theme we've encountered throughout this book, it's that human knowledge, while impressive, is simultaneously limited. Despite the fact that we often find ourselves caught in the certainty trap described by Ilana Redstone, we've seen that, in light of the preceding chapters, such a view of knowledge is difficult to justify. Blind confidence about the unquestionable truth of intellectual fashions betrays a stunning unwillingness by those who model it to acknowledge the profound limits of human understanding. Too often, even in the sciences, questions are treated as though they're settled and beyond dispute. The issue appears to be not so much the purported evidence for particular views as the attitudes of those advocating for their truth. One can't help but think that even a small amount of epistemic humility would go a long way to help heal the increasingly divisive gulf between people on issues that, not very long ago, it seems, they could discuss with civility and mutual respect.

That more diffidence in our public and private discourse is warranted was shown in what best characterizes human knowledge: namely, that while we have the remarkable ability to know the world around us, that same knowledge will always be the product of an ever changing social process. Yet even this accounts for only some of our epistemic limitations. We've also seen constraints resulting partly from our nature, from the fact that answers to questions only propagate more unanticipated questions, and from the heuristically generated methods we use to form judgments. Doubtless we could add to the list, but these establish that human beings perpetually exist suspended between necessary ignorance on the one hand and limited epistemic achievement (however grand we may view it) on the other.

To show this, we've explored many contentious issues, beginning with what constitutes justified knowledge. While the traditional view was straightforward and easy to understand, we noted a drawback in that it doesn't seem able to account for cases of justified true belief that still fall short of knowledge, as in lucky guesses. Though some proposals to fix this deficiency have merit, it has been argued that none of them succeed completely—and unless we're to surrender to radical skepticism, some forms of luck are going to have to be considered compatible with knowledge. Another rather central issue we discussed is whether we know the world directly via the senses or whether that knowledge is mediated in some fashion. While most philosophers acknowledge that we have some knowledge through the senses, they also recognize that they lead us astray at times and cause errors in judgment. Things aren't always what they appear to be, which is why commonsense realism (i.e., that what we sense is an accurate copy of the physical world) appears too simplistic. In opposition, we noted that phenomenalism holds that the physical world is the inferred totality of our sense data, and it doesn't exist apart from sense data. But some thinkers have taken this farther and ask: if the world isn't always what it appears to be, then how do we know if our senses ever give us an accurate understanding of the real world at all? The relativist/postmodernist answer to this is that everything, including science, is a human construction and therefore relative. Science and all human knowledge are held to be culturally or socially constructed, and they can be deconstructed to expose and eliminate the power structures holding them up.

However, we observed several objections that make such a social constructivism untenable, the first of which is that it's self-referential. That is, if these forms of relativism are to be proved, then a case has to be made from the available evidence, which would include various case studies. But since all knowledge is relative and wholly constructed, then it *itself* is incapable of supporting the grand claim that everything is relative. To say that all things are relative assumes that at least the person saying it has a "God's eye" view capable of making the relativity claim; i.e., in order to tell us things are relative, it has to assume at least *enough* objectivity to support the social constructivist claim. But that's precisely what it can't do, claiming as it does that no objectivity exists. As in all forms of relativism, its truth simultaneously implies its negation, with the consequence that it falls on its own axe.

As a way of navigating the tug between these competing approaches, critical realism acknowledges the reality of the thing known and that it's something other than the knower (thus realism), while also acknowledging that the knower is involved in the knowing process (thus critical). While accepting the fact that we know a reality "out there," separate from the knower, critical realism affirms the need for a critical reflection on what we say about reality and sees it as provisional. It's always possible that our judgments fail to represent the world as it is. Thus, knowledge, against postmodernism and constructivism, concerns realities independent of the knower. Yet critical realism also accepts, against commonsense realism, that knowledge is never completely independent and is in some ways modified by the knower and his wider social environment. This means that knowledge is always an approximation of the truth, not absolute truth. As Roy Bhaskar noted, because humans aren't just passive recipients of facts, a conversation regarding the prior social activity of science is important. This is because knowledge is a social product produced by prior social products. To recognize this is simply to recognize that we don't have an unbiased access to nature.

Bhaskar had contended that, in their social activity, human beings produce knowledge, which is a social product, much like any other, and is no more independent of its production and the people who produce it than any other of their productions. Their knowledge at any time includes antecedently established facts and theories, paradigms and models, methods and techniques currently available to the worker. We saw this in some detail in chapter two, where we noted that people (including scientists) have to rely on the expertise/testimony of others, given that knowledge of the world is much too vast to be contained in a single mind, group (however large), or committee. To underscore this, we observed in chapter eight the generally dismal record of expert predictions and the limits of what knowledge these can provide. The fact that scientists have to be trained shows that knowledge is a social product and can't be conceived as a purely individual acquisition. For any cognitive act to be possible, there has to be something that precedes it; some knowledge already established or already produced. Further, it follows that what is socially produced is socially changeable, as we have seen from the history of science. Yet the objects we discover in the social activity of science exist and act independently of men and would do so in a world without men. In saying this, Bhaskar was affirming that knowledge is *of* things that aren't produced by people at all. If humans ceased to exist, sound would continue to travel and heavy bodies fall to earth even though there would be no one to know it. These are the real things and structures that make our theories and observations possible. Thus, against the social constructivist, they're not structures imposed by men in their cognitive activity. It's this dual nature of knowledge, of the social and objective, that puts Bhaskar in the critical realist camp.

While it seems likely that most scientists are realists (in the sense of recommending belief in both the observable and unobservable aspects of the world described by the sciences), we've also detailed strong arguments for antirealism, which challenges realism on empiricist grounds and questions whether we're justified in our beliefs about unobservable entities. In doing so, antirealists such as Larry Laudan highlight the track record revealed in the history of science, which seems to demonstrate that many once popular theories that were believed to be true have been relegated to the dust bin—or, vice versa, that theories that weren't regarded as true are now seen to be true, thus disputing the realist notion of progress.

Another antirealist challenge concerned the realist use of abduction to makes its case for realism. Arthur Fine had noted that what antirealists question is whether acceptable explanations need to be true and whether the entities used in them need to exist. If not, then the usual abductive methods that lead us to good explanations can't be counted on to get us theories that are approximately true. For Laudan, the realist reliance on abductive reasoning commits the fallacy of affirming the consequent (the error of ignoring other possible causes with the power to produce the same effect). But the arguments for realism are usually based on this very sort of abductive inference, which means that the inference to realism as the best explanation is misguided, they say. Another way of articulating this is that we can't beg the question about the significance of explanatory power by assuming that it carries truth as well as explanatory power. Just because a theory has some true consequences doesn't entail that the theory is true; false theories as well as true ones could have true consequences. To argue that realism is true because it has true consequences is a monumental case of begging the question. Explanatory success, for the antirealist, doesn't entail truth.

In response, Richard Boyd pointed out that the issue between empiricists and realists over the legitimacy of abduction is a double-edged sword. It may highlight a sort of circularity in realism, but it's just as important to note that its prohibition would place a significant restriction on intellectual inquiry. If the fact that a theory provides the best explanation for some phenomenon isn't a justification for thinking it approximately true, then it's difficult to see how intellectual inquiry could proceed. Recall that the most extensive response to the antirealist objections came from Peter Lipton who, with Boyd, highlights the fact that these sorts of explanatory inferences are extremely common. The doctor, for instance, infers that his patient has the measles since this provides the best explanation for the symptoms. We construct causal scenarios and think about what they would explain and how well. The use of inference to the best explanation, Lipton argued, implies that our inferential practices are governed by explanatory considerations. Given our evidence and background beliefs, we infer what would—if true—provide the best of the competing explanations we can generate from that evidence (assuming, of course, that it's good enough to make an inference). A case in point concerns Ignaz Semmelweis' use of inference to the best explanation when trying to determine the cause of childbed fever, which we will recall had been killing infants and women. Nancy Cartwright had also pointed out that underdetermination, which the antirealist used to refute abduction, is a general feature of our knowledge and doesn't show anything peculiar to inference to the best explanation.

Beyond these philosophical issues, we also examined the judgment and decision-making research of Daniel Kahneman, Amos Tversky, and others. Based on empirical research, this field has documented various heuristics people use to reason quickly—and often with great efficiency and accuracy—that can lead to cognitive biases that skew their judgment. As we saw, humans appear to rely on a limited number of heuristic rules that reduce the complex tasks of assessing the likelihood of uncertain events and thus predict values through the use of simpler operations. While, again, these can be useful, they can also lead us into error, causing us (for example) to overestimate the frequency of rare events and underestimate the frequency of more common ones. Because most of these involve probability assessments—for which we're often intuitively unprepared—our predictions are commonly off base and swayed by completely irrelevant factors. Perhaps even more troublesome is that the same errors persistently show up in scientific literature, causing problems like the proliferation of statistically nonsignificant findings in published research.

Moving on from these issues, we ended our examination of knowledge by exploring various arguments for God's existence. Determining first that fideism is both philosophically and theologically indefensible, we discussed Alvin Plantinga's argument for Reformed Epistemology. Using his A/C model, Plantinga argued that theistic belief has sufficient warrant for it to be considered as knowledge. He based this on the idea that God has created human beings with a belief-producing process or source of belief, the *sensus divinitatis* (an immediate, natural knowledge of God), which works under various conditions to produce beliefs about God, including beliefs that immediately entail his existence. In response, Jeremy Koons challenged the idea that any belief can be properly basic in Plantinga's sense. Central to his critique is that our observation reports have an epistemic dependence on our background theories—which are inherently contestable and the proper subject for challenge and defense—in that their warrant depends on the warrant of the theories standing behind the observational terms embedded in our observational reports. In addition, other critics of Plantinga have been quick to point out that his argument could open the door to virtually any claim, meaning that if we're allowed to make judgments without evidential constraint, wouldn't anything be allowed?

Moving beyond Plantinga, we explored the resurgence of natural theology based (in part) on discoveries from within science. Based on the idea of complexity, or rather specified complexity, these arguments cited recent evidence from Big Bang cosmology showing that the universe is very finely tuned: so much so that even minor deviations in the cosmic constants would have resulted in an inanimate universe. As it stands, the universe appears to have been created with human beings in mind, given the improbability that it would have developed that way without intervention. While detractors, such as Quentin Smith, argued that these laws are uncaused and need no further explanation, theists such as William Lane Craig and Stephen Meyer insisted that the idea of such complexity being uncaused and coming from nothing takes more faith to believe than belief in a creator. Adding to the theist's case is the equally improbable development of living things on earth. Challenging the standard Darwinian account, theists (such as Michael Behe and Stephen Meyer) highlighted in great detail the mind-boggling complexity of even the simplest mechanisms in nature. Arguing that the standard Darwinist gradualism is outdated, in light of recent discoveries, these researchers rejected the idea that such mechanisms could have developed in a cumulative, step-by-step manner. Many biological systems, they contended, are irreducibly complex, meaning that they can't function without every part already in place and fully functioning.

Though Darwinian proponents such as Richard Dawkins insisted on the gradualist conception of biological evolution—i.e., that all biological forms came into existence by a gradual, cumulative, step-by-step transformation from simpler things, which consist of primordial objects sufficiently simple to have come about by chance—theistic proponents were quick to point out that evolution left to its own is more likely to break than to make things—thus making the probability of living things developing without guidance, or without an end in mind, inconceivably minute. Using inference to the best explanation (as they did with Big Bang cosmology), these theists contended that a grand designer both of the universe itself and life on earth constitutes the best explanation vis-a-vis alternative proposals.

As interesting as theistic arguments are in their own right, some have questioned their practicality, given their inherent epistemic limits. That is, even if valid, they at most could provide a knowledge of God's existence and perhaps some of his attributes, but they can't give any knowledge of who such a God is or what he desires for human beings. To supplement this more general knowledge, therefore, many scholars have formulated an argument for the historicity of Jesus' bodily resurrection from the dead. Appealing to a small list of core facts most scholars accept, they argue via abduction that God's having raised Jesus from the dead is the best explanation of the historical core vis-a-vis alternative explanations. Suggesting that we possess historically credible, multiply attested accounts of Jesus' death, burial, resurrection, and appearances, they further argue that we have justified knowledge that God forgives the world of its sins through the life, death, and resurrection of Jesus Christ. Thus, compared to the other theistic arguments we discussed, the resurrection hypothesis promised the most detailed validation not only of the existence of God, but also his specific intent for humankind.

What should be noted in all of these approaches is that their validity depends both on abduction generally and on the relative strength of available evidence, which implies that they each have varying levels of strength. This means that they need to be updated as our knowledge changes. Though it might be disconcerting to the religiously inclined, this also means that the arguments carry varying probabilities, but never certainty. While mystical arguments, including those from religious experience, often come with existential certainty, it was argued that they come at the cost of saying nothing about the real world. Fortunately or unfortunately (as we noted), Christianity in particular makes specific historical claims which are, in principle, open to factual assessment. Thus, it seems if one is going to claim any knowledge at all about God's existence—his attributes, or what he intends for human beings—that knowledge must bear the same restrictions and responsibilities as other types of knowledge. It must, in other words, be articulated along *a posteriori* lines and not presumed to be immune from evidence and probability assessment. This, of course, isn't to suggest that existential certainty can't be gained or that faith can't be certain, but only that, insofar as one's beliefs have conceptual content, they can't be independent of conceptual expression or exempt from criticism.

Articulating things in this way seems to follow from the very nature of human knowledge with which we began: namely, that we have the remarkable ability to interrogate nature and know many of its secrets, but also that our knowledge is a social product and necessarily limited. Yet, in the present author's opinion, such a fact shouldn't be a special cause for concern, for in it—as we sojourn on earth as God's creation—we can live out our vocations and serve our neighbor's ever-changing needs, while at the same time exploring new ways of expressing both the beauty of God's handiwork and of his own death as a Messianic pretender on a criminal's cross for the sins of the world.

Works Cited

Agrawal, Ajay and Joshua Gans, and Avi Goldfarb. *Prediction Machines: The Simple Economics of Artificial Intelligence.* Boston: Harvard Business Review Press, 2018.

Ashton, Kevin. *How to Fly a Horse: The Secret History of Creation, Invention, and Discovery.* New York: Doubleday, 2015.

Audi, Robert. *Epistemology: A Contemporary Introduction to the Theory of Knowledge.* London: Routledge, 2000.

Ayer, A. J. *Language, Truth, and Logic.* New York: Dover Publications, Inc., 1946.

Bauckham, Richard. *Jesus and the Eyewitnesses: The Gospels as Eyewitness Testimony.* Grand Rapids, MI: William B. Eerdmans Publishing Company, 2006.

Behe, Michael J. *Darwin's Black Box: The Biochemical Challenge to Evolution.* New York: The Free Press, 1996.

—*Darwin Devolves: The New Science About DNA That Challenges Evolution.* New York: HarperOne, 2019.

—*The Edge of Evolution: The Search for the Limits of Darwinism.* New York: Free Press, 2007.

Bergeron. Joseph W. and Gary Habermas. "The Resurrection of Jesus: A Clinical Review of Psychiatric Hypotheses for the Biblical Story of Easter," *Irish Theological Quarterly*, Vol. 80 (2), 2015, Pages 157-172. http://www.garyhabermas .com/articles/irish-theological-quarterly/Habermas_Resurrection%20of %20Jesus.pdf.

Berkhoff, Louis. *Systematic Theology.* East Peoria, IL: Versa Press, 2005.

Bhaskar, Roy. *A Realist Theory of Science.* London: Verso, 2008.

Blomberg, Craig L. "Orality and the Parables: With Special Reference to James D. G. Dunn's *Jesus Remembered*" in *Memories of Jesus: A Critical Appraisal of James D. G. Dunn's* Jesus Remembered, eds. Robert B. Stewart and Gary R. Habermas. Nashville, TN: B & H Academic, 2010, 79-127.

Boghossian, Paul. "Epistemic Relativism Defended" in *Social Epistemology: Essential Readings*, eds. Alvin I. Goldman and Dennis Whitcomb. New York: Oxford University Press, 2011. Pages 38-53.

Boyd, Richard N. "Realism, Approximate Truth, and Philosophical Method" in *The Philosophy of Science*, ed. David Papineau. New York: Oxford University Press, 1996. Pages 215-255.

—"The Current Status of Scientific Realism" in *Scientific Realism*, ed. Jarrett Leplin. Berkeley: University of California Press, 1984. Pages 41-82.

Brewer, William F. "What is Recollective Memory?" in *Remembering Our Past: Studies in Autobiographical Memory*, ed. David C. Rubin. Cambridge, UK: Cambridge University Press, 1995. Pages 19-66.

Burridge, Richard A. *What Are the Gospels? A Comparison with Graeco-Roman Biography*. Grand Rapids, MI: William B. Eerdmans Publishing Company, 2004.

Byrskog, Samuel, "A New Perspective on the Jesus Tradition: Reflections on James D. G. Dunn's *Jesus Remembered*" in *Memories of Jesus: A Critical Appraisal of James D. G. Dunn's* Jesus Remembered, eds. Robert B. Stewart and Gary R. Habermas. Nashville, TN: B & H Academic, 2010. Pages 59-78.

—*Story as History—History as Story: The Gospel Tradition in the Context of Ancient Oral History*. Boston: Brill Academic Publishers, 2002.

Cartwright, Nancy. "Fundamentalism vs the Patchwork of Laws" in *The Philosophy of Science*, ed. David Papineau. New York: Oxford University Press, 1996. Pages 314-326.

—*How the Laws of Physics Lie*. Oxford: Clarendon Press, 1983.

Catechism of the Catholic Church, Second Edition. Revised in Accordance with the Official Latin Text Promulgated by Pope John Paul II. New York: Doubleday, 1997.

Chakravartty, Anjan, "Scientific Realism" in The Stanford Encyclopedia of Philosophy (Summer 2017 Edition), ed. Edward N. Zalta, https://plato.stanford.edu/archives/sum2017/entries/scientific-realism/.

Cohen, Geoffrey L. "Party Over Policy: The Dominating Impact of Group Influence on Political Beliefs," *Journal of Personality and Social Psychology*, 2003, Vol. 85, No. 5, Pages 808-822.

Cohen, I. Bernard. *Revolution in Science*. Cambridge, MA: Harvard University Press, 1985.

Collier, Andrew. *Critical Realism: An Introduction to Roy Bhaskar's Philosophy*. London: Verso, 1994.

Copi, Irving M. and Carl Cohen. *Introduction to Logic*, Eleventh Edition. New Jersey: Prentice Hall, 2002.

Craig, William Lane. *Assessing the New Testament Evidence for the Historicity of the Resurrection of Jesus.* New York: Edwin Mellen Press, 1989.

—*In Quest of the Historical Adam: A Biblical and Scientific Exploration.* Grand Rapids, MI: Wm. B. Eerdmans Publishing Co., 2021.

—"The Caused Beginning of the Universe," in William Lane Craig and Quentin Smith, *Theism, Atheism and Big Bang Cosmology.* Oxford: Clarendon Press, 1995. Pages 141-160.

—"The Finitude of the Past and the Existence of God" in William Lane Craig and Quentin Smith, *Theism, Atheism and Big Bang Cosmology.* Oxford: Clarendon Press, 1995. Pages 3-76.

—"Theism and Big Bang Cosmology" in William Lane Craig and Quentin Smith, *Theism, Atheism and Big Bang Cosmology.* Oxford: Clarendon Press, 1995. Pages 218-231.

Creath, Richard. "Logical Empiricism" in The Stanford Encyclopedia of Philosophy (Winter 2021 Edition), ed. Edward N. Zalta, https://plato.stanford.edu /archives/win2021/entries/logical-empiricism/.

Dawkins, Richard. *River Out of Eden: A Darwinian View of Life.* New York: Basic Books, 1995.

—*The Blind Watchmaker: Why the Evidence of Evolution Reveals a Universe Without Design.* New York: Norton, 1996.

—*The God Delusion.* Boston: Houghton Mifflin, 2006.

Demarest, Bruce A. *General Revelation: Historical Views and Contemporary Issues.* Grand Rapids, MI: Zondervan Publishing House, 1982.

Dennett, Daniel. *Breaking the Spell: Religion as a Natural Phenomenon.* New York: Penguin, 2006.

—*Darwin's Dangerous Idea: Evolution and the Meaning of Life.* New York: Simon & Schuster, 1995.

Denton, Michael. *Evolution: A Theory in Crisis.* Chevy Chase, MD: Adler & Adler, 1985.

—*Evolution: Still a Theory in Crisis.* Seattle: Discovery Institute Press, 2016.

Dusheck, Jennie. "Misleading P-Values Showing Up More Often in Biomedical Journal Articles," https://med.stanford.edu/news/all-news/2016/03/misleading -p-values-showing-up-more-often-in-journals.html.

Edwards, Ward and Detlof von Winterfeldt. "On Cognitive Illusions and Their Implications" in *Judgement and Decision Making: An Interdisciplinary Reader,* Second Edition, eds. Terry Connolly, Hal R. Arkes, and Kenneth R. Hammond. Cambridge: Cambridge University Press, 2000. Pages 592-620.

Einhorn, Hillel J. "Learning from Experience and Suboptimal Rules in Decision Making" in *Judgment Under Uncertainty: Heuristics and Biases,* eds. Daniel Kahneman, Paul Slovic, and Amos Tversky. New York: Cambridge University Press, 1982. Pages 268-283.

Elga, Adam. "Reflection and Disagreement," *Social Epistemology: Essential Readings*, eds. Alvin I. Goldman and Dennis Whitcomb. New York: Oxford University Press, 2011. Pages 158-182.

Epstein, David. *Range: Why Generalists Triumph in a Specialized World.* New York: Riverhead Books, 2020.

Feldman, Richard. "Fallibilism and Knowing That One Knows," *The Philosophical Review*, Vol. 90, No. 2 (Apr., 1981), Pages 266-282.

Fine, Arthur. "The Natural Ontological Attitude" in *Scientific Realism*, ed. Jarrett Leplin. Berkeley: University of California Press, 1984. Pages 83-107.

Fischhoff, Baruch. "For Those Condemned to Study the Past: Heuristics and Biases in Hindsight" in *Judgment Under Uncertainty: Heuristics and Biases,* eds. Daniel Kahneman, Paul Slovic, and Amos Tversky. New York: Cambridge University Press, 1982. Pages 335-351.

—"What Forecasts (Seem to) Mean" in *Judgement and Decision Making: An Interdisciplinary Reader,* Second Edition, eds. Terry Connolly, Hal R. Arkes, and Kenneth R. Hammond. Cambridge: Cambridge University Press, 2000. Pages 353-377.

Fischhoff, Baruch, Ann Bostrom, and Marilyn Jacobs Quadrel, "Risk Perception and Communication" in *Judgement and Decision Making: An Interdisciplinary Reader,* Second Edition, eds. Terry Connolly, Hal R. Arkes, and Kenneth R. Hammond. Cambridge: Cambridge University Press, 2000. Pages 479-499.

Flannery, Austin, ed. *Vatican Council II: The Conciliar and Postconciliar Documents*, New Revised Edition. Collegeville, MN: Liturgical Press, 2014. Kindle Edition.

Flew, Anthony. "Malthus, Thomas Robert" in *The Encyclopedia of Philosophy*, ed. Paul Edwards, Vol. 5. New York: Macmillan Publishing Company, 1967.

Gagliardi, Mauro. *Truth Is a Synthesis: Catholic Dogmatic Theology.* Steubenville, OH: Emmaus Academic, 2020.

Gerhardsson, Birger. *Memory and Manuscript: Oral Tradition and Written Transmission in Rabbinic Judaism and Early Christianity with Tradition and Transmission in Early Christianity.* Grand Rapids, MI: William B. Eerdmans Publishing Company, 1998.

Gettier, Edmund L. "Is Justified True Belief Knowledge?" *Analysis*, Vol. 23, No. 6, 1963. Pages 121–123. *JSTOR*, www.jstor.org/stable/3326922.

Gigerenzer, Gerd and Daniel G. Goldstein. "Reasoning the Fast and Frugal Way: Models of Bounded Rationality" in *Judgement and Decision Making: An Interdisciplinary Reader,* Second Edition, eds. Terry Connolly, Hal R. Arkes, and Kenneth R. Hammond. Cambridge: Cambridge University Press, 2000. Pages 621-650.

Gerd Gegerenzer and Peter M. Todd. "Fast and Frugal Heuristics: The Adaptive Toolbox" in *Simple Heuristics That Make Us Smart*, eds. Gerd Gigerenzer,

Peter M. Todd, and the ABC Research Group. Oxford: Oxford University Press, 1999. Pages 3-34.

Gigerenzer, Gerd, Peter M. Todd, and the ABC Research Group, eds. *Simple Heuristics That Make Us Smart.* Oxford: Oxford University Press, 1999.

Goldberg, Sanford C. "If That Were True I Would Have Heard about It by Now," *Social Epistemology: Essential Readings,* eds. Alvin I. Goldman and Dennis Whitcomb. New York: Oxford University Press, 2011. Pages 92-108.

Goldman, Alvin I. "A Guide to Social Epistemology," *Social Epistemology: Essential Readings,* eds. Alvin I. Goldman and Dennis Whitcomb. New York: Oxford University Press, 2011. Pages 11-37.

—"Experts: Which Ones Should You Trust?" *Social Epistemology: Essential Readings,* eds. Alvin I. Goldman and Dennis Whitcomb. New York: Oxford University Press, 2011. Pages 109-133.

Goldman, Alvin and Bob Beddor, "Reliabilist Epistemology" in The Stanford Encyclopedia of Philosophy (Summer 2021 Edition), ed. Edward N. Zalta, forthcoming https://plato.stanford.edu/archives/sum2021/entries /reliabilism/.

Goldman, Alvin and Cailin O'Connor, "Social Epistemology" in The Stanford Encyclopedia of Philosophy (Summer 2021 Edition), ed. Edward N. Zalta, forthcoming https://plato.stanford.edu/archives/sum2021/entries /reliabilism/.

Gruber, Howard E. *Darwin on Man: A Psychological Study of Scientific Creativity.* Chicago: The University of Chicago Press, 1981.

Habermas, Gary R. "Jesus' Resurrection and Contemporary Criticism: An Apologetic" in *Criswell Theological Review,* Part 1, Vol. 4, No. 1 (Fall 1989). http://www.garyhabermas.com/articles/criswell_theol_review/1989-fall _jesusresandcontempcrit_pt1.htm.

—"The Minimal Facts Approach to the Resurrection of Jesus: The Role of Methodology as a Crucial Component in Establishing Historicity" in *Southeastern Theological Review,* 3/1 (Summer 2012), 15-26.

Hacking, Ian. "Experimentation and Scientific Realism," in *Scientific Realism,* ed. Jarrett Leplin. Berkeley: University of California Press, 1984. Pages 154-172.

Halverson, William H. *A Concise Introduction to Philosophy,* Fourth Edition. New York: Random House, 1981.

Hammond, Kenneth R. "Coherence and Correspondence Theories in Judgement and Decision Making" in *Judgement and Decision Making: An Interdisciplinary Reader,* Second Edition, eds. Terry Connolly, Hal R. Arkes, and Kenneth R. Hammond. Cambridge: Cambridge University Press, 2000. Pages 53-65.

Hardwig, John. "Epistemic Dependence," *The Journal of Philosophy,* Vol. 82, No. 7 (Jul., 1985), 335-349.

Hawking, Stephen and Leonard Mlodinow. *The Grand Design.* London: Bantam, 2010.

Hayek. F. A. *The Constitution of Liberty: The Definitive Edition.* Chicago: The University of Chicago Press, 2011.

—*The Fatal Conceit: The Errors of Socialism,* ed. W. W. Bartley III. Chicago: University of Chicago Press, 1989.

—"The Theory of Complex Phenomena: A Precarious Play on the Epistemology of Complexity" in *Studies in Philosophy, Politics and Economics.* London, UK: Routledge & Kegan Paul, 1967. Pages 22-42. https://bazaarmodel.net /ftp/Project-C/Bazaarmodel/Materiaal/Xtradetail/pdf/Theory%20of %20Complex%20Phenomena.pdf.

Helm, Paul. *Faith and Understanding.* Grand Rapids, MI: William B. Eerdmans Publishing Company, 1997.

Hetherington, Stephen. Internet Encyclopedia of Philosophy, https://iep.utm.edu /fallibil/.

Hitchens, Christopher. *God Is Not Great: How Religion Poisons Everything.* New York: Twelve Books, 2007.

Hodge, Charles. *Systematic Theology,* Vol. 1. Grand Rapids, MI: William B. Eerdmans Publishing Company, 1986.

Hoffrage, Ulrich and Ralph Hertwig. "Hindsight Bias: A Price Worth Paying for Fast and Frugal Memory" in *Simple Heuristics That Make Us Smart,* eds. Gerd Gigerenzer, Peter M. Todd, and the ABC Research Group. Oxford: Oxford University Press, 1999. Pages 191-208.

Horton, Michael. *The Christian Faith: A Systematic Theology for Pilgrims on the Way.* Grand Rapids, MI: Zondervan Academic, 2011.

Hospers, John. *An Introduction to Philosophical Analysis,* Third Edition. New Jersey: Prentice Hall, 1988.

Hume, David. *An Essay Concerning Human Understanding,* ed. Anthony Flew. La Salle, IL: Open Court, 1988.

Ichikawa, Jonathan Jenkins and Matthias Steup. "The Analysis of Knowledge" in The Stanford Encyclopedia of Philosophy (Summer 2018 Edition), ed. Edward N. Zalta, https://plato.stanford.edu/archives/sum2018/entries /knowledge-analysis/.

Ioannidis, John P. A. "Why Most Discovered True Associations Are Inflated," *Epidemiology,* Vol. 19, Number 5 (September 2008), 640-647.

—"Why Most Published Research Findings Are False," *PLoS Medicine* 2 (8) 0696-0701.

—"Why Science Is Not Necessarily Self-Correcting," *Perspectives on Psychological Science,* 7(6) 645-654.

Ioannidis, John P. A. and Marcus R. Munafo, Paolo Fusar-Poli, Brian A. Nosek, and Sean P. David. "Publication and Other Reporting Biases in Cognitive

Sciences: Detection, Prevalence, and Prevention," *Trends in Cognitive Sciences*, May 2014, Vol. 18, No. 5, 235-241.

Jones, W. T. *A History of Western Philosophy: Hobbes to Hume*, Second Edition. Fort Worth: Harcourt Brace Jovanovich Publishers, 1969.

Jungermann, Helmut. "The Two Camps on Rationality" in *Judgement and Decision Making: An Interdisciplinary Reader*, Second Edition, eds. Terry Connolly, Hal R. Arkes, and Kenneth R. Hammond. Cambridge: Cambridge University Press, 2000. Pages 575-591.

Kahneman, Daniel. *Thinking, Fast and Slow*. New York: Farrar, Straus and Giroux, 2011.

Kahneman, Daniel, Oliver Sibony, and Cass R. Sunstein. *Noise: A Flaw in Human Judgement*. New York: Little, Brown Spark, 2021.

Kahneman, Daniel and Amos Tversky. "Choices, Values, and Frames" in *Judgement and Decision Making: An Interdisciplinary Reader*, Second Edition, eds. Terry Connolly, Hal R. Arkes, and Kenneth R. Hammond. Cambridge: Cambridge University Press, 2000. Pages 147-165.

—"Intuitive Prediction: Biases and Corrective Procedures." Technical Report PTR-1042-77-6, Sponsored by Defense Advanced Research Project Agency, June 1977, Pages 4-5. https://apps.dtic.mil/dtic/tr/fulltext/u2/a047747.pdf.

—"On the Psychology of Prediction" in *Judgment Under Uncertainty: Heuristics and Biases*, eds. Daniel Kahneman, Paul Slovic, and Amos Tversky. New York: Cambridge University Press, 1982. Pages 48-68.

—"On the Study of Statistical Intuitions." *Cognition*, Volume 11, Issue 2 (March, 1982), Pages 123-141.

—"Subjective Probability: A Judgment of Representativeness" in *Judgment Under Uncertainty: Heuristics and Biases*, eds. Daniel Kahneman, Paul Slovic, and Amos Tversky. New York: Cambridge University Press, 1982. Pages 32-47.

Kelly, Thomas. "Peer Disagreement and Higher Order Evidence" in *Social Epistemology: Essential Readings*, eds. Alvin I. Goldman and Dennis Whitcomb. New York: Oxford University Press, 2011. Pages 183-217.

Kitcher, Philip. *The Advancement of Science: Science Without Legend, Objectivity Without Illusions*. New York: Oxford University Press, 1993.

—"Theories, Theorists and Theoretical Change," *The Philosophical Review*, Vol. 87, No. 4 (Oct., 1978), Pages 519-547.

Koons, Jeremy Randel. "Plantinga on Properly Basic Belief in God: Lessons from the Epistemology of Perception," *The Philosophical Quarterly* 61:245 (October 2011), Pages 839-850. https://faculty.georgetown.edu/koonsj/papers/Plantinga.pdf.

Krakauer, Jon. *Under the Banner of Heaven: A Story of Violent Faith*. New York: Anchor Books, 2004.

Krauss, Lawrence. *A Universe from Nothing: Why There Is Something Rather Than Nothing*. New York: Free Press, 2012.

Kuhn, Thomas S. *The Structure of Scientific Revolutions*, Fourth Edition. Chicago: University of Chicago Press, 2012.

Lackey, Jennifer. "Testimony: Acquiring Knowledge from Others" in *Social Epistemology: Essential Readings*, eds. Alvin I. Goldman and Dennis Whitcomb. New York: Oxford University Press, 2011. Pages 71-91.

Latour, Bruno and Steve Wooglar. *Laboratory Life: The Construction of Scientific Facts*. Princeton, NJ: Princeton University Press, 1986.

Laudan, Larry. "A Confutation of Convergent Realism" in *The Philosophy of Science*, ed. David Papineau. New York: Oxford University Press, 1996. Pages 107-138.

—*Progress and Its Problems: Towards a Theory of Scientific Growth*. Berkeley: University of California Press, 1977.

—*Science and Values: The Aims of Science and Their Role in Scientific Debate*. Berkeley: University of California Press, 1984.

—"The Demise of the Demarcation Problem" in *Physics, Philosophy and Psychoanalysis*, eds. R. S. Cohen and L. Laudan. Dordrecht: R. Reidel Publishing Company, 1983. Pages 111-127.

Licona, Michael R. *The Resurrection of Jesus: A New Historiographical Approach*. Downers Grove, Illinois: IVP Academic, 2010.

Lipton, Peter. *Inference to the Best Explanation*, Second Edition. London: Routledge, 2004.

—"Is The Best Good Enough?" in *The Philosophy of Science*, ed. David Papineau. New York: Oxford University Press, 1996. Pages 93-106.

Lennox, John C. *God's Undertaker: Has Science Buried God?* Oxford: Lion, 2009.

Leplin, Jarrett. "Introduction" in *Scientific Realism*, ed. Jarrett Leplin. Berkeley: University of California Press, 1984. Pages 1-7.

—"Truth and Scientific Progress" in *Scientific Realism*, ed. Jarrett Leplin. Berkeley: University of California Press, 1984. Pages 193-217.

List, Christian. "Group Knowledge and Group Rationality: A Judgment Aggregation Perspective" in *Social Epistemology: Essential Readings*, eds. Alvin I. Goldman and Dennis Whitcomb. Oxford: Oxford University Press, 2011. Pages 221-241.

Locke, John. *An Essay Concerning Human Understanding*, 2 Vols., collated and annotated by Alexander Campbell Fraser. New York: Dover Publications, Inc. 1959.

Longino, Helen, "The Social Dimensions of Scientific Knowledge" in *The Stanford Encyclopedia of Philosophy* (Summer 2019 Edition), ed. Edward N. Zalta, https://plato.stanford.edu/archives/sum2019/entries/scientific-knowledge-social/.

Markie, Peter, "Rationalism vs. Empiricism" in The Stanford Encyclopedia of Philosophy (Summer 2019 Edition), ed. Edward N. Zalta, https://plato.stanford.edu/archives/fall2017/entries/rationalism-empiricism/.

McGrath, Alister E. *A Fine-Tuned Universe: The Quest for God in Science and Theology.* Louisville: Westminster John Knox Press, 2009.

—*A Scientific Theology,* Vols. 1-3. Grand Rapids, MI: William B. Eerdmans Publishing Company, 2002.

—*Darwinism and the Divine: Evolutionary Thought and Natural Theology.* West Sussex, UK: Wiley-Blackwell, 2011.

McMullin, Ernan. "A Case for Scientific Realism" in *Scientific Realism,* ed. Jarrett Leplin. Berkeley: University of California Press, 1984. Pages 8-40.

Meyer, Stephen C. *Darwin's Doubt: The Explosive Origin of Animal Life and the Case for Intelligent Design.* New York: HarperOne, 2014.

—*Return of the God Hypothesis: Three Scientific Discoveries That Reveal the Mind Behind the Universe.* New York: Harper One, 2021.

—*Signature in the Cell: DNA and the Evidence for Intelligent Design.* New York: Harper One, 2009.

Montgomery, John Warwick. *Tractatus Logico-Theologicus.* Bonn: VKW, 2002.

Musgrave, Alan. "NOA's Ark—Fine for Realism" in *The Philosophy of Science,* ed. David Papineau. New York: Oxford University Press, 1996. Pages 45-60.

Nielsen, Kai. "Can Faith Validate God-Talk?" in *New Theology,* No. 1, ed. Martin E. Marty and Dean G. Peerman. New York: Macmillan, 1964.

Nisbett, Richard E., Eugene Borgida, Rick Crandall, and Harvey Reed. "Popular Induction: Information Is Not Necessarily Informative" in *Judgment Under Uncertainty: Heuristics and Biases,* eds. Daniel Kahneman, Paul Slovic, and Amos Tversky. New York: Cambridge University Press, 1982. Pages 101-116.

Nisbett, Richard E. and David H. Krantz, Christopher Jepson, and Geoffrey T. Fong. "Improving Inductive Inference" in *Judgment Under Uncertainty: Heuristics and Biases,* eds. Daniel Kahneman, Paul Slovic, and Amos Tversky. New York: Cambridge University Press, 1982. Pages 445-459.

Ott, Ludwig. *Fundamentals of Catholic Dogma: A One-Volume Encyclopedia of the Doctrines of the Catholic Church, Showing Their Sources in Scripture and Tradition and Their Definitions by Popes and Councils.* Rockford, IL: Tan Books and Publishers, Inc., 1960.

Paley, William. *Natural Theology,* ed. Frederick Ferrè. Indianapolis: Bobbs-Merrill, 1963.

Pannenberg, Wolfhart. *Systematic Theology,* Vol. 1, trans. by Geoffrey W. Bromiley. Grand Rapids, MI: William B. Eerdmans Publishing Company, 1988.

Papineau, David. "Does the Sociology of Science Discredit Science?" in *Relativism and Realism in Science,* ed. Robert Nola. Dordrecht: Kluwer Academic Publishers, 1988. Pages 37-57.

—"Introduction" in *The Philosophy of Science,* ed. David Papineau. New York: Oxford University Press, 1996. Pages 1-20.

—*Reality and Representation.* Oxford: Basil Blackwell, 1987.

Peterson, Michael, William Hasker, Bruce Reichenbach, and David Basinger. *Reason & Religious Belief: An Introduction to the Philosophy of Religion.* New York: Oxford University Press, 1991.

Pettit, Philip. "Groups with Minds of Their Own" in *Social Epistemology: Essential Readings,* eds. Alvin I. Goldman and Dennis Whitcomb. New York: Oxford University Press, 2011. Pages 242-268.

—"The Strong Sociology of Knowledge Without Relativism" in *Relativism and Realism in Science,* ed. Robert Nola. Dordrecht, 1988. Pages 81-91.

—"When to Defer to Majority Testimony—And When Not," *Analysis,* July 2006, Pages 179-186.

Pieper, Francis. *Christian Dogmatics,* Vol. 1. Saint Louis: Concordia Publishing House, 1950.

Plantinga, Alvin. *Knowledge and Christian Belief.* Grand Rapids, MI: William B. Eerdmans Publishing Company, 2015.

—"Is Belief in God Properly Basic?" *Nous,* 15 (1): 1981, Pages 41-51.

Polanyi, Michael. *Personal Knowledge: Towards a Post-Critical Philosophy.* Chicago: The University of Chicago Press, 1974.

Polkinghorne, John. *One World: The Interaction of Science and Theology.* London: SPCK, 1986.

—*Reason and Reality: The Relationship Between Science and Theology.* London: SPCK, 1992.

—*Science and Creation: The Search for Understanding.* London: SPCK, 1988.

—*Science and the Trinity: The Christian Encounter with Reality.* New Haven: Yale University Press, 2004.

Putnam, Hilary. "The Analytic and the Synthetic" in *Mind, Language and Reality: Philosophical Papers, Volume 2.* Cambridge: Cambridge University Press, 1975. Pages 33-69.

—"What is Realism?" in *Scientific Realism,* ed. Jarrett Leplin. Berkeley: University of California Press, 1984. Pages 140-153.

Quine, Willard Van Orman. "Two Dogmas of Empiricism" in *From a Logical Point of View: 9 Logico-Philosophical Essays.* Cambridge, Mass: Harvard University Press, 1953. Pages 20-46.

Rescher, Nicholas. *The Limits of Science,* Revised Edition. Pittsburgh: University of Pittsburgh Press, 1999.

Romero, Felipe. "Can the Behavioral Sciences Self-Correct? A Social Epistemic Study," *Studies in History and Philosophy of Science,* Part A (2016), 60, Pages 55-69.

Rorty, Richard. *Philosophy and the Mirror of Nature.* Princeton, NJ: Princeton University Press, 1979.

Rosenzweig, Phil. *The Halo Effect...and the Eight Other Business Delusions That Deceive Managers*. New York: Free Press, 2007.

Ross, Lee and Craig A. Anderson. "Shortcomings in the Attribution Process: On the Social Origins and Maintenance of Erroneous Social Assessments" in *Judgment Under Uncertainty: Heuristics and Biases*, eds. Daniel Kahneman, Paul Slovic, and Amos Tversky. New York: Cambridge University Press, 1982. Pages 129-152.

Ross, Michael and Fiore Sicoly. "Egocentric Biases in Availability and Attribution" in *Judgment Under Uncertainty: Heuristics and Biases*, eds. Daniel Kahneman, Paul Slovic, and Amos Tversky. New York: Cambridge University Press, 1982. Pages 179-189.

Russell, Bruce, "A Priori Justification and Knowledge" in The Stanford Encyclopedia of Philosophy (Summer 2020 Edition), ed. Edward N. Zalta, https://plato.stanford.edu/archives/sum2020/entries/apriori/.

Rysiew, Patrick, "Naturalism in Epistemology" in The Stanford Encyclopedia of Philosophy (Summer 2020 Edition), ed. Edward N. Zalta, https://plato.stanford.edu/archives/fall2020/entries/epistemology-naturalized/.

Saad, Gad. *The Parasitic Mind: How Infectious Ideas Are Killing Common Sense*. Washington DC: Regnery Publishing, 2020.

Sapolsky, Robert M. *Behave: The Biology of Humans at Our Best and Worst*. New York: Penguin Books, 2017.

Slovic, Paul, Baruch Fischhoff, and Sarah Lichtenstein. "Facts Versus Fears: Understanding Perceived Risk" in *Judgment Under Uncertainty: Heuristics and Biases*, eds. Daniel Kahneman, Paul Slovic, and Amos Tversky. New York: Cambridge University Press, 1982. Pages 463-489.

Smith, Quentin. "Atheism, Theism, and Big Bang Cosmology" in William Lane Craig and Quentin Smith, *Theism, Atheism and Big Bang Cosmology*. Oxford: Clarendon Press, 1995. Pages 195-217.

—"The Uncaused Beginning of the Universe" in William Lane Craig and Quentin Smith, *Theism, Atheism and Big Bang Cosmology*. Oxford: Clarendon Press, 1995. Pages 108-140.

Sowell, Thomas. *A Conflict of Visions: Ideological Origins of Political Struggles*. New York: Basic Books, 1987. Page 200.

—*Discrimination and Disparities*. New York: Basic Books, 2019.

—*Knowledge and Decisions*. New York: Basic Books, 1996.

Swinburne, Richard. "Plantinga on Warrant," *Religious Studies* 37, Pages 203-214.

—*The Existence of God*. Oxford: Clarendon Press, 1979.

Tabor, James D. *Paul and Jesus: How the Apostle Transformed Christianity*. New York: Simon & Schuster Paperbacks, 2012.

Taleb, Nassim Nicholas. *The Black Swan: The Impact of the Highly Improbable*. New York: Random House Trade Paperbacks, 2010.

Tatsioni, Athina, Nikolaos G. Bonitsis, and John P. A. Ioannidis, "Persistence of Contradicted Claims in the Literature," *JAMA*, December 5, 2007, Vol. 298, No. 21, Pages 2517-2526.

Taylor, Shelley E. "The Availability Bias in Social Perception and Interaction" in *Judgment Under Uncertainty: Heuristics and Biases,* eds. Daniel Kahneman, Paul Slovic, and Amos Tversky. New York: Cambridge University Press, 1982. Pages 190-200.

Tetlock, Philip E. *Expert Political Judgement: How Good Is It? How Can We Know?* Princeton, NJ: Princeton University Press, 2005.

Tetlock, Philip E. and Dan Gardner. *Superforecasting: The Art and Science of Prediction.* New York: Broadway Books, 2015.

Tversky, Amos and Daniel Kahneman. "Availability: A Heuristic for Judging Frequency and Probability" in *Judgment Under Uncertainty: Heuristics and Biases,* eds. Daniel Kahneman, Paul Slovic, and Amos Tversky. New York: Cambridge University Press, 1982. Pages 163-178.

—"Belief in the Law of Small Numbers" in *Judgment Under Uncertainty: Heuristics and Biases,* eds. Daniel Kahneman, Paul Slovic, and Amos Tversky. New York: Cambridge University Press, 1982. Pages 23-31.

—"Causal Schemas in Judgments Under Uncertainty" in *Judgment Under Uncertainty: Heuristics and Biases,* eds. Daniel Kahneman, Paul Slovic, and Amos Tversky. New York: Cambridge University Press, 1982. Pages 117-128.

—"Evidential Impact of Base Rates" in *Judgment Under Uncertainty: Heuristics and Biases,* eds. Daniel Kahneman, Paul Slovic, and Amos Tversky. New York: Cambridge University Press, 1982. Pages 153-160.

—"Judgement Under Uncertainty: Heuristics and Biases" in *Judgement and Decision Making: An Interdisciplinary Reader,* Second Edition, eds. Terry Connolly, Hal R. Arkes, and Kenneth R. Hammond. Cambridge: Cambridge University Press, 2000. Pages 35-52.

Van Fraassen, Bas C. *The Scientific Image.* New York: Clarendon Press, 1980.

—"To Save the Phenomena" in *Scientific Realism,* ed. Jarrett Leplin. Berkeley: University of California Press, 1984. Pages 250-259.

Warfield, Benjamin B. *The Inspiration and Authority of the Bible.* Grand Rapids, MI: Baker Book House, 1948.

Weatherall, James Owen, Cailin O'Connor, and Justin P. Bruner. "How to Beat Science and Influence People: Policy Makers and Propaganda in Epistemic Networks." https://www.journals.uchicago.edu/doi/full/10.1093/bjps/axy062.

Weaver, Warren. "Science and Complexity," *American Scientist*, 36:536 (1948), https://people.physics.anu.edu.au/~tas110/Teaching/Lectures/L1/Material /WEAVER1947.pdf.

Wheelan, Charles. *Naked Statistics: Stripping the Dread from the Data.* New York: W. W. Norton & Company, 2013.

Wigner, Eugene. "The Unreasonable Effectiveness of Mathematics in the Natural Sciences," *Communications in Pure and Applied Mathematics*, Vol. 13, No. 1 (February, 1960). Pages 1-14.

Wright, N. T. *The Resurrection of the Son of God.* Minneapolis: Fortress Press, 2003.

Zaltman, Gerald. *How Customers Think: Essential Insights Into the Mind of the Market.* Boston, MA: Harvard Business School Press, 2003.

Zeckhauser, Richard J. and W. Kip Viscusi. "Risk within Reason" in *Judgement and Decision Making: An Interdisciplinary Reader,* Second Edition, eds. Terry Connolly, Hal R. Arkes, and Kenneth R. Hammond. Cambridge: Cambridge University Press, 2000. Pages 465-478.

Zollman, Kevin J. S. "The Communication Structure of Epistemic Communities," *Philosophy of Science*, 74(5): 574-587.

Index

CPSIA information can be obtained
at www.ICGtesting.com
Printed in the USA
LVHW041125180723
752783LV00012B/19/J

9 781956 658583